Risk and misfortune

HEALTH, RISK AND SOCIETY

Series editor
Graham Hart
MRC Medical Sociology Unit, Glasgow

In recent years, social scientific interest in risk has increased enormously. In the health field, risk is seen as having the potential to bridge the gap between individuals, communities and the larger social structure, with a theoretical framework which unifies concerns around a number of contemporary health issues. This new series will explore the concept of risk in detail, and address some of the most active areas of current health and research practice.

Forthcoming titles include:

Living with HIV: identity and social risk
Gill Green & E. J. Sobo

Risk landscapes and heart disease
Charlie Davison, George Davey Smith, Stephen Frankel

Food and health: the mass media and the social production of risk
David Miller, Jacquie Reilly, Sally Macintyre

Sexual risks and strategies: constructing and interpreting gay male sexual behaviour
Graham Hart & Paul Flowers

Risk and misfortune

A social construction of accidents

Judith Green
London School of Hygiene and Tropical Medicine

UCL
PRESS

© Judith Green 1997

First published in 1997 by UCL Press

UCL Press Limited
1 Gunpowder Square
London
EC4A 3DE
UK

and

1900 Frost Road, Suite 101
Bristol
Pennsylvania 19007-1598
USA

The name of University College London (UCL) is a registered
trade mark used by UCL Press with the consent of the owner.

British Library Cataloguing-in-Publication Data
A catalogue record for this book is available from the British Library.

Library of Congress Cataloging-in-Publication Data are available.

ISBNs: 1-85728-560-3 HB
        1-85728-561-1 PB

Cover design by Jim Wilkie
Printed and bound in Great Britain by
T. J. International Ltd, Padstow, Cornwall

Contents

This book is dedicated to Rebecca Green.

Preface

In recent years interest in the subject of risk has increased enormously. Although estimates of risk have long been a feature of modern life, and there exists a large technical literature on the topic, it is only relatively recently that sociologists and other social scientists have engaged conceptually with risk. For sociologists of health and illness, the interest in risk lies in its potential to bridge the gap between individuals, communities, and the larger social structure which constructs, contextualizes and determines exposure to harm. There are now a number of examples of empirical and theoretical work which render risk more problematic than previously considered. The series, *Health, Risk and Society* intends to offer an integrative and cohesive approach to health and risk, providing fresh and challenging insights to current health problems and the way in which we conceptualize them.

If our aim is to establish a body of literature that unifies sociological interest in both risk and health studies, then we could not have a better start to the series than *Risk and misfortune: a social construction of accidents*. Referring to an "archaeology of accidents", Judith Green has provided an exemplar of this innovative approach to the understanding of risk through her detailed historical, theoretical and empirical analysis of accidents. If risk is concerned with the likelihood of exposure to a given harm, and an accident is an unforeseen event (at least in its specific timing), then consideration of the two – the risk of an accident occurring – sets us off on a fascinating epistemological and conceptual journey. Comprehensive in its breadth and depth, *Risk and misfortune* will prove invaluable to any reader who has for a moment considered what constitutes an accident or mishap, the notion of "responsibility" for misfortune, and the extent to which "accident prevention" is possible.

Graham Hart
Series Editor
Health, Risk and Society

Acknowledgements

If the student of accidents has few academic sources to draw on, this is more than compensated by the wealth of primary data. Most people have a fund of "accident stories" and this book owes a great debt to the many people who have shared theirs with me over the past few years. I am particularly grateful to those who were kind enough to take part in interviews and discussion groups about their experiences. Apart from consenting to have their stories recorded, many of them also passed on articles to read and contributed to the arguments here. Many friends and colleagues have also made useful comments, suggested books to read or debated the issues. They include Wayne Parkin, Jackie Pearce, Gil Thornhill, Paul Kelly, Steven Wibberley, Laurence Pearl and Sarah Nettleton. Christine Jenner and Anne Heller have both helped to provide time to write, for which I am very grateful. Thanks are due to Nicki Thorogood, who has been an unstinting source of both academic and social support, and who made useful comments on an earlier draft.

This book is based on a PhD thesis, and special thanks are due to my supervisor, David Armstrong, who has known exactly when to be encouraging and when to be challenging, and whose advice has always been invaluable. The Department of General Practice and Primary Care at King's College School of Medicine and Dentistry funded the first two years of the PhD, and I would like to thank Professor Roger Higgs for early encouragement, and colleagues at the Department of General Practice of UMDS for their support. Graham Hart, as series editor for UCL

Press, has made useful suggestions on how to turn a PhD into a readable book. Any failings in that respect, or any other, are of course entirely my own.

The tables in Chapter 6 listing cases of mountain accidents and advice to walkers and climbers are reproduced with kind permission of the Lake District Search and Mountain Rescue Association.

In the excerpts reproduced in Chapter 7, the following conventions are used:

  . . . words omitted by author
  –   at the end or beginning of utterance indicates interrupted speech
  [ ]   enclose words added by author

Chapter 1

Introduction

What is an accident?

Milk is spilt, a car crashes, a woman unintentionally becomes pregnant, a small boy wets himself. The range of events that we describe as accidents is vast and disparate, including the serendipitous chance meeting or interesting discovery, but more usually some kind of misfortune, often trivial but occasionally tragic. Indeed, the word "accident" covers a seemingly infinite range of possible misfortunes that, as we say, will happen and have to be expected from time to time. Such misfortunes are perhaps universal to human society, but ways of classifying, understanding and managing them clearly are not. This book is an attempt to examine accidents sociologically, in order to understand how some misfortunes have become classified specifically as "accidents" in the late twentieth century.

At one level this is perhaps a rather trivial question, as we all have a knowledge of what accidents are and in everyday conversation we use the term, on the whole, unproblematically. As a description of certain kinds of misfortune, we use the word "accident" in two rather different ways. First, it is used to denote certain kinds of outcome: as a synonym for "injury", as in "an industrial accident", or to describe a car crash. The work colleague who comments that she "was involved in a car accident yesterday" or the parent who says "my daughter had an accident at school today" is marking the event in terms of its outcome: perhaps damage to the car, or injury to the person. Secondly, though, it is also used as a moral term,

1

denoting lack of intent or motivation on the part of the agent: "it happened by accident". In this sense, the term "accident" is used to describe a causal sequence. Similar outcomes (such as a death, injury or material damage) can be produced by events that are clearly not accidents, such as homicide, war or wilful damage. It is the process preceding the outcome that is critical.

So, in everyday conversation, how are particular kinds of misfortune defined as accidents? They are defined through their ascribed cause or, rather, lack of cause. We do not decide that an accident has occurred by observing what happened, but by investigating how it happened. There are two factors that apparently characterize the process by which accidents are seen to occur. The first is that an accident should be an unmotivated event; neither the victim nor any other agency, human or divine, willed it to happen. Ironic usage clearly illustrates this, as in the title of Dario Fo's (1980) play *The accidental death of an anarchist* or the gangster's "we could arrange for you to have an accident". In general, no-one can be blamed for the occurrence of an accident. It is this feature that distinguishes accidents from wilful damage and neglect. The arrangement of physical objects and temporal sequences that precede an accident must be seen to be purely coincidental: they cannot have been willed. The causation of accidents is apparently arbitrary and not logical.

Secondly, and following from this, an accident is unpredictable as a unique event. Although the epidemiology of accidents can be mapped through aggregation and examination of their incidence, the occurrence of a particular accident cannot be foreseen. The victim, in an ideal accident, has no previous knowledge of the misfortune and therefore cannot be held responsible. From an early age we learn to negotiate claims to the accidental in order to disclaim responsibility for its consequences: anyone caring for children will recognize the bid for clemency "I didn't do it on purpose – it was an accident."

Contested accidents

The first clue that accidents are not as unproblematic as they seem at first sight is that this working definition, which we all use with competence, apparently applies only to an "ideal type" of accident. In practice, not all accidents are held to be unwilled and unpredicted. There are many events that are defined as "accidental", but in which some blame is apportioned: road traffic accidents caused by a driver over the legal alcohol limit, or falls over loose paving stones that should have been maintained by a local authority. Indeed some have argued that the contemporary victim is loathe to accept that any misfortune "just happens" and is increasingly willing to hold others not only morally but also legally culpable (Fox 1980, Douglas & Wildavsky 1983). The classification of any event as "accidental" is certainly often provisional: misfortunes are only described as accidents until responsibility can be apportioned. Even a brief review of media coverage of disasters (the "accidents" that affect many people) and the calls for their investigation demonstrates how the definition is negotiated rather than given, with different parties sometimes in open conflict over how a particular event should be categorized. In some there are clear political interests, such as questions about the extent to which the "profit motive" outweighs health and safety concerns. What is notable is that even when explicit political interests are absent, the label of "accident" neither absolves responsibility nor halts debate around it. In 1989, for instance, a tragic accident occurred on the Thames in London when a pleasure cruiser, the *Marchioness*, capsized when hit by a sand dredger, with the loss of 51 lives. Despite being described by one commentator as "truly an accident" (Lee 1992: 134), the report of the Marine Accident Investigation Branch of the Department of Transport (DOT/MAIB 1991) found several factors that contributed to the tragedy, including the design of the vessels and their lack of adequate lighting, and did attribute responsibility in its conclusions: "it is inescapable that those in charge of the navigation of both vessels concerned must bear a large measure of the responsibility; but they share it with those who provided them with each vessel . . ." (DOT/MAIB 1991: 44).

Ideal accidents may, then, be blameless and unpredictable events, but accidents in practice are potentially surrounded by moral enquiry. Even if blame cannot be apportioned in a direct way (there is no agent with a duty of responsibility to the victim), there may still be a more generalized moral accountability. In one of his essays on *Three forms of sudden death*, the pathologist Gonzalez-Crussi provides an example. He describes a bizarre accident that caused the death of several homeless men in the subways of New York City's underground train system:

> With their bladders full to capacity. . . they had released a stream
> of urine, which formed a continuous arched jet between their

3

bladders and the train tracks. As soon as the stream touched the tracks, the thousands upon thousands of volts of electricity needed to move New Yorkers around, conveniently harnessed in the tracks, found an alternative route in the salt-rich fluid, and flowed for a fraction of a second into the body of the unwary vagrants. Diagnosis: struck by lightning, underground. (Gonzalez-Crussi 1986: 66–7)

Every unexpected death in New York City, like in other modern cities, has to be classified as one of three classes: suicide, homicide or accident, "the mark", says Gonzalez-Crussi, respectively "of dishonor, pity or indifference impressed upon it by the living" (ibid.: 65). He is struck, though, not by the bizarre way in which these men met their death, but by the reaction to it of the living, which was not the "indifference" suggested by a verdict of accidental death, but "a certain sanctimoniousness, a certain urge to remonstrate that all was as it should be, that death by electrocution was a means of divine reproof" (ibid.: 69). On the one hand, he implies, accidents are a matter of indifference: they are unforeseen occurrences, misfortunes that "just happen", which cannot be helped and for which therefore no-one can be blamed. On the other hand, accidents are apparently at the centre of moral debate: although they "just happen", some people are seen to deserve them. Both other agents and the victim can, then, be held responsible for accidents, either in the sense of being blamed directly for some kind of negligence, or in a more diffuse way as being "the kind of person who deserves an accident".

If accidents in practice are not necessarily blameless events, neither are they unambiguously unpredictable. In folk wisdom there are "accidents waiting to happen": potentially dangerous situations recognized as making an accident inevitable eventually, even if its timing cannot be predicted. In the late twentieth century, there is a growing risk assessment industry that attempts to objectify such situations through measuring both the probability (or risk) of them leading to an accident and the extent of damage likely to be caused.

The process by which some misfortunes become classified as accidents is not, perhaps, as transparent as first suggested. If in practice they are neither necessarily unmotivated nor necessarily unpredictable, there is considerable space for negotiation or even conflict over legitimate classification. One source of potential conflict implied by the above is that between professional and "lay" definitions of an accident. There are many formal (or "expert") bodies of knowledge that refer to accidents. Many of these attempt explicitly to impose some order on the apparent chaos of accidents as a "lay" category of misfortune. English legal discourse, for example, specifies the duties of certain kinds of people to prevent accidents happening and to identify what redress can be sought if these duties are breached. It is very much a professional discourse, presented as utilizing rather different principles than those current in everyday usage: "principles of duty, breach and damage . . . are legal constructs which do not always correspond with ordinary and 'common sense' conceptions of the 'causes' of accidents and attributions of fault by the injury victim" (Genn 1987: 4).

Medicine, too, has developed professional bodies of knowledge about accidents which concern the distribution of accidental injuries, the treatment of those injuries and, more recently, how they should be prevented. Like legal discourse, medical knowledge situates itself as specifically counter to common sense, in that accidents are seen to be predictable and thus preventable, rather than as random misfortunes we can do nothing about. Legal and medical discourses intersect in forensic medicine, which attempts to identify fatal accidents retrospectively from the patterns of wounds and other signs they leave on the body (Simpson & Knight 1985: 68).

Here, then, is adequate justification for sociological interest in accidents, for an answer to the question "what is an accident?" may not be as trivial as first suggested. There are several, sometimes contradictory, discourses that concern accidents, and the potential conflict between them provides a rich field for sociological enquiry into how such conflict is managed.

The social construction of accidents

How should such sociological enquiry proceed? One method might be to begin by developing some sociological classification of accidents in the tradition of Durkheim's classic study of *Suicide*. Durkheim suggested that such a foundation was a necessary one:

Since the word "suicide" recurs constantly in the course of conversation, it might be thought that its sense is universally known

> and that definition is superfluous . . . if we follow common use, we
> risk distinguishing what should be combined, or combining what
> should be distinguished, thus mistaking the real affinity of things.
> (Durkheim 1963: 41)

In 1992 accidents accounted for more than twice as many fatalities as
suicides in the Registrar-General's annual returns for England and Wales
(OPCS 1994b), but they have, in contrast, received relatively little attention from sociologists. An initial problem is that following Durkheim's
advice, and discovering the "real affinity" of those disparate events we call
accidents, may be rather difficult. The word "accident" is also widely
used, far more so than "suicide", in everyday conversation, but it refers
not only to the fatalities recorded by the Registrar-General, but also to a
wide range of other, everyday misfortunes. That the word "accident"
describes such a seemingly disparate range of events poses the first challenge for a sociology of accidents. Defining the field of study by first discovering the "real affinity" between these events is problematic: there are
no obvious dimensions along which a classification could be developed.
Our working definition of an unmotivated and unpredictable event was
seen to be negotiable, and in conflict with professional bodies of knowledge. Before an adequate sociology of accidents can be developed, a fundamental question is perhaps how the "reality" of accidents is socially
constructed.

If there has been comparatively little sociological interest in accidents,
this is in part because accidents are widely assumed to be "given", a natural and obvious category of events which, unlike suicide, do not warrant
close examination. It is perhaps a truism to note that the accidental, like
any other category, is a socially constructed one. Accidents are so often
taken as "givens", or inevitable features of the universe that it is perhaps
worth stating the social construction of their classification as a starting
point. There is no natural category of events which are accidents. This is
not of course to suggest that accidents or the human suffering that results
from them are not "real", merely that in modern cosmologies certain
misfortunes are selected and described as "accidents" and others not, and
that there is nothing inevitable about this classification.

Apart from those clues which suggest that the contemporary classification of accidents is somewhat problematic, even the most cursory glance
at anthropological and historical evidence about other cosmologies provides evidence that there are other ways to classify misfortune. Although

the kinds of misfortunes we call "accidents" (unmotivated and unpredict-able chance events) may always have happened, they are not in all times and places labelled as "accidents" or understood in the ways we under-stand them. Evans-Pritchard, for instance, in his account of Azande cos-mology (Evans-Pritchard 1937), described a belief system within which accidents cannot happen, because all misfortunes are potentially attribut-able to witchcraft. Mead (1931), in her account of child-rearing in Manus culture, similarly described a social system which can allow no "acci-dents", here because of what she saw to be the physical dangers of the environment, rather than any all-embracing cosmology:

> The Manus world, slight framework of narrow boards above the changing tides of the lagoon, is too precarious a place for costly mistakes. The successful fashion in which each baby is efficiently adapted to its dangerous way of life is relevant to the problem which parents here [North America] must face as our mode of life becomes increasingly charged with possibilities of accident. (Mead 1931: 5)

A combination of early discipline and refusal to sympathize with the accidental outcomes of childhood clumsiness ensured, claimed Mead, that the children of the Manus grew up "physically dextrous, sure footed, clear eyed [and] quick handed" (Mead 1931: 21). Mead's suggestion that Western children might benefit from a similar upbringing to protect them from accidental harm has not been adopted: the prevention of accidents in contemporary Britain is centred on a rather different understanding of what constitutes a risk and how it should be managed.

Why a sociology of accidents now?

A modernist answer

Apart from anthropological accounts of other cultures, which demon-strate that it is not inevitable that some misfortunes will be seen as acci-dents, sociology has traditionally largely ignored accidents as a legitimate object of study. So why is it possible now to attempt such a study? A first, pragmatic, answer perhaps lies in the relative growth in importance of accidental injury as a cause of death, disability and distress. With decreasing mortality, particularly childhood mortality, in the West, accidents account for an increasing proportion of deaths and, given their distribution throughout the lifespan, a disproportionate number of life years lost. Accidents were found to be the cause of over 10,000 deaths in England and Wales in 1992 (OPCS 1994b). Accidents have been the leading cause of childhood death for over 25 years in Britain (Jackson 1977) and it has been estimated that some 10,000 children each year are permanently disabled by accidents (CAPT 1989). Each year around one in five children needs hospital treatment for accidental injury (Sibert et al. 1981). Minor accidents, causing distress or pain at the time, are perhaps a universal experience. There is evidence that these misfortunes are not randomly distributed, but affect certain classes of people more than others. In the 1970s, for instance, the chance of dying from an accident in childhood was three and a half times greater for boys born to families in social class V than for those born into families of social class I (DHSS 1980), and there is evidence that differences in morbidity between social classes persist (Alwash & McCarthy 1987). Although there has been some sociological work that has addressed questions of the social structure of accidental injury (see for instance Roberts et al. 1992, 1993), the sociology of health and illness generally has viewed accidents as a rather marginal category of disease, and has left questions about the social distribution of accidental injury to epidemiologists.

This epidemiological interest in accident rates, "risk factors" for various kinds of accident and suggestions for managing these risks has been reflected in policy. Since the middle of the twentieth century there has been a growth in "accident prevention" as a professional activity, aimed at changing the beliefs and behaviour of the population to reduce its risks for accidental injury. The forms that this health promotion has taken warrant sociological interest, both in accounting for the emergence of accident prevention and in assessing its likely impact on the population.

A "postmodern" answer?

A second reason why it may be possible to write a sociology of accidents now, after so much apparent neglect, lies in the debate about recent social transformations and how we characterize the social order (if indeed it is an "order") of late twentieth-century Western societies. It has been widely argued that we inhabit, or at least are on the threshold of, a "postmodern" epoch, "a new social totality with its own organizing principles" (Featherstone 1988), and that the logics of contemporary culture and society represent a radical break from the "modern", or that historical period between the end of the seventeenth century and the end of the nineteenth (see, for instance, Lyotard 1986, Featherstone 1988, Bauman 1992). "Postmodernity" refers to those features of material culture, art, intellectual thought and patterns of consumption that represent a radical (it is argued) departure from modernist conceptions about the world. For Bauman, modernism can be characterized primarily by the attempt to impose structure on the physical and social universe. Modern society, he argues, arose from the "discovery that human order is vulnerable" (Bauman 1992: xi) and the response to that discovery, which was to " . . . problematise contingency as an enemy and order as a task . . . an incessant drive to eliminate the haphazard and annihilate the spontaneous . . . The dream of order and the practice of ordering constitute the world – their object – as chaos" (ibid.: xi).

"Postmodernity", for Bauman, is the abandonment of such efforts, and the denial of any one universal reason, and the acceptance of contingency. Others, such as Giddens (1991), have preferred the phrase "late" or "high" modernity to characterize contemporary developments in institutional forms, seeing in them the extension of modernist logic rather than a complete transformation of it. For Giddens, one of the central features of "high modernity" is the uncertainty it engenders in the individual. With a fracturing of any certainty about scientific explanations of the world, and a lack of consensus about what counts as "truth" or who can be trusted to deliver it, the individual is faced with an endless task of assessing opinion and making decisions in a rapidly changing environment. Thus high modernity is " . . . characterised by widespread scepticism about providential reason, coupled with the recognition that science and technology are double-edged . . . Such scepticism is not confined to the writings and ponderings of philosophers and intellectuals" (Giddens 1991: 28).

Scientific rationality, with its promise of potentially all-embracing explanation, comes to pose as many problems as it solves, and there is widespread doubt about the abilities of "experts" to provide solutions. Such doubts create anxiety, for we all become individually responsible for calculating the likely consequences of our actions, rather than merely relying on expert opinion to guide decisions. Not only has the pace of change increased, but the directions that it might take are unpredictable and uncertain. For Giddens, living in high modernity is like "riding a juggernaut" (Giddens 1991: 28). In Lyotard's (1986) phrase, the "grand narratives" of science are no longer legitimate and there is no consensus about the progress of human knowledge. Postmodern institutions are reflexive, in that they contribute to and construct the very objects they seek to describe. Thus sociology does not merely analyze the world (in, say, tracing shifting gender relations) but constructs it, as social actors act upon the "knowledge" produced.

It is not intended to contribute here to the debates about periodization, characterization or the possibilities of a "postmodern" sociology. They have been introduced, though, because there are two facets of those debates that have opened a space for the possibility of a sociology of accidents, and have implications for how it might proceed.

First, the role of "contingency" in these characterizations of modern and postmodern is an interesting one. If the modernist project was one of imposing order and (as Bauman suggests) banishing the random and disordered, then, at the most superficial level, accidents clearly have a problematic status as a legitimate object of study within modernist sociology, being by definition both random and unpredictable. It is, then, hardly surprising that there is no developed "sociology of accidents". However, if the experience of uncertainty and contingency is a widespread characteristic of postmodern society, then the accident (in its "modernist" construction), is surely the paradigmatic case of uncertainty, and there is now every incentive to examine how such uncertainty is understood and managed. In a "risk society" (Beck 1992), in which we are constantly engaged in assessing and managing risks in all areas of our lives, the accident is still the ultimate indicator that risk assessment has gone wrong. An exploration of how we reduce uncertainty from accidental causes will perhaps be a helpful example to illustrate the more general case of how such uncertainty is more widely managed.

Secondly, the debate about how to characterize postmodern society has raised political questions about the relationship between social institutions and the individual in contemporary society. These questions make possible an examination of apparently trivial activities such as "accident prevention". Foucault's notion of "governmentality", or the "conduct of conduct" (Gordon 1991: 2) is one account of how political relationships have shifted with the advent of neo-liberalism. In *Discipline and punish* (1979), Foucault contrasted two forms of power. The first was sovereign power, based on the monarch's absolute right to govern and evidenced in punishment such as torture, which destroyed the physical body. The second, "disciplinary" power, is a more pervasive, individualizing strategy of power, which operates upon bodies and populations through the mundane and trivial constitution of everyday activities such as the organization of the school room, prison, or medical examination. Governance in the late twentieth century depends not on power in the sovereign sense, but on disciplinary power. Foucault's account of power turns liberal assumptions about progress on their head: to reform the criminal rather than torture them, or to look after the mentally ill in the community rather than chain them in an asylum are not necessarily the marks of a more civilized, humane society. Instead, they are evidence of different discourses of power, in which "reform" aims to change and transform the criminal rather than destroy, as the subjects of reform are engaged in the work of their own transformation. The implications of this analysis of power for a study of accidents are that it becomes possible to see techniques such as accident prevention not as an inevitable development of epidemiological knowledge (and as such sociologically rather uninteresting), but as a strategy of power which produces individuals. At one level, engaging in accident prevention seems a mundane, even unquestionable, activity. Seen as an aspect of "governmentality" though, it becomes a route to examining how, through everyday risk management, we constitute ourselves as individuals in the late twentieth century.

Risk, modernity and misfortune: an outline of the argument

In exploring how accidents have come to be understood and managed in contemporary society, this book is, then, an exploration in the sociology of knowledge. As Berger and Luckman (1979) suggest in their classic treatise on *The social construction of reality*, such an enterprise ought to "*concern itself with everything that passes for 'knowledge' in society*" (Berger & Luckman 1979: 26, emphasis in original), and focus on "common sense" reality as well as professional theories of accidents and what they are. The concern is with how accidents have come to appear as an inevitable part of the universe in the late twentieth century: how they have been reified, in Berger and Luckman's term, as if "they were something other than human products" (Berger & Luckman 1979: 106). With a focus on how accidents "have come" to be understood, this book is also about transformations. Given that it is not inevitable that some misfortunes are classified as accidents, the first task is to identify the point at which they entered discourse: when it became possible to have an accident. Foucault describes the process of mapping points such as these as one of "rediscovering the connections, encounters, supports, blockages, plays of forces, strategies and so on which at any given moment establish what subsequently counts as being self-evident, universal and necessary." (Foucault 1991: 76).

In attempting to "rediscover" some of the clues to how accidents have come to be "self-evident, universal and necessary" in everyday talk in the late twentieth century, a number of clues have been followed up. Chapter 2 examines the literature on accidents in the social sciences. It is not a large literature, as the study of accidents has not been a legitimate one for classical sociology. In those discourses that do address accidents, such as Freudian psychology, or epidemiology, the accident is rendered "non-accidental", as a misfortune that was neither random nor unpredictable on serious reflection.

Chapter 3 examines the emergence of the accident in Western thought. At the end of the seventeenth century, accidents form a leftover category of misfortunes. They were the remnants of a cosmology that increasingly relied upon rational explanation and probability to describe the causation and distribution of misfortune. Accidents mark the boundary of explanatory power: some misfortunes "just happen", and there is no gain in examining them too closely. By the early twentieth century, in anthropology and developmental psychology, the existence of such a leftover category was definitional of a self-conscious rational modernity: to believe that "accidents just happen" was what separated the modern European adult from the child, the "primitive" and their medieval ancestors.

Medicine is one key discourse that situated the accident at the margins of what is known. Chapter 4 will trace the development of accidents as a nosological category, the growth in epidemiological interest and the social production of accident statistics. Although the ideal accident is essentially amoral (no-one meant it to happen), the production of medical knowledge about accidents is an inherently moral enterprise.

In the late twentieth century there has been a dramatic transformation in how accidents are classified, discussed and managed. Ideally, accidents should no longer happen. In an era of ever more sophisticated risk assessment, the accident apparently occupies a rather different conceptual space than it did in the first half of the century: as an event that is predictable, and ultimately preventable. The rise of health promotion, and its advocacy of "accident prevention", is one facet of this contemporary construction of accidents, which will be addressed in Chapter 5.

In Chapter 6 it is suggested that the emergence of a discourse of "risk" in the late twentieth century can illuminate both the transformation of the accident and the emergence of accident prevention. From being marginal misfortunes, accidents move centre stage in a "risk society", for they are both a sign of inadequate risk management and the ultimate problem upon which risk management can demonstrate its effectiveness.

Chapter 7 is a more grounded examination of how accidents are produced in everyday talk. Data from interviews and discussion groups are used to explore how "taken-for-granted" knowledge about accidents is created in social interaction, and how risk management produces not only a strategy for reducing accidents, but also a strategy for demonstrating social competence in the late twentieth century.

The accident is a key element in our classification of misfortune. Talk about accidents is commonplace, as a way of describing both events and causation. Television programmes about accidents are enormously popular in Britain, whether they focus on "true stories" of survivors or on the emergency services that deal with accidents. An increasing number of professionals claim some expertise in the management of accidents: health and safety officials, health promoters, risk assessors. In a society that is perhaps obsessed by risk and its management, the accident is central. That an accident has happened (whether in a nuclear reactor or a domestic kitchen) denotes that risk has not been adequately managed. That we hold an enquiry, set up new safety measures for nuclear power stations or install a cooker guard demonstrates our enduring faith in the possibilities of risk management to reduce accidents. Given the ubiquity of accidents and their importance to understanding the "risk society" in which we live, it is surprising that so few sociologists, even those writing specifically on risk, have addressed them explicitly. This book does not seek to redress this neglect, it is not a definitive sociology of accidents. It does, though, uncover some traces of the accident in what has been written over the last three hundred years and what is said today in order to examine transformations in the social construction of accidents. In that sense, this is offered as a step towards an archaeology of accidents.

Chapter 2

Accidents and social science

Introduction

Until recently, sociology has largely ignored accidents as a legitimate subject of study. This chapter explores the marginal place that accidents have had in both empirical research in sociology and in classical social theory, and suggests that this neglect is not mere coincidence but an inevitable outcome of the ways in which accidents have been constructed. When they have been studied, accidents have been redefined as "non-accidental", as something other than our initial working definition of random misfortunes in Chapter 1 suggested.

When the accident does appear in sociological writings, it is as a given, and the concern has been with how it is caused or how we react to it. The sociology of health and illness has largely been concerned with accidents tangentially, as marginal cases of disease. Although the sociology of health and illness has arguably taken its lead from medicine in its marginalization of accidents as legitimate objects of study, a more significant reason for this neglect lies perhaps in the historical concerns of social theory, which have been largely in the arenas of social life that are both patterned and motivated. As the accident is constructed as neither, it has had little place. More recently, sociological theory has focused on chance as a legitimate area of enquiry, most notably from a "postmodern" perspective. Accidents, in that they are constructed as a paradigmatic "chance" event, therefore become a legitimate subject of study. However, retrospective attempts to reconstruct a history of accidents prove rather problematic.

Large-scale accidents: disasters and the social distribution of knowledge

Disasters are one particular kind of accident that has received some attention from sociologists and organizational theorists. Barry Turner's study of disasters (Turner 1978) established a base for a social theory of accidents in his argument that such events could be understood through a study of how knowledge is socially distributed. Although noting that there was no precise definition of a disaster, he suggested that they would include specific types of accident, such as "an unusually large-scale accident, an unusually costly accident, an unusually public accident, an unusually unexpected accident, or . . . some combination of these properties" (Turner 1978: 26).

Another property of a disaster was that it was an event: "concentrated in time and space, which threatens society, or a relatively self-sufficient sub-division of a society, with major unwanted consequences as a result of the collapse of precautions that had hitherto been accepted as adequate" (Turner 1978: 62).

Traditionally, Turner claimed, social scientists had only been interested in such accidents as examples of social pathology: events that caused massive disruption to communities. The focus was on how communities coped with the aftermath, and the implication was that the factors contributing to the original accident were not a legitimate area for sociological study (Turner 1978: 39). Turner argued that a social understanding of these large-scale accidents was possible. Disasters are produced through an interaction of social, technical and organizational processes and arise from an absence of some kind of knowledge or, more specifically, from "disjunct information". Thus it was the social distribution of relevant knowledge that held the key to a social theory of disasters, which happen on the general principle that "disaster = energy + misinformation" (Turner 1978: 195).

He examined the preconditions of three disasters: the Aberfan tip collapse, the Hixon level crossing accident and the fire at the Summerland Leisure Centre. The knowledge needed to avoid all three disasters existed, claimed Turner, but was not distributed in a way that enabled it to be acted upon. Thus, the tribunal charged with inquiry into Aberfan noted that the knowledge about procedures necessary to stabilize tips had existed for years, but had been collectively neglected. In mining, attention was directed to the more clearly defined area of underground safety, distracting attention from above-ground hazards, such as unstable tips. The Hixon level crossing incident (in which a 150-ft vehicle took longer to cross a level crossing than the 24-second warning given of an oncoming train) happened despite, again, the availability of the knowledge needed to foresee such an eventuality. Although the knowledge about the time a long vehicle would take to cross a level crossing was known, it was not known by the same agencies responsible for setting the timed warning. Adequate knowledge was not concentrated in any individual who had the insight to foresee its possible implications.

Within such an explanatory framework, an understanding of the social distribution of knowledge and, by implication, ignorance is seen as the key to understanding causation. If accidents are seen as being caused by ignorance or error, it is not enough merely to identify inadequate knowledge, or irrational behaviour in the face of adequate knowledge about safety. A rather more sophisticated model of ignorance is needed. There have been attempts to theorize the social relations of production of that ignorance. As Smithson (1985) has noted, ignorance is not simply the absence of knowledge, but is socially produced. Workers, for instance, are encouraged to concentrate on only "relevant" information necessary for the performance of their occupational role and to avoid the distraction of "irrelevant" inputs. Knowledge itself is not always socially desirable. Tombs (1991), for instance, in his work on safety in the chemical industry, makes the point that managers may be reluctant to pass on information about shop floor hazards to workers because of fears about the political purposes to which such information might be put by trade union officials.

It may well be possible to analyze the causes of all large-scale disasters in terms of the social relations of the production of safety knowledge, and indeed inquiries into disasters routinely comment on the availability of knowledge about hazards and the inability of relevant managers to act on this information. The problem of accident prevention is thus often framed as one of better "management", and much of the commentary on disasters has been in the management literature (see for instance Ansell & Wharton 1992). Jackson and Carter (1992), drawing on Turner's work, comment on the 1986 case of the US space shuttle Challenger, which exploded 73 seconds after its launch. Investigation into this accident found that the knowledge needed to prevent it was not only known, but passed on to the management team responsible for the launch. Engineers had warned that the "O" ring seals in the rocket booster joints performed poorly in low temperatures, and should not be relied on if the seal temperature fell below 53°F. Although the night before the launch was a cool one, and the seal temperature was predicted to fall below this, the decision was made to continue with the launch, with tragic results (Jackson & Carter 1992: 50). This example illustrates the strength of "authoritative" beliefs about safety (held by the management team) and the difficulties in changing them. Simple "knowledge" about risks is not enough to prevent accidents; attention must also be paid to the political and social relations within which such knowledge is situated.

Jackson and Carter see closer attention to the social distribution of legitimate knowledge also as the key to more effective accident prevention. Using post-structuralist methods of textual deconstruction as a model, they suggest that a more pluralist approach to studying accidents in complex systems (such as the Challenger launch, or Turner's example of the Hixon level crossing) would avoid a "rational" emphasis on one, authoritative interpretation that excludes all others until it is proved (disastrously) wrong. A deconstructive approach, they argue, would provide "a safety net of competing interpretations, all of which are the subject of a test of plausibility and that can therefore be legitimated" (Jackson & Carter 1992: 52), so improving the chance that the potential failures of safety systems can be identified.

Are some disasters "inevitable"?

The "better management" argument presupposes that accidents can be prevented, if only enough safeguards are in place to ensure that information is translated into legitimate knowledge. Charles Perrow's argument undermines even this assumption. Perrow's (1984) argument went further than Turner's in his claim that accidents are not only analyzable in hindsight, but that they are predictable, even if the form they take may not be. Indeed in some systems they are "inevitable" or "normal". Systems, argued Perrow, can be modelled as consisting of six components known by the acronym DEPOSE; namely, Design, Equipment, Procedures, Operators, Supplies and Equipment & Environment. In some systems, these components display an "interactive complexity", in that there are many cross-cutting relationships between them, and the system is "tightly coupled", in that there is little slack to allow for shut-downs when one component fails. Accidents in such systems are not only possible, but inevitable. The relevant question then becomes not how they can be avoided, but whether the system in question (such as nuclear energy production) has benefits that are worth the risk. *Post hoc* construction of accident causation, notes Perrow, often identifies "operator error" as the cause, yet operators are often faced with the inevitable but unexpected and mysterious interaction of parts of the system for which they are unprepared. Indeed, with some complex systems, with many technical and organization components that could potentially interact, it would be impossible to prepare workers for all eventualities. It is only possible in retrospect to identify the preventative action that should have been taken. "Accident reconstruction" claimed Perrow "reveals the banality and triviality behind most catastrophes" (Perrow 1984: 9).

Perrow, in claiming that some accidents are inevitable (in folk wisdom, that there are "accidents waiting to happen"), is, however, almost a lone voice. In general, the literature on accidents has concentrated on the questions of why and how some accidents happen, as if they could have been avoided. As a general class of events accidents are represented as a given; a natural category, the constitution of which is obvious. The question of how and why some misfortunes become labelled as accidents has received less attention.

Accidents as a facet of capitalist relations of production

One notable exception is Karl Figlio (1985), who has attempted to account for the social category of accidents, rather than their causation. Figlio's argument was a broadly Marxist one: that the appearance of events that could be called accidents was intimately tied to the rise of capitalist relations of production. Accidents, he claimed, could not have happened before contractual working relationships developed, for they are essentially acts of negligence. Intentional injuries, where compensation could be claimed if motivation could be proved, have, Figlio claimed, a long history, but it was not until the Workmen's Compensation Act of 1897, which established routine procedures for claiming compensation for injuries caused during employment, that compensation could be claimed without proving malicious intent.

A transitional stage was a fatality requiring a "deodand" payment. This literally means "a gift to God", and was a forfeit paid to the Crown to the value of the object found to be "responsible" for the fatality, which could be an inanimate object or an animal. It persisted in English law until the early nineteenth century when it was reputedly abolished because of the large payments potentially arising from railway accidents (Jervis 1986: 3), although it had virtually fallen into disuse by the nineteenth century. Figlio sees the fatality requiring a deodand payment as "an ambiguous accident, unforeseen and not malicious, yet somehow implying intent". Before the rise of industrialism there was a belief, argued Figlio, that everything had a cause, so there could logically be no merely "accidental" occurrences. Once the idea of negligence had entered master-servant law in the nineteenth century, replacing notions of complete responsibility, it became possible, Figlio argued, to conceive of the notion of an accidental injury. The concept of "negligence" enabled outcomes that were not directly and maliciously intended still to be held as someone's responsibility; in short, accountability became divorced from culpability. One could be responsible for injuries to another without having deliberately meant them to happen. Within a "contract" relationship, events such as injuries in the workplace could be seen as the result of negligence of contractual obligations as well as motivated action, and the notion of an "accident", which was not intended to happen, but for which responsibility could be apportioned, became possible.

Others have also assumed a linkage between the notion of an accident and the history of economic relations. In her study of disability Blaxter (1976), for instance, claims "there may be no practical difference in condition between a man . . . whose chronic back pain is due to a lifetime's manual work and one whose back injury is caused by a single identifiable accident" but "for reasons concerned with the economic value of the work ethic . . . most industrialized societies have chosen to treat the work injured rather differently from the rest" (Blaxter 1976: 183). For the respondents in Blaxter's study of people with disabilities, such differences were a source of problems, as similar injuries were compensated by different benefits, depending on what the cause was found to be, and some of those who were disabled as a result of workplace "accidents" were reluctant to accept the relevance of concepts such as negligence or fault (Blaxter 1976: 186). Turner (1989) also examined the relationship between relations of production and the notion of accidents, but turned Figlio's causal relation on its head. In charting the rise of the managerial class in Australian mines, she tied the emergence of this new class to a new discourse of safety that arose at the end of the nineteenth century. This new discourse centred on the visible bodies of miners, making it essential that they could be seen and their safety ensured at all times, necessitating a managerial function concerned with monitoring and co-ordinating this visibility. The discourse of safety, and an associated one of accidental injury, was not merely the result of new forms of managerial surveillance but one that altered the relations of production within mining, establishing a new alliance of managers with the capitalist class and differentiating them from the labourers.

Whether it is claimed that industrial relations of production enabled us to conceptualize accidents or that, conversely, a discourse of safety was a facet of emergent industrial relations, there is perhaps a problem in this terminological slippage from "accident" to "industrial injury". It becomes tautological to argue that industrial injuries could only happen once industrial modes of production were established, even if the processes and ideologies surrounding those connections may be fertile ground for research. Focusing exclusively on one kind of accident risks begging the question: "why were such injuries categorized specifically as accidents?" Figlio's essay opened the field of enquiry into the social construction of accidents, charted the inclusion of industrial injuries into the larger group of misfortunes that we call accidents and analyzed the shift in ideas of responsibility, with the inclusion of negligence as an act of responsibility. These new departures described by Figlio (1985) and Turner (1989) do not, though, account for the place accidents have had in our classificatory frameworks of misfortune. The comments of Blaxter's respondents suggest that we still distinguish acts for which no blame can reasonably be apportioned from others, even if the former category has been shrunk, at least in legal terms, by the removal of negligent acts. These are the events that are (at least provisionally) labelled as "accidents", and they form a set which is larger than that of industrial injuries. Understanding how accidents are constructed as a category of misfortune may involve more than an account of how negligence is constructed in legal discourses.

The accident as a marginal category of disease

A considerable proportion of the events we classify as accidents results in injury, and has implications for our health. If there is no recognizable "sociology of accidents" as yet, with the few exceptions noted above, there is a thriving sociology of health and illness which could perhaps serve as a starting point to an exploration of the social construction of at least these accidents. A thorough review of work in the field of health and illness is outside the scope of this book, but there are three traditions in the discipline that might suggest it had something to say about the social construction of accidents.

Social constructionism and lay health beliefs

The first tradition is social constructionism. During the 1980s, the sociology of health and illness was characterized by a growing trend towards social constructionism (Bury 1986). This involved first a problematizing of medical reality (Wright & Treacher 1982: 9), in which the objects of medical knowledge (such as parts of anatomy or diseases) were seen not as natural categories, discovered and explained by medicine, but as products of medical practice. So disease categories such as asthma (Gabbay 1982) or mental illness (Ingleby 1982) are examined not as static concepts with an external reality, but as products of the social relations of medicine.

Related to this, a second tradition in medical sociology is an interest in "lay" accounts of health and illness. If professional medical accounts of disease have no privileged place as descriptions of reality, then it becomes possible to see lay accounts as equally rational conceptions of the world, rather than mistaken or ill-informed beliefs. There is a considerable body of work on general lay health and illness beliefs, and there have been some social scientific analyses of professional discourses about accidents: Cooter's (1993) work on how the emergent medical specialty of orthopaedics came to take an interest in accidents, for instance, or Scheppele's arguments about tort law and accidents (Scheppele 1991). But, with the exception of the work of Helen Roberts and her co-workers (Roberts et al. 1992, 1993), there has been little on how accidents are constructed in everyday life.

In terms of examining how illnesses are constructed in everyday life, a useful starting point might be the approach adopted by Cornwell (1984a, 1984b) in her study of "public" and "private" lay accounts of illness. Cornwell noted that ideas of fate, destiny and luck were as important to her respondents as biomedical explanations in accounting for the experience of illness. Although, in general, good health was constructed as a morally worthy state and ill health as discreditable, the moral content of the illness depended on the circumstances: whether it was internally or externally caused; whether it was avoidable or unavoidable and whether blame could be attached. For those illnesses that were unavoidable and to which no blame was attached, explanations centred on luck, fate and destiny: good health was a coincidence. In these accounts, accidents appear to have a rather ambivalent status. First, they are ambiguous categories of ill health, being not strictly "illnesses", which meant that moral attribution was potentially problematic. However, as a category of health problems that were externally caused, Cornwell claims that accidents were "not problematic, in the sense that it was not difficult for people to admit to having had them . . . [their] 'otherness' could be taken for granted" (Cornwell 1984a: 189).

In Cornwell's study, accidents are only a marginal category of the misfortunes her respondents discuss, but her approach does suggest at least that the features which characterize accidents can be examined as ways of understanding the world, rather than as misconceptions. Despite Cornwell's assertion that accidents are "not problematic" they emerge as rather ambiguous: incurring perhaps a morally discredited state in "public" accounts yet not in themselves blameworthy. In private accounts, Cornwell's respondents did not differentiate disabilities resulting from accidents, such as workplace injuries, from those resulting from other illnesses.

Health and moral meaning: the accident as an ideal disease

Cornwell's study also raises the important issue of how moral meaning attaches to misfortune. This is the third theme in the sociology of health and illness that has some bearing on the sociology of accidents. Illness, as an arena of moral debate, has received considerable attention in research. In his classic study on the moral meaning of illness, Zola (1972), for instance, reported that students described illness with terms loaded with ideas about moral responsibility: "on nearly every level, from getting sick to recovery, a moral battle raged". This construction of illness as "moral battle" has been reviewed as metaphor by Sontag in her work on the symbolic meanings of cancer and tuberculosis (1979) and more recently AIDS (1989). According to Sontag, the notion of cancer as a "moral battle" derives from the metaphors that surround the illness. The word "cancer" is a metaphor for insidious evil that, she argues, renders the disease as equated with the sufferer. Comparing the "myths" that surrounded tuberculosis in the nineteenth century, which constructed the symptoms to be expressive of the sufferer's personality (sensitive, refined, interesting and therefore romantic), she argued that in the late twentieth century cancer is seen to be the outcome of certain personality traits, rather being an expression of them. Thus "the cancer personality is regarded, more simply, and with more condescension, as one of life's losers" (Sontag 1979: 49). These metaphors, she argued, are as punitive as ancient concepts of illness as punishment for wrongdoing, and they are essentially dysfunctional: "the healthiest way of being ill is the one most purified of metaphorical thinking" (Sontag 1979: 4).

If we accept the social constructionist argument that there is no essential reality of disease (whether cancer or AIDS) and that these categories are products of specific social practices, it is difficult to envisage the domain of illness being "stripped" of its metaphoric meanings, as these in part create our understandings of disease. However, in her attention to the specific meanings of certain illnesses, Sontag pointed to the potentially infinite range of moral meanings that could attach to illness. Zola's respondents talked largely about infectious disease, and here there is some evidence to suggest that illness resulting from this kind of disease is no longer constructed in moral terms, or at least not so starkly as Zola suggested. Pill and Stott (1982), in contrast, suggested that germ theory was now the dominant ideology of causation and responsibility for the lay public, despite efforts of health educators to persuade people to feel more responsible for their own illness and health. Unlike Zola's American students, their working-class British respondents did not see illness in terms of blame and responsibility. Pill and Stott attributed this contrast in part to the provision of free health care at the point of delivery in Britain, but more significantly as an inevitable result of a generation of propaganda around the success of antibiotics in halting the epidemic diseases that were prevalent before the Second World War. Germ theory is essentially an "amoral" theory, in that germs are seen to be random, and no responsibility can be attributed to the ill.

This is the classic Parsonian model of modern illness – a state that is undesirable, but which incurs no moral culpability and towards which the physician is ideally to be "value neutral", his or her role being "specifically limited to concern with matters of health" (Parsons 1951b). The ideal physician relates to patients in terms of their symptoms and prognosis, rather than any personal attributes (Gerhardt 1979). This Parsonian model of the physician's role has been criticized as limited (Szasz & Hollander 1956, Gallagher 1976), romantic (Frankenberg 1974) and as primarily reflecting the physician's idealistic account (Bloor & Horobin 1975). Furthermore, empirical research in a number of settings suggests it has little validity as a depiction of the reality of medical encounters: Roth (1972) and Jeffrey (1979), for instance, describe the explicit moral evaluations made of accident and emergency department attenders, and Daniels (1987) describes how the bureaucratic environment in which military psychiatrists work constrains their exercise of morally neutral medicine. Despite the many and varied critiques, and more recent reformulations (Gerhardt 1979) it is, though, a model that apparently still holds some force as a normative ideal, against which these physicians found in research and in practice are measured. The "ideal" doctor still separates moral views from the provision of clinical care, and there is an enduring myth that matters such as medicine and hygiene in modern society are to do with the rational control of disease rather than the moral and social order (see for instance Douglas 1984: 29). This very neutrality is seen as evidence of the progress of Western medicine and its maturity as a science, and individual physicians who express moral censure do so at risk of public and professional isolation. As an example, the profession's response to HIV infection and AIDS in Britain, and to a lesser extent, the United States, is illustrative. Despite the view that there has been a "moral panic" (see, for instance, Patton 1985: 12), the public reaction of the medical profession has been cautious and characterized by an anxiety not to appear morally judgemental, under the rationalization that such judgements may "drive the disease underground" (Bayer et al. 1986, Smith 1987). Research and debate centres on risk factors, epidemiology, prevention and cure, and although the media coverage may engage in a moral debate in contrasting "innocent victims" and "blameworthy carriers", we would not expect the medical profession to endorse such views in public. We are still, by and large, disturbed by clinicians who do not match Parson's value-neutral ideal – by the surgeon who refuses to treat smokers or the dentist who refuses to treat children who eat too many sweets (Bunting 1994). In an ideal medical encounter, we expect to be judged solely on medical, not moral, criteria.

This is not, of course, to suggest that medicine does not have a sophisticated role in constructing and reinforcing moral boundaries, and indeed there has been much debate about this aspect of the medical profession in terms of its social control function (see, for example, Szasz 1961; Zola

1972, 1975; Illich 1976). Rather, it is merely to suggest that there is an enduring normative construction of medicine as morally neutral, and illness, at least in "public" accounts, as being the result of chance factors ("germs") as well as heredity, environment and behaviour (or "lifestyle"). Despite the rise in what Crawford has called "victim blaming ideologies" which hold the sufferer, rather than external social factors to be responsible for illness (Crawford 1986), we are not often (at least not yet) held accountable for our illnesses, even if we may be seen as sometimes culpable of contributory negligence.

Within such a normative account of medicine as rational and value-neutral, the accident may appear initially to be the ideal medical misfortune. In terms of the way in which accidents are apparently defined (as unmotivated and unpredictable), impaired health arising from accidental injury ought to be an "ideal" illness. Indeed, Figlio (1985) has suggested that the accident forms an archetypal model for modern understandings of illnesses.

Within Cornwell's, and others', accounts of lay beliefs though, accidents are suggested as being morally rather more ambiguous. In general they have been constructed as marginal to ideas about health and illness, which are the central concerns of medical sociology. The reasons for this focus may lie partly in the continuing dependence of medical sociology on the structures of Western medicine: we have no "sociology of misfortune" that might include an examination of the accidental, but a "sociology of health and illness" within which the accident occupies a similar place as it does in nosology. In these terms accidents are reduced to injuries, with research concerned with how medical and psychological causes and sequelae are managed and conceptualized.

The dominance of medicine over the substantive concerns of medical sociology cannot, however, be held solely to blame for the neglect of the accident in social theory, and it is worth reviewing the origins of some of sociology's "core theory" in order to examine some of the theoretical disincentives to the development of such a study. Classical sociology was concerned with questions of social order – how was society possible? It was also concerned with demonstrating that answers to these questions could be found through rigorous study, modelled on the emergent "rationality" of the natural sciences. Many of the founders of modern sociology were "self-consciously rational" (Wilson 1970: 1) and sociology has been overtly, and perhaps inevitably, concerned with providing rational explanations for the behaviour of people (agency), the ordering of societies (structure) and the relationships between the two. Popper (1960) is possibly a notable exception, in his argument against what he called "historicism" in the social sciences. He advocated a less ambitious role for sociology, with a focus on "a more detailed analysis of the logic of situations" (Popper 1960: 149), given his belief that the "human or personal factor will remain the irrational element in most, or all, social institutions" (ibid.: 157). However, Popper's advocacy of a "piecemeal social engineering" (ibid.: 67) role for sociology (in contrast to that of elucidating laws of social development) came from outside the discipline and perhaps has had little intrinsic appeal for social theorists. Until recently, the concerns of grand theory have been of structures and patterns. The "accidental", almost by definition, has been largely perceived as meaningless as a type of social action because it is unmotivated, and as irrelevant as explanation of events. Medical sociology may have developed no adequate theory of misfortune for our purposes, but the main traditions of social theory have provided little incentive.

Social theory and the accident

Durkheim and the positivist tradition

To begin with the classic example of Durkheim's more positivist writings, it is difficult to see what part the accidental could play. Part of the Durkeimian project, for instance, was explicitly concerned with uncovering social laws to make sense of social behaviour. Although Durkheim was concerned with supposedly "irrational" facets of social behaviour such as religion and suicide, his concern was to demonstrate regularities at the social level that rendered individual irrationality comprehensible, and his methodological premises have no room for the accidental. Durkheim claimed that "our principle objective is to extend scientific rationalism to human behaviour. It can be shown that the behaviour of the past, when analyzed, can be reduced to relationships of cause and effect" (Durkheim 1950: xxxix).

The capricious accident can furnish no useful data for such a project. Although *The rules of sociological method* (1950) represent only a small, and perhaps atypical, part of Durkheim's work, the sentiments expressed here have had an enduring impact on the positivist tradition. Durkheim's sociology here and in *Suicide* (1963) relied on the kind of vital statistics that were well established by the end of the nineteenth century. Social facts, he claimed, were:

> represented with considerable exactness by the rates of births, marriages and suicides, that is by the number obtained by dividing the average annual total of marriages, births and suicides by the number of persons whose ages lie in the range in which births, marriages and suicides occur. Since each of these figures contains all the individual cases indiscriminately, the individual circumstances that might have had a share in the production of the phenomena are neutralized and, consequently, do not contribute to its determination. The average, then, expresses a certain state of the group mind. (Durkheim 1950: 8)

Those that do not reveal such objectivity of observation are presumably not worthy of further investigation. The vital statistics available to Durkheim did not include the sophisticated analyses of accident rates that were produced from the middle of the twentieth century, but since then there has of course been considerable scope for a positivist sociological analysis of accidental injuries in terms of such social division as class, gender and ethnicity. These studies have been largely the domain of epidemiologists and, as we will see in Chapter 5, the rise of epidemiology in the second half of the twentieth century was tied to the presentation of accidents as not really "accidents" in that they were as predictable on an aggregate level as any disease.

The few exceptions in sociology have also explicitly challenged the concept of accidents as random, morally neutral misfortunes. In the debate about how far workplace accident rates can be seen as indicators of economic recession, for instance, such events have been referred to as "industrial injuries", to indicate that there is nothing "accidental" about their causation (see Nichols 1989, 1991; Tombs 1990, 1992). The accident has to be reconceptualized as something "other" before it can be used in any positivist sociological enquiry. In the tradition of Durkheim, apparently accidental events will only reveal their structured causes after appropriate investigation: "facts most arbitrary in appearances will come to present, after more attentive observation, qualities of consistency and regularity that are symptomatic of their objectivity" (Durkheim 1950: 28). It is at this point, though, that they cease to become accidents.

Weber and Pareto

If our concern is with an exploration of the meaning of accidents and with how they are constructed as a category of misfortune, then the Weberian tradition in sociology could perhaps more reasonably be expected to provide a theoretical starting point, as Weber is the theorist associated with an approach that centred on understanding meaning as it is constructed by social actors. Given the suggestion that accidents are somehow defined outside the bounds of rational behaviour and understanding, Weber's problematization of rationality (Wilson 1970; Schroeder 1987) may perhaps be helpful. However, a major legacy of Weber's work has been a prioritization of the rational as an essential feature of the modern world and a conceptualization of non-rational behaviour or belief as characteristic of pre-modern society or as simply uninteresting as a subject of social enquiry. Belief in accidental cause appears as anachronistic within a modern rational cosmology, an example of merely ritualistic action in that it does not constitute proper social action. Action is only properly social, Weber claimed, "in so far as, by virtue of the subjective meaning attached to it by the acting individual (or individuals), it takes account of the behaviour of others, and is thereby orientated in its course" (Weber 1978: 4). Only action so orientated is seen as a fruitful object of sociological inquiry. Accidents, by definition, do not result from this kind of motivated behaviour and describing a misfortune as an "accident" rules it outside the bounds of an outcome of rational calculations. Characterizing modernity as rational, and characterizing rationality as an economic cost-benefit calculus, renders the accident a leftover; an event of little interest.

It is, however, not enough to associate Weberian sociology merely with an interest in understanding social action and with modern rationality. Sica (1988) has claimed that Weber was much interested in the place of irrationality in social life, at times giving primacy to notions such as personality and erotic love that exist in tension with rational incentives, but that later theorists such as Parsons have neglected this area of his work. Sica argues that this neglect, together with the relative neglect of Pareto's writings on the irrational, have impoverished social theory. "With Vilfredo Pareto's death in 1923", he claims, "the century's last major social theorist to set irrational factors as central to communal life was silenced" (Sica 1988: 1). Pareto was concerned to rehabilitate the "accidental" in social life, as a reaction to macro theory (specifically Marxism) that aimed to explain short-term change and behaviour as well as broader social change: "The notion that great historical occurrences are attributable to small personal causes is now almost wholly discarded, but it is frequently replaced by another error, that of denying the individual any influence at all on circumstances" (Pareto 1976: 123).

Our concern to attribute rationality to all human decision-making results, argued Pareto, in *post hoc* rationalizations of what are essentially sentiment: "a large number of human actions are not the outcome of reasoning. They are purely instinctive actions . . ." (Pareto 1976: 124). Like instinctive actions, accidents apparently "just happen", but possibly with far-reaching social consequences. Theoretically, though, events that "just happen" are not amenable to analysis. At the moment they are analyzed and mapped on to a pattern, they cease to be accidents.

Sica argues that the neglect of Pareto's work on the place of the irrational in social life, at least in North American sociology, has as much to do with extra-intellectual causes as with quality of scholarship. Whereas Weber was concerned to make his ideas accessible through seminars and popular lectures, Pareto was more introverted, and suffered from purported associations with Fascism in Italy. The neglect of Weber's more sophisticated work on irrational influences is attributed to the difficulty in reading many of his works and the fact that the interest was never made explicit, but can only be inferred from the tension in the writing and biographical knowledge. Although Weber did prioritize the "irrational" as a force for change (in, for instance, his notion of "charisma"), his legacy has been the study of social behaviour as rational behaviour, and a placing of rationality at the heart of the modern. The result of this somewhat biased legacy, claims Sica, is that sociology and non-experimental psychology have not "assumed their rightful place as interpreters of all social behaviour that surfaces within modern societies. They remain fixed too securely to a scholastic vision, leaving interpretation of the most interesting (which often means non-rationalized) behaviour to theologians, psychiatrists and journalists . . ." (Sica 1988: 30). Thus, he argues, such questions as why people might behave in apparently irrational ways, or what factors contribute to making life meaningful have been neglected, although they are potentially legitimate areas of sociological interest. One such area is the accident.

As a specific category of misfortune, then, the accident seems to have been neglected: considered by definition, and inevitably, not worthy of proper sociological enquiry. Any positivistic enquiry, in the spirit of Durkheim, relies on an argument that accidents are not accidents: in aggregate, they are patterned and predictable. Any sociological enquiry rooted in a Weberian empathetic sociology is a nonsense, as "accidents" cannot constitute meaningful action. In academic study the meaning of the personal and individual misfortune is undermined: for it is demonstrably not unique, nor should it have been unexpected.

Freud and the non-accidental accident

If positivist sociology has, at least partially, undermined one assumed element of the lay construction of accidents (their unpredictability as random, individual misfortunes), then the Freudian tradition in psychological theory has explicitly challenged the other: their lack of motivation. In his work on mishaps, losses and "slips of the tongue" (the accidents of everyday life and of speech), Freud argued that the minor mishaps that we label meaningless and accidental are signs of the ordered rational workings of the unconscious: they are only superficially "accidental", with the real meaning lying beneath the surface to be revealed by the analyst. The most mundane of everyday mishaps can be rendered meaningful through an examination of unconscious motives: "Whoever forgets articles in the doctor's office, such as eye glasses, gloves, handbags generally indicates that he cannot tear himself away and is anxious to return soon" (Freud 1938: 155f.).

The "real" meaning of this apparently accidental event is that the patient wishes to remain with their analyst. The losses of personal possessions dear to us are not trivial accidents but are the effects of the unconscious working out perhaps difficult relationships or represent the manipulation of meaningful symbols. This attribution of rationality to the seemingly irrational is, for Freud, a comfort: "It is consoling to think that the 'losing of objects' by people is merely the unsuspecting extension of a symptomatic action, and is thus welcome at least to the secret intention of the loser" (Freud 1938: 154).

That the inexplicable has been brought within the realm of the explicable is an advance in knowledge: for Freud, there can be no mere coincidences left to clutter a universal explanatory framework. "Slips of the tongue", apparently accidental mistakes in spoken language, likewise reveal more meaning than the patternings of superficially correct speech:

> in the psychotherapeutic procedure which I employ in the solution and removal of neurotic symptoms, I am often confronted

31

> with the task of discovering from the accidental utterances and
> fancies of the patient the thought contents, which, though striving
> for concealment, nevertheless unintentionally betray themselves.
> (Freud 1938: 64)

Thus proper names with unpleasant associations may be forgotten,
or substitutions made (such as "mother" for "sister") that reveal unconscious, and therefore more "truthful" attitudes or desires. Although this
explanation of "Freudian slips" has entered lay theories of accident causation, it seems doubtful whether it has changed the definitions that operate
to include or exclude events from the category of accidents. It has merely
excluded a certain group of happenings from the category; we may cease
to see as accidents that for which there is now a rational causal explanation, even if that explanation relies on appeal to unconscious motivation.
As the Freudian unconscious has become part of lay theories of causation
it has become possible to see motivation as being hidden from the actor.
Denial of motivation is no longer enough to make a successful claim for a
speech accident to have happened (indeed the very denial might furnish
definitive proof of unconscious motivation). Denial merely places the
speech accident on the negotiable boundary space of morally loaded and
motivated actions.

Injuries as well as speech accidents are evidence of unconscious motivation. Freud is quite clear on the implications of his view for treatment of
the sufferer: "When a member of my family complains that he or she has
bitten his tongue, bruised her finger, and so on, instead of the expected
sympathy I put the question, 'why did you do that?'" (Freud 1938: 131).

If the "accident" is not really an "accident", victims cannot expect the
sympathy normally due to those who cannot be held responsible for their
injury. The Freudian legacy meant that accidental injuries could be seen
not as the random outcomes of coincidence, but as demonstrations of
underlying unconscious thought processes. Such unconscious motivations
could be those of the accident victim, as in this analyst's report: "The only
way in which Allan could get relief from his guilt was by inviting punish-
ments and hurts from outside . . . he became accident-prone" (Wolff
1969: 88).

Equally, though, we could be the victim of some other agent's unconscious:

> A patient, while driving to work . . . suddenly struck an elderly
> man with his left, front fender and knocked him to the ground . . .

On the basis of his associations to the various circumstances of what happened, it was possible to discover that the chief, unconscious, motive for the mishap was the patient's wish to destroy his father. (Brenner 1964: 293)

Such analyses have had perhaps little effect on the field of accident research, even if they persist in the psychoanalytic literature. An editorial comment, preceding the paper from which the above quote was taken, suggested that such work may be difficult to integrate with the rising epidemiological approach in medicine, in that it was anecdotal, and not supported by "rigorous and systematic research . . . [and] controls are non-existent" (Haddon et al. 1964). Freud's work may have shifted the boundaries of the accidental in everyday discourse (for instance, using the name of one's previous lover to the new one may no longer be forgivable as a purely accidental utterance) but it does not seem to have dispersed the category of events that are deemed to be accidental, as Brenner (1964) claimed it might. This approach could be seen as an attempt to make the unpredictable in some way predictable; providing rational meaning for the seemingly irrational. However, in everyday discourse there is still a heterogeneous group of events that, with a workable consensus, we agree to categorize as "real" accidents: events with no motivation and that can be understood only as random misfortunes.

Remedying neglect?

This brief review of the place of accidents and the accidental in various disciplines (organizational theory, medical sociology, classical social theory and the Freudian tradition in psychology) has suggested perhaps a "neglect" that can now be remedied as we have identified a gap in the literature. In Chapter 1, it was suggested that the development of a "postmodern" sociology in the late twentieth century had made it possible to study accidents: that the rationalist assumptions of sociology's core had been fractured by a questioning of such "grand theory".

One aspect of these shifts has been an attempt to accommodate chance as a legitimate area for enquiry in sociological theory. Smith (1993) reviews the major traditions in social theory, particularly Weberian ones, and concludes that chance (like the accidental) has been treated as a residual category. From the 1980s onwards, though, he claims, the work of writers such as Foucault and Giddens has recognized the potential importance of chance as an explanatory concept. He attributes the shift in focus to the undermining of the structural functionalist consensus in sociology in the 1960s and to a renewed interest in the mechanisms of change rather than stability. From the middle of the 1970s "late modernity" provided an added incentive, in terms of both the cultural environment and methodologies developed to understand that environment. The cultural factors are those of fragmentation, with an attendant focus on difference and ambiguity. Smith argues that chance itself becomes a more significant feature when there are fewer certainties to describe social life. Furthermore, sociologists, in reacting to these new "conditions for chance" have developed more flexible approaches that must encompass the fragmentary and arbitrary in social life, as well as the patterned and structured elements that were reviewed above. Foucault (1984), for instance, is cited as elaborating a conceptual framework within which chance holds a dominant place, and Smith quotes examples of recent work that has involved chance as an explanatory variable.

So if chance is no longer a residual category, how has it been conceptualized? Social chance, argues Smith, refers not to the merely random or coincidental nature of much social life as it is actually experienced, but to what he refers to as "unforeseen chance". This combines the unforeseen impacts of causal sequences and the unforeseen consequences of interactions. A sociology of chance, he implies, is properly concerned with the social distribution of such events: in what circumstances are unforeseen consequences likely to arise, and which developmental processes are they likely to generate? Accepting chance as a legitimate explanatory concept does not, he argues, deny the significance of structure or agency, but rather adds to them, to produce a more adequate model of social development.

An archaeology of accidents

The implications of such a sociology, in which "chance" events such as accidents are integrated into social explanation, are potentially rather disturbing. Accidents, perhaps, retain a power to disturb simply as a reminder of the limits of rational cosmologies, and of our tenuous control over the worlds that they describe. Rorty (1986) finds in this a more fundamental reason for the neglect of accident and accidental explanation in social theory. In reviewing Foucault's *Archaeology of knowledge*, he suggests that if we do as Foucault bids, and "accept the introduction of chance as a category in the production of events" (Foucault 1972: 23, quoted by Rorty 1986: 48), then this would provide a glimpse of an impossible, or at least untenable, culture:

> If we once could feel the full force of the claim that our present discursive practices were given neither by God, nor intuition of essence nor by cunning of reason, but *only* by chance, then we would have a culture that lacked not only a theory of knowledge, not only a sense of progress, but *any* source of what Nietzsche called "metaphysical comfort". (Rorty 1986: 48, emphasis in original)

Rorty is perhaps taking an extreme view of the consequences of a Foucauldian "archaeology", which rejects any notion of progress, or continuity, or the search for historical origins, but it is one shared by critics of social constructionism. Writing on the sociology of health and illness, Bury notes, for instance, the danger that "reality is portrayed as a contingent and haphazard affair" (Bury 1986) in such accounts.

However, an examination of "accidental" causes does not necessarily preclude a theory of knowledge, but merely encourages a scepticism about any assumed "causal" or evolutionary progression. What is suggested here is not a prioritization of the accidental as determinant of social life, but rather an examination of the rules by which some events or causes have been relegated to the status of "accidental". The very act of observing a group of accidents dissolves them, in either the statistical patterning of epidemiological enquiry, or in a Freudian search for meaning. We only observe the apparently irrational in order to discover the rational "true" motivation, whether in the spirit of Durkheim, or that of structuralist theory, which attempts to uncover deep patternings underpinning superficial discontinuities. Until recently there has been no place in social theory to take the accident as a legitimate category of misfortune and examine its place in the way we make sense of the world. Rather than seeing the accident as epiphenomenal of a deeper rationality or as irrelevant in the grand sweep of social explanations, it might be helpful to focus on the accident itself as an ideal type of event: that which, by consensus, is morally neutral and that lies both outside the bounds of rational explanation and on the boundary of our concerns about health and illness.

Smith's outline of what could be called the rehabilitation of chance in sociology is an interesting one, which suggests accidents as a significant set of what we choose to define as "chance" events. In some ways it serves perhaps as a belated answer to Popper's call for a less ambitious project for sociology that accounts for the specifics of social situations, including the personal element. However, it does raise the question of how certain events or outcomes come to be defined as "chance". To argue that chance events are somehow a more central feature of our cultural life in late modernity and that therefore sociological theory must, if it is to be useful and relevant, encompass it, risks a rather circular argument, for it is impossible to test empirically whether chance has become more significant or whether by theorizing it, we make it so. Sociology is one discourse that helps produce "late modernity", with its fragmentation and ambiguity, and can logically have no privileged position in accounting for how it is constituted. It thus becomes rather difficult to argue, as above, that the accident has been "neglected" in traditional social theory, as this supposes there was a pre-existing category of "chance" events, produced by some other discourse.

So, at one level, it appears that there has been a neglect of the accidental as a lay category of misfortune in the social sciences. The two features that apparently describe accidents in lay discourse (their unpredictability and their moral neutrality) have been explicitly challenged in the professional accounts of psychology, and marginalized in classical sociological theory. Only in more recent sociological writings has there been a legitimate space to analyze events constructed as "chance" happenings. However, there is a logical problem with merely characterizing the silence of earlier literatures as "neglect", as this implies that accidents somehow exist outside discourse, as a "natural" category, regardless of how social actors choose to classify or analyze them. An examination of attempts to construct a "history" of accidents indicates how problematic such a notion of remedying the neglect might be.

Reconstructing medieval misfortunes

The interpretation of one historical source – evidence from the coroners' courts of medieval London – may illustrate the difficulties of such assumptions. A "history" of accidents might start with an attempt to trace the events we would label as accidents today in terms of how they were classified and conceptualized in earlier periods. Sharpe's transcriptions (Guildhall MS 126) and translations (Guildhall MS 126, Sharpe 1913) of the calendar of fourteenth-century coroners' rolls from the City of London are one example of such a project, in that they provide some information on one particular group of misfortunes, those of people found *ex alia morte quam recta morte sua* ("lying dead of a death other than their rightful death"), for whom a coroner and jury had to be called. In early English law, it has been argued, the overriding principle was of compensation, rather than punishment or reform: a wrong was not a wrong because it was inherently immoral, but because it caused a loss to someone else, and must be compensated. The reform of the subject was not at issue, only the peace of a community potentially disrupted by an act such as theft or injury. Holdsworth (1936: 51) has claimed that it was not until the thirteenth century that morality became a significant issue. Until then, intent was not relevant, but rather the consequences (intended or other) of one's actions. The law, as Holdsworth put it, was "regarding not the culpability of the actor, but the feelings of the injured person whose sufferings may be traced ultimately to the act" (ibid.: 52). There was, therefore, no logical need for the law to differentiate accidental injuries from "purposeful" ones. If an act led (however indirectly) to an injury, the actor was responsible for recompensing the injured or their kin and their motivation was not at issue. Culpability extended also to material possessions and animals, and these could be held "responsible" for a death, in that a particular object or animal constituted the immediate cause. In such cases, their value could be deemed "deodand", or payable to the Crown as "compensation" to God. Anything moving could be held deodand, including weapons used to murder, or objects that caused fatal injuries.

Elements of this earlier compensation principle are still in evidence in Sharpe's translation of the fourteenth-century coroners' rolls, although Hunnisett (1961: 21) claims that by then the coroner had a duty to distinguish felonious and other fatalities, and that those caused by misadventure would "invariably" result in a pardon for the person found responsible, although this would require a further enquiry (ibid.: 77). Although this suggests a legal discourse of morality and intent, within which the accidental would have a place as explanation of events that were not intended, it is perhaps unhelpful to fall into the trap of seeing here echoes of our modern obsession with a specifically moral enquiry. As Foucault has warned, in another context (that of uncovering knowledge about wealth), it is misleading to extrapolate backwards towards supposed origins on the basis of superficial similarities:

> ... there does exist in the seventeenth and eighteenth centuries a notion that is still familiar to us today, though it has lost its essential precision for us. But "notion" is not really the word we should apply to it ... it is more a matter of a general domain ... this domain is that of *wealth*. It is useless to apply to it questions deriving from a different type of economics ... useless also to analyze its various concepts ... without taking into account the system from which they draw their positivity ... We must therefore avoid a retrospective reading ... (Foucault 1989: 168)

To avoid a "retrospective reading" of these misfortunes it might, then, be more productive to avoid a chronological exercise in identifying early examples of accidents and attempt instead to account for the essential dimensions of this medieval classification of misfortunes.

The case of Elyas Ide illustrates the problems of a retrospective reading. This seaman, having drunk considerable amounts of beer, suffers a fatal fall while attempting to climb the mast of a ship. At his inquest: "They [the jury] attribute his death solely to his drunkenness, the rope and, further, find that neither the ship nor anything belonging to it was moving or being moved, except the rope" (Sharpe 1913: 177).

Two central issues exercise the jury here: to which objects can the death be directly attributed, and were they moving at the time? As the ship is not moving, it cannot be held to be the cause. The rope the seaman is attempting to climb is moving, so that can legitimately be held deodand and is found to be the only cause of Elyas Ide's death. The rope is therefore appraised at 10s., which must be paid as deodand. Sharpe makes an editorial note that this is "another instance of objects, animate and inanimate, being made to bear the guilt of homicide, which would more justly have been ascribed to beer" (Sharpe 1913: 12ff.). In similar vein is the case of William Borefaunt, a skinner, who: "stood drunk, naked and alone, on top of the stair in the aforesaid rent for the purpose of relieving nature when by accident he fell foremost to the ground and forthwith died. The stair appraised at 6d for which William de Brykelworth, one of the Sheriffs will answer" (Sharpe 1913: 276).

The important distinction made by these medieval juries is not, however, between fatalities for which the victim could be held as negligent and thus, to our modern morality, somewhat responsible as this man may have been, and those which are blameless, but is rather that made between fatalities which have some discrete object that can be held to be the cause (such as a rope or stairs) and those with no such object. Sharpe's comment implies that this reflects a kind of irrational animism, a shifting of "rightful" blame from victim to object. To see the deodand as animism is to read these accounts with a modern (or at least post-seventeenth-century) gaze. The juries of these medieval cases found *infortunia* to be the cause of most of these misfortunes. Sharpe translates *infortunia* variously as "mischance" (Guildhall MS 126: 5) and more specifically as "accident': as in "Robert Page shot the aforesaid Robert Palfreyman with a certain arrow by accident in the left hand side" (Guildhall MS126: 269). The cautious Robert Page is then reported to have "fled forthwith", presumably knowing that the jury would have been interested not in his motivation (whether he meant to kill or not), but in whether his arrow caused the death, in which case the responsibility would be his. The *infortunia* here is not the misfortune of the modern accident, which derives its character from opposition to other, more culpable acts. It is rather "misadventure": a concept that seems to encompass a lack of object, rather than a lack of motivation. Felonies may have been differentiated from these "misadventures" at some later date, after the inquest was over, but motivation was not a central issue for the jury. Sharpe translated "infortunia" as "accident" in those cases that looked (in 1913) like "accidents". Today, it is no more possible to translate the Latin transcripts in a way that reflects how the actors at the time conceptualized misfortune. We have only the implication, from what it was considered important to record, that motivation (which is so central to both our ideas about accidents and about justice) was less important than identifying the immediate cause of fatalities.

If it is not possible to reconstruct an earlier classification of misfortune through an examination of how medieval juries dealt with deaths that we would see as "accidental", it may be more profitable to look for the conditions that made our classification possible. The question then becomes not "How have accidents been seen through history?", with a consequent focus on why they may have been neglected in sociology, but rather "When did it become possible to have an accident?" The answer to such a question may lie in an examination of the history of a discourse of accidents, rather than in a history of the events that we would today label as "accidental".

At what point, then, did it become possible to speak of accidents? In some respects the silence of the social theorists of the late nineteenth and early twentieth centuries was broken by the 1930s, when accidents appear in the accounts of social anthropologists. Here, accidents (or a belief that they happen) serve as an indicator of a specifically "modern" way of thinking about the world. In an attempt to understand the essential difference between "moderns" (the anthropologists) and "primitives" (the objects of their study), a belief in accidents – events that are unpredictable and have no moral culpability – is central. The next chapter will trace the emergence of a conceptual space in which the "accidental" could happen.

Chapter 3

Modernity and the emergence of accidents

The classical social theorists were silent about accidents, and other disciplines claimed that accidents were not really accidents. At what point did it become possible to talk about accidents? Two literatures from the early twentieth century in which accidents do appear are the writings of the European anthropologists, who were concerned to delineate the "primitive" cultures they studied from those of Europe, and those of developmental psychologists. The accident, or a belief that it could happen, proved to be a useful indicator of both the difference between the primitive and the modern in anthropology, and between the child and the adult in psychology. This chapter traces the appearance of the accident in this discourse of modernity, and identifies two conditions of its possibility; namely a consensus about rationality and the emergence of probabilistic thinking.

Anthropological accounts: the accident defines modernity

In 1923, Lévy-Bruhl presented "primitive mentality" as essentially irrational, in that it was governed by ideas (such as belief in supernatural forces) that would be held as illogical and contradictory by Western standards of the time. It was the primitive's attitude to the events that we might label accidents that Lévy-Bruhl saw as definitive of this irrationality. The

41

primitive had no conception of chance, or coincidence, because all events were invested with meaning.

> From disease and death to mere accident is an almost impercept-
> ible transition . . . primitives as a rule do not perceive any differ-
> ence between a death which is the result of old age or disease and
> a violent death . . . Therefore every death is an accidental one,
> even death from illness. Or to put it more precisely, no death is,
> since to the primitive mind nothing ever happens by accident,
> properly speaking (Lévy-Bruhl 1923: 43)

Lévy-Bruhl collected accounts from missionaries in Africa and North America to demonstrate the primitive's different perceptions of chance events. All misfortunes, whether illness, accidents or bad weather hap-pened for a reason and had a decipherable cause, be it the breaking of a taboo or the action of witches or of angry ancestors. The victim of an "accident" in such systems had none of the status Lévy-Bruhl saw as belonging to a modern victim, such as the right to sympathy or at least not to be held culpable. Indeed, in primitive society, the victim was likely to be secluded, outcast or persecuted as the bearer of mystic infection. The logic of supernatural causation is self-sustaining: the continued appear-ance of misfortune demonstrates the continued action of witches or the necessity to respect taboo. One of Lévy-Bruhl's examples was that of three women on a river bank, one of whom is pulled into the water by an alliga-tor and eaten. Here, argued Lévy-Bruhl, two beliefs that the "modern" mind would hold to be contradictory were held simultaneously by primi-tives. One is that alligators do not attack, and that it is therefore quite safe to draw water where they swim. The second is that sometimes people do get eaten by alligators.

> . . . to the native mind what has occurred cannot be accidental.
> First of all, alligators would not have attacked the women of their
> own accord. Therefore someone must have incited this one to
> do it. Then, too, it knew exactly which woman to drag under the
> water . . . The only thing to find out was *who* had done it . . .
> (Lévy-Bruhl 1923: 50)

To hold two apparently contradictory beliefs was, for Lévy-Bruhl, evi-dence of the essential "irrationality" of primitive mentality.

Evans-Pritchard's description of Azande cosmology has acquired the status of a "classic" case study of these irrational beliefs described by Lévy-Bruhl. It might be useful to examine how Evans-Pritchard described Azande explanations of misfortune and the accidental, given that their cosmology has been seen as not "rational", or at least not rational in the same way that modern scientific discourse is held to be, and to examine the place of accidents within that cosmology. Evans-Pritchard concurred with Lévy-Bruhl's theory that there is something quite different about "primitive mentality", and he described the Azande's views on witches to be irrational, despite their seductiveness. He noted how powerful this dominant discourse could be: "I, too, used to react to misfortunes in the idiom of witchcraft and it was often an effort to check this lapse into unreason" (Evans-Pritchard 1937: 99). According to Evans-Pritchard, all misfortune, for the Azande, was the result of witchcraft. Witchcraft was an invisible substance that witches could send flying through the night to attack others. Witchcraft could be inherited, and one did not necessarily know that one was a witch. Only by consulting an oracle could the identity of a witch be discovered. A belief in witches was a ubiquitous and comprehensive explanatory system that functioned to explain misfortunes that arose "not only from miscalculation, incompetence and laziness, but also from causes from which the African, with his meagre scientific knowledge, has no control" (ibid.: 64). Only misfortunes that clearly resulted from the breaking of a taboo (such as not observing appropriate restrictions on when sexual intercourse could occur) were exempt from these explanations.

While concurring with the theories of natural causation that we might describe as "rational" (that for instance a leg is broken because a tree branch fell on it), an Azande would also have expected an explanation of "why me, and why now?", a question not perhaps amenable to rational explanation. The Azande would not only have asked the question, but would also have expected to find the answer. Accidents, like other kinds of misfortune (such as illness or lack of success in hunting) were seen to be explicable in personal and moral terms as well as those of natural cause and effect. The Azande recognized a plurality of causes, relating to different levels of explanation, and witchcraft operated at the social level of explanation. In a hunting metaphor, witchcraft was "umbaga", or "the second spear", which had as great a part to play in the death of a hunted elephant as the first spear. Thus the "natural" causes of a misfortune such as the immediate cause of injury or lack of foresight were accepted, but not as a complete explanation: "It is the particular and variable conditions of an event and not the general and universal conditions that witchcraft explains" (Evans-Pritchard 1937: 69). As an example, Evans-Pritchard described one potential misfortune that we might classify as an accident; that of a granary collapsing while someone was sitting underneath, sheltering from the sun. The legs of the granaries were often weakened by termites, and a collapse could perhaps kill those sitting beneath. The immediate cause of the collapse (and so the death) may be clear, but there would still be a need to understand why the granary had to collapse at the very moment when someone was underneath:

> To our minds the only relationship between these two independently caused facts is their coincidence in time and space. We have no explanation of why the two chains of causation intersected at a certain time and in a certain place, for there is no interdependence between them.
> Zande philosophy can supply the missing link . . . Witchcraft explains the coincidence of these two happenings. (Evans-Pritchard 1937: 70)

The Azande would have fully expected to discover why such a misfortune befell them and who they could rightly have blamed – and indeed exacted vengeance from. For Evans-Pritchard, this lack of belief in the coincidences that cause accidents as normal misfortunes which warrant no further investigation marked the Azande as irrational: primitive in comparison to modern societies.

Developmental psychology and the accident

It was not only the social anthropologists of the 1920s and 1930s who used a belief in accidents as an indicator of superior mental abilities. Piaget, writing in 1930 on the development of children's causal logic, described children's views of physical causality in terms rather similar to those of Lévy-Bruhl: "The child fills the world with spontaneous movements and living 'forces'; the heavenly bodies may rest and move as they please . . . trees swing their branches spontaneously to make a breeze, water flows by virtue of a force residing in it" (Piaget 1930: 114).

The young child attributed animistic motives to physical objects and, even in later stages of development when mechanical cause and effect was understood, Piaget argued that "the child feels a very definite repugnance for the ideas of physical necessity and chance" (Piaget 1930: 117). Until seven or eight years old, he or she feels that there are no chance events in the world. Everything has a reason, has been willed and is entirely moral. Only after this stage do they admit that "there are things which serve no useful purpose and events due solely to chance encounters" (ibid.: 277). As an example of children's lack of understanding of chance, he cites an experiment involving a "fixed" guessing game. In this game, a set of counters all marked with an "X" are placed in a bag. The children are asked to draw a counter after first guessing if it will be marked "X" or "O". Although this instruction might lead them to believe that the set was mixed, the children, reported Piaget, are not at all surprised by the result: that all the counters they draw are the same, and none have an "O". They would have expected such a result from a normal, mixed, set of counters (Piaget & Inholden 1975: 95–115). Children's inability to conceptualize the rules of random chance also, argued Piaget, indicates an immature moral viewpoint. Until the age of 10, he argued, the child is as likely to evaluate moral culpability through the effects of an action (for instance the extent of damage it caused) as whether the action was intended or not (Piaget 1932: 118). The child is thus perceived as essentially a primitive, still to learn those modern modes of explanation and moral accountability which suggest that the "accidental" carries a lesser burden of blame than an intended action, and that some events "just happen".

Although Piaget was writing in the 1930s, and many of his findings about children's conceptual development have been contested (see, for example, Donaldson 1978), the idea that development can be measured in terms of ability to accept the accident has, to some extent, persisted in psychological research. One study (Kister & Patterson 1980) looked at whether there were developmental trends in the understanding of the causes of misfortune, and whether children used notions of "imminent justice" to explain misfortunes such as accidents, illness and loss. This is the idea that misfortune strikes as a direct result of wrongdoing. The authors hypothesized that "as the rational causes for an event become more salient, the child should be less inclined to explain that event in terms of imminent justice". They asked the children in the study about contagious ailments (a cold), a non-contagious ailment (toothache), an accident (a scraped knee) and a non-health misfortune taken from one of

Piaget's studies. This was the story of a boy who, after disobeying his mother, walks over a bridge which then collapses. The children were asked whether these misfortunes could be the direct result of imminent justice: that is, whether they were caused directly as a result of bad behaviour. Younger children, the findings suggested, were more likely to believe in imminent justice as a cause of misfortune than the older children. The authors concluded that: "the decline in imminent justice thinking during childhood is caused by the child's growing awareness of the actual causes of events (in this case the causes of illness)" (Kister & Patterson 1980). The growing understanding of the "actual" cause of events is demonstrated by their increasingly accurate use of the concept of contagion as they grow older. Younger children overextended this concept, for instance attributing headaches to contagion, or not understanding the effects of distance on contagion. Here, growing faith in the rational causes of disease (such as germ theory) is seen as replacing earlier moralistic accounts, in which behaviour is seen as having direct outcomes such as accidents or illnesses.

The legitimacy of rationality

In these accounts from the early twentieth century, accidents are unproblematic. That some misfortunes "just happen", and that there can be no profit in examining the cause, is so obvious as to need no explanation. Only the primitive or the child would seek an explanation for mere coincidence, or be unsurprised if the rules of chance are broken. There are two, connected, explanatory models that render the accidental misfortune as obvious and natural in these writings from the 1930s. One is rationality, a set of beliefs about cause and effect, which holds some effects to be the inevitable and natural outcomes of certain causes. The other is probability, a set of beliefs about the predictability of events. In the accounts of Lévy-Bruhl, Evans-Pritchard and Piaget a belief in accidents characterized the developed mind, for which some misfortunes "just happen". They are unproblematic because, in the early twentieth century, it seems that rationality itself is unproblematic.

This is not to argue that by 1930 there had been no debate about the nature, or universality, of rationality. The "modern" set of beliefs contrasted by Lévy-Bruhl to primitive mentality had certainly not been, in 1923, universally described as rational. As well as those philosophers who had seen rationality as an impoverishment of the human spirit (such as Nietzsche or Rousseau, and, to a certain extent, Weber), others had explicitly questioned the assumption that apparently rational behaviour can be so described. Two hundred years earlier, Hume (1739), for instance, had argued that human action is intrinsically irrational, given that causal relationships are based only on impressions and expectations rather than any direct observation of the link between two events. The expectation that, for instance, pain will be experienced on touching a fire is based solely on our past experience of the succession between the two: we cannot directly perceive the causal relationship, which is merely inferred from repetition: "objects have no discoverable connexion together; nor is it from any other principle but custom operating in the imagination, that we can draw any inference from the appearance of one to the existence of another" (Hume 1739: 184). Further, he argued, we have no rational basis for assuming that this relationship will continue into the future; our avoidance of fire is based on habit not rational decision-making. There is no essential difference between the attribution of chance or of "cause" as the reason for an event, except the latter is merely more probable, in that it has happened more often. Rationality as a basis for reasoning is undermined, as "all probable reasoning is nothing but a species of sensation" (ibid.: 183). However, this view of human behaviour had little impact and few disciples: Russell noted that Hume's ideas were a "dead end" in philosophy and represented the "bankruptcy of eighteenth century reasonableness" (Russell 1946: 698). "To refute Hume", claimed Russell, "has been, ever since he wrote, a favourite pastime among metaphysicians" (ibid.: 685).

The fate of critics

As well as such critiques of rationality, there had been attempts at the development of alternative explanatory systems from within the scientific community. One interesting one was the thesis of the Austrian biologist Paul Kammerer, better known for his controversial work in the early twentieth century on Lamarckian evolution. Kammerer's thesis, published in 1919, set out his ideas on "seriality". This was an attempt to analyze scientifically the common-sense notions of "lucky days" or "one thing after another" as well as repetitions in nature (such as the recursive shapes of leaves) in terms of a principle of "seriality" which, he argued, coexisted with linear natural laws:

die Serie (Multiplizität der Fälle) dar als eine gesetzmäßige Wiederholung gleicher oder ähnlicher Dinger und Ereignisse – eine Wiederholung (Häufung) in der Zeit oder im Raume, deren Einzelfälle, soweit es nur sorgsame Untersuchung zu offenbaren vermag, nicht durch dieselbe, gemeinsam fortwirkende Ursache verknüpft sein können. (Kammerer 1919: 36)

the seriality (multiplicity of causes) presents itself as a systematic repetition of the same or similar things and events – a repetition (building-up) in time or in space, with specific causes which may be interlinked, in so far as it is possible to discover by careful investigation, not through the causes working together in a linear way.

However, the publication of this thesis had negligible impact on the scientific community and no lasting influence. The work has never been translated into English, or reprinted. Perhaps more significantly, it has been claimed that Kammerer's publication of his thesis was a major setback to his career in academic science: "friends implored him to postpone publication until after the meeting of the University Senate which was to decide his appointment. In keeping with his temperament, Kammerer refused the compromise. That was the end of his hopes for a professorship . . ." (Koestler 1975: 41).

Even by the early twentieth century, then, rationality was not universally held to be the sole explanation of either human behaviour or of natural events in modern thought, and there were attempts to theorize the universe in ways in which the "accidental" might have a role. However, there are some indications that rationality had a dominance and legitimacy in the early decades of the twentieth century that was secure enough to marginalize the ideas and legacies of those who challenged it or suggested alternative paradigms for scientific investigation.

In the light of the fate of Kammerer's thesis, it is interesting to compare a (remarkably) similar work by Carl Jung, first published some thirty years later. In his book *Synchronicity: an acausal connecting principle* (1955), he argued that natural laws, being only statistical truths, have limited value in explaining natural phenomena as individual events. Chance happenings and coincidences are considered meaningless in terms of the experimental method, which seeks regular patterns, but sometimes incidents seem to fall beyond the bounds of possibility, and suggest some kind of meaningful, even if not causal, connection. He cited as an example a day when fish were mentioned or appeared on six separate occasions within twenty-four hours; more than would be expected by mere chance (though the cynic might note the day was Friday, and Jung was at the time working on the fish as a symbol) and suggesting, he argued, some meaning beyond that of "mere" coincidence. Rather than assuming, as a rational method would, that such a large number of coincidences was the result of the random play of chance, Jung proposed a second principle, that of "synchronicity", to operate alongside the causal one. This principle (very like Kammerer's concept of "seriality") asserted that "the terms of a meaningful co-incidence are connected by simultaneity and meaning" (Jung 1955: 95), and occurs in such situations as dreams that are premonitions of future events, or when a psychic state and a corresponding objective process occur simultaneously.

This theory, as an attempt to understand events that have no obviously rational cause, never generated the further research that Jung had hoped for, and had little influence beyond the margins of academia: it was described by one biographer as a "curious sideline" in terms of his contribution to psychological theory (Fordham 1966: 130). It did not, however, have the devastating effect on his career and prestige that his predecessor's, Kammerer's, project did for him, and it is still referenced in popular texts on chance and coincidence (see, for instance, Richards 1985).

Although comparing the fate of two texts separated by thirty years can prove little, it does suggest one possible line of enquiry for situating the accident in terms of the rationality that made it a "natural" category. If the status of rationality as unquestionable is central to the construction of some misfortunes as accidents, it may be worth tracing some of these debates about rationality in order to situate historically the point at which it became possible to speak about accidents. By the middle of the twentieth century there were several sources of criticism of rational explanatory systems that had rather more credibility than those of the early twentieth century.

Rationality undermined?

First, it must be noted that the term "rationality" itself has been used in so many contexts over the last century that its meaning has been highly contested: indeed it could be argued that it has little meaning left. "Rational" behaviour has been variously conceptualized, for example, as being based on an economic model of human behaviour, in which actors seek to maximize the satisfaction of their preferences (see Hindess 1988); in a Weberian sense as describing a "disenchantment" of the modern world, in which magical and supernatural forces no longer have any meaning, and as relating to the objectivity of scientific logic (Popper 1974) which describes the world in a way that can be tested. The diverse meanings attached to the concept perhaps make it more useful as an ideological label rather than any precise description of actions or beliefs. In the writings of Lévy-Bruhl and others in the 1930s, the implication was that "rationality" could be used to describe first a cosmology that assumes a universe governed by known or knowable laws that predict the behaviour of the material environment and, second, perhaps, the extension of that assumption to the social world as a normative ideal.

This "classic" view of rationality is perhaps best represented by the writings of Karl Popper, first published in the 1930s. Popper is one of the philosophers who was concerned to refute Hume's claim that human action is essentially irrational, and he situated rationality explicitly at the heart of scientific and, by implication, social progress. He argued that first there is a psychological need to discover regularities in the world: "expectation may arise without, or before, any repetition" (Popper 1974: 24), so our beliefs in causal relationships cannot be based on appearance and habit, as Hume had suggested. Second, there is a rational basis for accepting scientific statements, since they are empirically testable and have been subject to critical examination. The basis of this testing is the notion of "falsifiability': theories can only be accepted if they are capable of being falsified (Popper 1959). Although he accepted that chance may play a part in the causation of events, Popper suggested that the proper level of analysis would be regular underlying structure. Thus water molecules tumbling over a waterfall may appear to move randomly, but on aggregate their behaviour is structured by the known laws of fluid dynamics. Science, he argued, is properly directed at these underlying structures, not at the accidental and unknowable. Despite Popper's arguments elsewhere (Popper 1960) that the social sciences should have the particular and local as a legitimate object of study, he here dismissed chance in human behaviour as simply uninteresting: "It may be said that some of our decisions are snap decisions, taken without deliberation, since we often do not have time to deliberate . . . But are snap decisions really so very interesting? Are they really characteristic of human behaviour – of *rational* human behaviour?" (Popper 1974: 228, emphasis in original).

Although Popper's characterization of scientific knowledge as built on falsifiable theory has been seen as an idealization of the process of the production of scientific knowledge (see, for instance, Kuhn 1970, Wright 1979), and indeed random systems may now be legitimate objects of scientific inquiry, such ideas of rationality dominated in the 1930s and survive, perhaps, as a normative ideal in much scientific discourse today.

The social production of rationality

Criticism of this orthodox account of the primacy of rationality came from several sources. First, there were those who agreed that Western rationality had achieved hegemony as a normative ideal, but that this had been the outcome of social processes rather than the inherent superiority of rational argument itself. Feyerabend (1987), for instance, argued that this hegemony had been the result of economic and military colonization rather than the objective superiority of rational argument. "Western science" he claimed "has infected the whole world like a contagious disease" (Feyerabend 1987: 297).

Historians, also, have undermined the assumption that rationality has any innate or logical primacy as explanation, even where the growth of rationality has been seen as an indicator of progress. Thomas (1978), for instance, in *Religion and the decline of magic*, charted how the Reformation in England gradually eroded seventeenth-century beliefs about the efficacy of magic with the introduction of "rational" religious beliefs. Medieval beliefs were characterized by rites and practices designed, claimed Thomas, to facilitate direct divine protection or intervention. Such rituals as blessing with holy water, the churching of women and perambulation to bless the crops were attempts to alter the social and physical world through magical means. The new Protestant theology was aggressively rationalist and pushed out Catholic ritual and the remaining pagan rites that had persisted in Christian guise. Thomas found no wholly convincing argument for the demise of such beliefs, but offered some partial explanations in the rise of experimental science and corresponding advances in technology; the growing dominance of the Protestant ideal of trying self help before the invocation of supernatural aid; and the move from agrarian to industrial production. Thomas was cautious about these explanations, but the significance here of his presentation of modernity as a rational belief system, contrasted with earlier "superstitious" beliefs, is that it is dependent on an examination of social processes, rather than on the self-evidently superior explanatory power of rationality.

Moral critiques

If attempts to delineate the particular historical and social circumstances necessary for a belief in rationality are one source of debate around the universality and "obviousness" of rational belief systems, then Feyerabend's suggestion that other cosmologies may have a more "functional" approach to misfortune provided a second: a moral questioning of how far rationality could provide meaning for misfortune. In his essay *Farewell to reason*, Feyerabend idealistically contrasted the functional value of the cosmologies of pre-colonized peoples with those whose only recourse is to rational explanatory systems. Western science, he claimed:

> not only destroyed spiritual values which gave meaning to human lives, it also damaged a corresponding mastery of the material surroundings without replacing it by methods of comparable efficiency. "Primitive" tribes know how to deal with natural disasters such as plagues, floods, droughts – they had an "immune system" that enabled them to overcome a great variety of threats to the social organism. (Feyerabend 1987: 297)

In this view, Western rationality has been successful, but such success is to be deplored not celebrated. Such sentiments echo to some extent Weber's description of the "disenchantment" of the modern world, and continue in anthropological debates around the limits of Western rationality in terms of its ability to provide solace or spiritual meaning for misfortune. Although modern rational explanations can encompass what Evans-Pritchard called the "general and universal", they fail completely, it can be argued, at the level of the "particular and variable conditions" of a misfortune. Although anthropological debate about cosmologies such as that of the Azande later questioned the extent to which witchcraft beliefs were in any sense "functional" for society (see, for instance, Gillies 1976), what was notable in Evans-Pritchard's descriptions was the relative paucity of the explanations he could offer as alternatives. In this case, for instance, he took issue with a boy who has a festering wound from an injury "caused" by stubbing his toe on a tree stump:

I always argued with the Azande and criticized their statements, and I did so on this occasion. I told the boy that he had knocked his foot against the stump of wood because he had been careless, and that witchcraft had not placed it in the path, for it had grown there naturally. He agreed that witchcraft had nothing to do with the stump of wood being in his path but added that he had kept his eyes open for stumps, as indeed every Zande does most carefully, and that if he had not been bewitched he would have seen the stump. (ibid.: 65–6)

Just as Lévy-Bruhl could offer no explanation of the misfortune of being eaten by an alligator other than the coincidences one might statistically expect if a "rational" approach to the dangers of alligators is adopted, Evans-Pritchard could not really begin to engage with this boy's need to know why this stump surprised him in the bush, and why the cut was taking so long to heal. We moderns, too, it has been argued, may understand the general laws which dictate that a certain event has happened because of the random play of coincidence, but may still want to know why a misfortune has afflicted our lives at a particular moment. A rationality cosmology, though, can provide no answer.

The shortcomings of rational explanatory systems in terms of their ability to provide meaning for personal misfortune has been well documented (see, for instance, Comaroff & Maguire 1981, Greil et al. 1989). Comaroff and Maguire described the "search for meaning" engaged in by parents of children diagnosed as having leukaemia. Despite the advances brought by scientific rationality which led to increasing understanding of the disease and its treatment, there was a gap in explanation at the level of the meaning of misfortune. Faced with uncertain prognosis, both of outcome and duration, the parents attempted to discover all they could about the aetiology and prognosis of the disease. Their search went beyond the limits of medical knowledge as they wondered why this had happened to them and what their children's individual chances were, reflecting on possible environmental causes that may have affected their children and examining statistical forecasts to guess at the prognosis for their child. The need to understand the "coincidence" of "why me" may well, they suggested, be universal.

Evans-Pritchard noted an Azande saying: "Death has always a cause, and no man dies without a reason" (Evans-Pritchard 1937: 111). In their cosmology a plurality of causes was recognized. In a rational discourse there are no legitimate explanations that address the particular causes of misfortunes at particular times; these are merely the result of "coincidence". In the second half of the twentieth century, the assumption that this, rationally derived, explanation was adequate had been challenged.

Relativist critiques

A third challenge to the consensus around rationality was also engendered in part by the anthropological writings of Evans-Pritchard and others, and centred on questions of relativity: to what extent was it possible to judge the rationality of a culture such as the Azande by using the criteria of another? This debate started in the 1960s, when Winch (1964) contested that Azande beliefs were not illogical (as Evans-Pritchard, claiming that they did not accord with objective reality, had implied) but rather that our definitions of rationality are social constructions that may have no relevance outside the Western cultural tradition. To evaluate Azande beliefs from the standpoint of Western science is thus a pointless ethnocentric exercise. Considerable debate followed, and has continued ever since (see, for instance, Wilson 1970, Bloor 1976, Hollis & Lukes 1982, Overing 1985, Lash & Whimster 1987, Hindess 1988). In essence, one refutation of Winch's "relativist" argument was that rational scientific explanations were superior because they were empirically testable, and that it was therefore reasonable to judge other beliefs by them. Others pointed to the technical superiority of modern Western culture to demonstrate the theoretical superiority of modern scientific thought (see, for example, Taylor 1982). Others still made broader philosophical attacks on the kind of relativism Winch was suggesting (see Lukes 1982, Hollis 1982), arguing that a "strong" programme of relativism was undermined by the self-evident universality of certain beliefs held by all people, irrespective of culture, and by the paradox that relativistic logic should be reflexive, so making a strong relativist position logically untenable. Horton (1970) argued that the debate about the application of Western rational criteria to African practices may be misinformed not because the protagonists could never understand African beliefs, but because they were ill informed about Western science and theory.

It is not intended to detail here the various positions in these debates about rationality and relativity, or to assess their merits. The significance of the debate is twofold. First, it is largely a debate about other cultures, and interpreting the findings of anthropologists: even by the middle of the twentieth century, a rational ideological hegemony could still be assumed in the West. Winch (1964), for instance, considered apparently "irrational" practices in the West (such as a belief in astrology or attendance at a Black Mass) to be safely dismissed as such, unlike the beliefs of the Azande. Such modern practices, he claimed, took their meaning from contemporary scientific modern practice, and could not be understood other than in relation to those rational practices.

Second, the very existence of the debate is perhaps the most salient issue for this argument. In 1964 it was possible for Winch to question that assumption of rationality which Evans-Pritchard could take for granted in 1937. In 1937 accidents were unproblematic because rational explanation was unproblematic, and any challenges were marginalized.

Postmodern critiques

The fourth, and most recent, attack on the notion of rationality is perhaps the inverse of Feyerabend's assumption: that rationality (as embodied by Western science) is not inevitably all conquering, but that it is inherently precarious, and liable to dissolution. If the "rationality debate" of the 1970s and 1980s assumed, to a large extent, a rational hegemony in the West, then the most recent attack has undermined even this. This is (loosely) the starting point of many "postmodern" theorists, who focus on the heterogeneity of current ideas and possible world views, sometimes implicitly contrasting the "postmodern" with earlier times when ways of thought were supposedly more integrated. As Smart puts it: "It is argued that the modern *episteme* was fragmented from its inception – that it 'exploded in different directions'" (Smart 1990).

Such arguments celebrate not the dominance of rationality but the heterogeneity of current intellectual thought. Lyotard, for instance, examines the concerns of the scientific community, which he claims are fragmented and discontinuous, with paradox being at the very centre of the notion of scientific thought. He cites quantum theory, the uncertainty principle and Mandlebrot's work on fractal patterns as evidence that scientists are no longer concerned to situate themselves within a linear progression and no longer seek representations of the world as it is, for the world has been exposed as an unstable system:

55

Postmodern science – by concerning itself with such things as undecidables, the limits of precise control, conflicts characterized by incomplete information, *"fracta"*, catastrophes, and pragmatic paradoxes – is theorizing its own evolution as discontinuous, catastrophic, non-rectifiable and paradoxical. (Lyotard 1986: 60)

With this crisis in the "hard" sciences and the postmodern critique, claims Lyotard, the whole question of rationality is an open one: "there is no reason, only reasons" (Lyotard, in van Reijen & Veerman 1988).

One example of what Lyotard describes as "undecidables" in science is the interest in theories of chaos in the natural sciences, which are directed at what might be called the "accidental" outcomes of natural laws, such as the water cascading apparently randomly over Popper's waterfall. Whereas Popper dismissed these phenomena as scientifically uninteresting, "chaos" theories attempt to reconcile deterministic and probabilistic explanations of apparently "chaotic" systems which do not have outcomes that are exactly predictable (Percival 1992). The weather is a familiar example of such a system: in the medium term we can predict that for instance the summer in Britain will be hot and mainly dry and that the winter will be cold, but in the short term (tomorrow) we can only make probabilistic predictions based on the possible trajectories of current conditions. Whereas classical Newtonian physics treats such local randomness as "noise", and provides a mathematical term for the uncertainty that results, chaos theory posits a new set of laws which determine the patterning of these trajectories. Thus weather conditions may appear random, but are determined not by linear laws linking variables together, but by "strange attractors" which are represented as the shapes that pattern the field of all possible weather states (Palmer 1992). In a simplified model of a weather system with only three determining variables, this attractor will have a three-dimensional shape. Although the trajectory of individual weather conditions appears random if we try to predict outcomes with linear laws, the field of possible outcomes is clearly patterned. Such an attractor has a regular "shape": it represents the regular laws that determine the system. An analogy could be made with the unconscious "deep structures" of the structuralists, which pattern the apparent trivia of cultural life such as characters in folk tales, or the kinds of food we eat.

The current scientific interest in non-linear systems, it could be argued, is evidence of a desire to extend rational explanation to new areas of the physical environment (such as turbulence and short-term climatic change), previously thought to be outside the remit of theory, as much as it is evidence of a theoretical crisis. If Lyotard is citing the interest in such subjects as evidence of a "crisis" in science, it is perhaps equally possible to see it as evidence of confidence and expansion. Chaos theory in some senses extends the possibilities for rational science (one that integrates stochastic and deterministic laws) as much as it undermines its base.

Indeed, it has been claimed that science in the West is characterized by few competing schools of thought (Kuhn 1970: 209), and if there is any one unifying theory it is surely that of scientific causal logic. We assume the universe and everything in it is ordered and potentially predictable, even if our models are not yet sophisticated enough to predict accurately in the short term.

Rationality and the accident

For now, it may be useful to put these recent challenges of modern multiple rationalities to one side (we will return to them in Chapter 6), and place "rationality" at the level of an ideology of periodization rather than empirical description of systems of knowledge, and see how the accident could be seen to emerge as a category of misfortune necessitated by that discourse. The idea of rational hegemony may be in decline or may be mythical, but the ideological force of rational ideas in our understanding of the world has been a powerful one. In general, in the first half of the twentieth century the persistence of other explanatory frameworks is seen as anachronistic, and the superiority of rational explanation was assumed in contrast with other times and places that were or are less "rational". One of the defining features of this rational view was seen as the acceptance of the limits of rational explanation: that is, that there can be "accidents", events whose causation is coincidental and thus could not be predicted.

Against a consensus about rationality the accident, then, was a given. That accidents happened was taken for granted, uninteresting and hardly the subject of scholarly enquiry. Only in domains that defined the boundaries of rationality (the verdicts of medieval coroners, the minds of primitives and the moral evaluations of children) were accidents noteworthy – and that was for their absence.

There is, then, a case for the importance of an ideology of rationality for constructing the idea of an accident. It may now be useful to return to the concept of probability as the other strand identified as contributing to making accidents possible. If it became possible to talk about accidents in 1930 (if only as events given significance by their absence from other, non-rational, arenas), how did they become linked, as categories of misfortune, to a rational view of the universe? What conditions made possible Lévy-Bruhl's view that only the modern mind could comprehend that accidents happen?

The emergence of the accident

The *Oxford English Dictionary* (*OED*) gives three versions of the main meaning for the word "accident". The first is an obsolete sense: "an occurrence, incident, event". The second and third are those contemporary ones with which we are concerned here: "anything that happens without foresight or expectation" and "an unfortunate event, a disaster, a mishap". A medical definition is also noted as obsolete: "an occurring symptom". If we look at how writers from the early seventeenth century in England used the word "accident" there is no notion of an unmotivated act. The second and third definitions that we recognize today do not seem to have occurred before the end of the seventeenth century. How did it become possible to describe some misfortunes as arising without foresight or expectation?

Logically, and following from the discussion of rationality above, the conditions of possibility for accidents to happen are first the emergence of a rationalist view of causation, in which the patternings of events are seen to be determinable and predictable, and second a corresponding belief in probability to explain the particular distribution of events. An accident appears in the gaps left by a rationalist cosmology, at the limit of deterministic laws, but where superstition no longer has a legitimate part to play.

These gaps in rationalist explanations emerge between what is known for sure (that is, that which is subject to deterministic laws, such as those describing the motions of planets around the sun, or gravity on the earth) and that which is known statistically (that is, that which is subject to the laws of probability, such as the chance of reaching a certain age or of dying of a certain disease). At a local, or individual level, there is little that can be known for sure. Rationalist laws governing most of the areas of life in which misfortunes are likely to occur are statistical, not determinist.

The probability of various life events and kinds of death can be known, and thus the chance of them happening to an individual, but this is of little use in explaining personal misfortunes. As probability may, then, be important to an understanding of accidents, the work of Hacking (1975) on the emergence of probability in the West is taken as a starting point.

Hacking and the emergence of probability

Hacking (1975) regarded John Graunt's 1662 publication of his *Natural and political observations on the Bills of Mortality* (Graunt 1662) as the first extensive set of statistical inferences made in the West. These observations on the Bills of Mortality were an attempt to define the risk of dying from various causes and laid the foundations of the modern science of population statistics. Hacking (1975) situated Graunt's work in the context of emerging ideas about probability, evidenced by Pascal's use of probabilistic reasoning to establish a pragmatic rationale for the belief in God; Leibnitz' application of probability to legal problems and Huygens' publication of the first textbook on probability which all appeared in the second half of the seventeenth century. That a science of probability became possible in the West at this point in the mid-seventeenth century was, claimed Hacking, to do with the dual nature of the emergent concept of probability; it was at the same time "aleatory" and "epistemic". That is, it referred to both stable frequencies (an event is "probable" because such events have a statistically calculable chance of occurring) and to degrees of belief (an event is possible because we know that such an event can occur). This concept replaced the "probabilism" of the sixteenth century, which referred to the approvability of an opinion: a probable happening or opinion was one attested to by eminent or respected authorities. This "probabilism" of the sixteenth century was despised by the discoverers of the new probability, such as Pascal. To account for why a new concept of probability entered European discourse towards the end of the seventeenth century, making possible the science of statistics, Hacking examined shifts in scientific thought, and emergent concepts of evidence and deduction.

Evidence and deduction

Evidence, as we now understand it, argued Hacking, appeared only by the end of the seventeenth century. Previously, "evidence" was rooted in authority: the testimony of learned authorities. The distinction between such testimony and the evidence of things (empirical evidence) is relatively recent. In 1662 the *Port-Royal logic* described the distinction as being one of external evidence (the testimony of authorities) and internal evidence, from the existence of things. This book on the "art of thinking" arose from conversations between a group of philosophers, who believed they could set down "all that was of any use on logic" in one day (Arnauld & Nicole 1851: XIV). The result, published by Antonie Arnauld and Pierre Nicole, remained a key textbook for two hundred years. The idea of internal evidence was a new one, rooted in the idea of causal inference: that one could infer one thing from another. Such internal evidence was different from the "signs" of the Renaissance period, which were based on verisimilitude. Although signs were things and not written testimony, argued Hacking, and were utilized as evidence, this was on the basis of their similarities, or correspondences with what they signified. Thus nature (in the signs of the stars, or the climate, or the symptoms of disease) could be "read" in the same way as the testimony of learned authorities. The relationship of a bodily sign with a corresponding disease was not conceptualized as a causal one, though: the disease did not "cause" the sign, but was signified by it. Probability, argued Hacking, only became possible once signs were conceptualized as internal evidence, from which causal chains could be inferred, rather than as merely the testimony of the natural world.

Thomas Lodge (*c.*1558–1625), a poet and author who went on to study medicine, published his *Treatise of the plague* in 1603. This text neatly illustrates the testimony of authorities and the evidence of signs in its advice on avoiding and curing the plague. Lodge claims to have: "faithfully gathered out of the most approved Authors, (especially out of certaine notes which I received from Valenolaeus sonne, now Doctor of Phisique in Arles in Province) a true Methode how to know and cure the Plague" (Lodge 1603: A4).

As well as such authority, he also cites the signs of the plague in nature. Plague can be authoritatively predicted:

> If the Winter be hot and moist, and observe not his natural temperature and when the Spring time is dry without rain ... Moreover, if at that time there appears any increase of such crea-

tures as engendered of putrification, as wormes of the earth, flies, gnattes, eales, serpents, toads, frogs and such like foretelling corruption and putrification on the earth and waters, and when the aire the same day changes from faire to foule, and from clear to cloudy. . . . (Lodge 1603: C2)

This notion of the sign included the idea that it could be believed because it could be trusted: the appearance of toads and frogs heralding the arrival of a plague epidemic was to be believed because this had happened before in nature. It now became possible to argue deductively, from observed effects to hypothetical causes. Internal evidence, the basis of new probabilistic reasoning, could be distinguished when conventional signs were finally separated from natural signs. The former are the arbitrary signs chosen at will, such as the names of stars and substances which were once thought to have intrinsic meaning. As an example of the possibilities open when internal evidence can be distinguished from the external evidence of authority, Hacking quoted Hobbes from *Human nature* (1650), who somewhat preempted Hume:

the signs are but conjectural; and according as they have often or seldom failed, so their assurance is more or less; but never full and evident: for although a man has always seen day and night to follow one another hitherto, yet can he not hence conclude they shall do so eternally; experience concludeth nothing universally. If the signs hit twenty times for one missing, a man may lay a wager of twenty to one on the event, but may not conclude it for truth. (Hobbes 1650, cited in Hacking 1975)

As the modern notion of probability became possible, the science of statistics could emerge as the study of quantitative facts about the state and its population. As an example, Hacking cites the City of London's weekly tally of christenings and burials from 1603, which was kept to detail the current state of the plague. It was not until Graunt's notes on the Bills of Mortality were published in 1662 that anyone made such use of them. Until then, when the data could be seen as "evidence" from which conclusions could be drawn, these data were merely "signs" of the plague, correspondences to it, and not data that could be examined in this way: "Once it became possible for a Graunt or a Petty to look at the data as data, and not as a 'signature' of the plague, it was possible to draw a great many inferences" (Hacking 1975: 106).

Cause and motivation

Hacking's argument is important for a study of accidents because these new ways of conceptualizing evidence and probability also provided new ways of thinking about cause and how it was to be attributed. It might, then, be useful to revisit some of the seventeenth-century writings examined by Hacking, together with a sermon by a preacher of the period, Samuel Ward (1577–1640), to trace how this new discourse of probability, together with the emergent consensus around rationality, could also produce the accident as a marginal category of misfortune.

First, the word "accident" itself, in terms of the meanings defined by the *OED* above, rarely occurs in these writings. Most often the word accident referred simply to a happening, undistinguished in cause from any other. Writing on the plague in 1603, Thomas Lodge used the word in this "obsolete" sense of an "occurring symptom": "The most troublesome or dangerous accidents in this Sicknesse are weakness of vertue, faintings of the heart, soundings, raving or frenzie . . ." (Lodge 1603: K2). Accidents were here the deteriorations or "events" in the course of the illness and nothing more.

So what were happenings with no discernable motivation or will, those we would categorize as accidents, called in the early seventeenth century? It appears that there was simply no need to distinguish them from those more culpable acts or those with some definable motivation. In 1622 Samuel Ward, for instance, in a sermon entitled *Woe to drunkards*, listed the many misfortunes that befall those who drink. These were attributed to the direct judgement of God, to whom drunkenness is an odious sin, punished by all manner of untimely ends. He listed numerous examples of such misfortunes, including deaths from diseases we would describe as arising from alcohol use, such as a man who "having surcharged his stomacke with drinke, hee fell vommiting, broke a Veyne, lay two days in extreme paine of body & distresse of mind, till in the end recovering a little comfort, he died" (Ward 1622: 24–25). Other misfortunes included injuries sustained while drunk, including a "man 85 yeares old, or thereabout, in Suffolk, overtaken with Wine [who] going downe a paire of staires . . . fell, and was so dangerously hurt, as hee dyed soone after, not being able to speake from the time of his fall to the time of his death" (Ward 1622: 29).

Although drunkenness itself is implied to be an intermediate cause of this and other fatalities, it was not the ultimate cause, which was God's retribution. Misfortunes that were not associated with the victim's own drunkenness were therefore also subsumed under the same explanatory framework: thus a woman who had persuaded three men to stay to drink some more was "suddenly taken speechlesse and sicke, her tongue swolne in her mouth, never recovered speech, the third day after dyed" (Ward 1622: 20). Her misfortune, though not "caused" directly by the action of alcohol was attributed to the moral culpability incurred by encouraging others.

We would now perhaps divide such misfortunes into three distinct categories with very different moral content. First, effects of disease which result directly from alcohol use. Second, injuries arising from drunkenness. These would perhaps be seen as somewhat blameworthy. Third are true "accidents'; injuries sustained by people who may be drinkers but who were not inebriated at the time. Those injuries not attributable to the causal effects of alcohol use we would have no ready explanation for, but within the moral universe of Ward's God there was no need for such a category since the judgement of God was an all-embracing explanation. The sin of drunkenness is the ultimate cause of all the misfortunes to which drinkers are prone, through the intervention of a righteous God. There was no need, within such a universal explanatory framework, for a category of events for which no cause was known.

Patterns and leftovers

By the 1660s, however, a dramatic change had occurred. With the emergence of the possibility of using data as evidence, we find the beginnings of the concept of a category of events that are not regular and that do not fit within a predictable pattern. At this point, what we are here defining as "rational" ways of thinking are beginning to gain precedence, and the study of disease and mortality was no exception. Graunt, writing on the Bills of Mortality in the second half of the seventeenth century, had an approach to investigating causality that we would recognize as essentially "rational':

> . . . among the several casualties some bear a constant proportion unto the whole number of Burials; such are the chronic diseases, and the diseases whereunto the City is most subject; as for example Consumption, Dropsies, Jaundice, Gowt, Stone, Palsie, Scurvy,

rising of the Lights, rickets, aged, agues, Feavers, Blood Flux, and Scowring: nay, from Accidents, as Grief, Drowning, Mens' making away themselves and being killed by several accidents &c do the like, whereas Epidemical and Malignant diseases, as the Plagues, Purples, spotted Feaver, Small Pox and Measles do not keep that equality, so in some Years or Months there died ten times as many as in others. (Graunt 1662: 18)

Using the new possibilities of probabilistic reasoning, Graunt differentiated a certain group of diseases (consumption, etc.) as being perhaps unpredictable in their effect on individuals, yet predictable in their effect on the population of London as a whole. There were also, though, diseases that have no such apparent pattern; the "Epidemical and Malignant" diseases. So here, although "accident" still referred to a group of happenings distinguished by the suddenness of their effect or the externality of the cause of death, rather than their exclusion from a pattern, there was the notion of happenings that do not "bear a constant proportion to the whole". He brings accidents into that pattern: they are made predictable on a magnified scale, yet there is also the notion equivalent to ours of cases that do not fit *yet*. This notion is perhaps a vital condition of possibility for "accidents" as we know them to occur, as a temporary categorization of a lack of cause, waiting for inclusion through aggregation, which constructs individual misfortunes as part of population rates. The events that did not fit in Graunt's scheme are the epidemics, for which he had not established a predictable pattern from his study of the Bills of Mortality. Graunt later listed some of the events that we might now label as accidents, claiming that it is not worth examining them too closely as they are not amenable to the discovery of regular patterns:

We shall say nothing of the numbers of these that have been Drowned, Killed by falls from Scaffolds, or by carts running over them &C, because the same depends on careful Trade, and Employment of men and upon matters that are but circumstantial to the Seasons, and Regions we live in; and affords little of that Science and Certainty we aim at. (Graunt 1662: 23)

Graunt's project in these *Observations* quoted above was in some senses emblematic of the beginnings of the process of rationality, although tentative in that it excludes cases which will not exhibit "Science and Certainty". It was an attempt to calculate the risk of various kinds of death in an "objective" way, untainted by the subjective fears people have of different risks. He appealed to empirical evidence to calculate the exact chance of death from various causes:

> . . . whereas many persons live in great fear, and apprehension of some of the more formidable and notorious diseases following; I shall only set down how many died of each: that the respective numbers, being compared to the total 229250, those persons may the better understand the Hazard they are in . . . (Graunt 1662: 16)

This use of empirical evidence (the essential substance of this new rationality, as well as probability) contrasts neatly with Lodge's appeal to medieval "proof" quoted above: that of learned authority. It is not merely that Graunt's "science" was true whereas Lodge's was not, but that between 1603 and 1662 it became possible to frame an argument in terms that became recognized as having a rational appeal to logic and evidence. Graunt's "Hazard" was not an unpredictable danger, but a calculable "risk", which could be understood and mapped, if not yet manipulated and managed. At this point, the accident becomes possible. A conceptual space has opened to define the boundaries of what could be calculated and explained, and it was here that the accident could happen.

This is not to argue, of course, that all misfortune was suddenly attributed to causes that were amenable to rational enquiry. Writing in his diary on 10 October, just after the fire of London in 1666, John Evelyn provides an explanation for this and the plague of the preceding year similar in tone to that of Samuel Ward: "[this] dreadful conflagration added to the plague and warr, the most dismal judgements that could be inflicted, but which indeede we highly deserv'd for our prodigious ingratitude, burning lusts, dissolute Court, profane and abominable lives (Evelyn 1819: 377).

But Graunt's "science" means that it was now possible to interpret evidence of plague (the mortality statistics) not just as God's judgement, but as data to be examined for inherent regularities. By the end of the seventeenth century the political economist and administrative reformer William Petty (1623–87), could confidently dismiss arbitrary or non-rational causes as having no relevance to his projects. Comparing the mortality rates between two Paris hospitals, he notes that given *l'hostel Dieu* had a mortality rate double that of *Le Charité*, then "it follows that half the said Numbers did not die by natural necessity, but by the evil administration of that hospital" (Petty 1687: 11).

Indeed, Petty's confidence in his methods leads him to a scathing condemnation of the arbitrary as a possible explanation of trends in his data. Reviewing fluctuations in the population of London, he wrote:

> what reason to assign the like increase from 1604 to 1642 I know not, unless I should pick out some Remarkable Accident happening in each part of the said period and make that to be the Cause of this Increase (as vulgar People make the cause of Man's Sickness to be what he did last eat). (Petty 1699: 27)

"Remarkable Accidents", random happenings, were now apparently causes not worthy of serious consideration. Using the new-found rationality in political statistics, Petty could then separate what had for Graunt been irregular features, such as plague years, and place them neatly into the larger pattern of predictable population shifts. He predicted, for instance, the time it would take for London's population to double by calculating population increases based on Bills of Mortality and "including some allowance for Wars, Plagues and Famines, the effects whereof, though they may be Terrible at the Times and Places where they happen, yet in a period of 360 years is no great matter in the whole Nation" (ibid.: 18).

When Ward and Lodge were writing at the beginning of the seventeenth century they had no need to appeal to the accidental as a cause of mishap. By the end of the century, Petty's "Remarkable Accident" was not only a necessary part of the rational world view, to explain that which did not fit a pattern, but also a despised one that could be dismissed as irrelevant to the emerging scheme or put to one side until a place could be found. Accidents were essentially the remnants of an emerging classificatory system: the leftovers that demonstrated its boundaries.

A marginal category

The limits to this new cosmology, in which death rates and the behaviour of populations were as worthy of study as the physical laws that were seen to govern the universe, necessitated a category of events that could not be explained. These were the random, unimportant events that could be concealed by the aggregation of Vital Statistics or dismissed as simply unimportant as single events – as the causes given merely by "Vulgar People". Misfortunes such as death and disease gained a new meaning beyond that of individual tragedy: they could now be interrogated as evidence for the predictable and patterned behaviour of populations. Some misfortunes, however, could not be so neatly described by the predictions of the mortality reports, as a universe governed by natural laws is fallible. In the new order, it is first the epidemics that lie outside such patterns, then, when they are incorporated as temporary deviations through the analysis of populations over time, there remain only the violent or "unnatural" deaths, a diverse category defying any description other than that of a remainder. Deaths from intentional violence have some moral meaning but others are merely happenings. These "accidents" emerge as a necessary category of event, falling on the boundary of what is explicable through the new sciences of statistics and population studies.

There is, however, a tension here. Belief in "accidental" causes, in the 1930s, demonstrated a self-conscious modernity. Tracing the emergence of rationality and probability in the West points to the possibility (or perhaps, even, necessity) for a category of "accidental" events and explanations. However, although "accidental cause" can only be understood as a concept in relation to the rational, already we have Petty dismissing such explanations as uninformed. The modern belief in a rational universe would hardly have been sustainable without a belief that some misfortunes just happen, yet accidents stand as a challenge to these emerging modern explanatory systems, to be brought within the laws of determinism and probability where possible (through Freudian psychology, or ever more detailed epidemiological study). This is perhaps the paradox that underpins both the relative neglect of accidents as misfortunes and the difficulty in developing a sociology of accidents: they are specifically defined as being unworthy of study, as being what is left over after we have explained all we can. The accidental in social life appears from the events deemed worthy of no further enquiry; the remnants of our explanatory system.

In the early years of the twentieth century, then, the modern era was described as being dominated by a rationalist cosmology. This cosmology dominated an understanding of events in the material and social world, including misfortunes, until the consensus was fractured by both scientific criticisms (of the assumption of rationality in models of belief and behaviour) and moral criticisms (of rationality itself). Against a rational consensus, the accident is notable only when absent. For Evans-Pritchard, the absence was noted in his description of Azande thought, which countenanced no meaningful distinction between what we would call an accident and any other kind of misfortune. He described a cosmology in which all misfortunes – damage to property, personal injury, failure in hunting – were amenable to the same types of explanations and remedies. There was an agent (witchcraft) potentially responsible for all unwelcome events, so there is no logically possible category of events for which the cause cannot be explained, or which are apparently unmotivated. It is only when there are supposedly rational causes for most misfortunes that a marginal category can arise: that of events for which we cannot logically explain why they happened when they did. They are a despised "given" of a rational cosmology, unworthy of scientific study unless absent.

Chapter 4

Medicine and morality

Introduction

So far, two potential answers to the question "When did it become possible to have an accident?" have been suggested. The first answer was the late seventeenth century, when the emergence of modern rational explanatory systems in the West enabled some misfortunes to be classified as "accidental", in that they were ideally neither motivated nor predicted. Indeed within a cosmology that has been characterized as "rationalist", the accident becomes not only possible, but also perhaps necessary. The accident produced by this discourse is an unintended and morally neutral misfortune, one that sits outside available explanatory laws and describes a category of leftover misfortunes, which are inexplicable.

The second answer is perhaps to pose a slightly different question: "When did it become possible to talk about accidents?" This, it has been suggested, was in the early twentieth century, when a self-conscious "modernity" enabled accidents to be spoken of, as indicators of that modernity and, in some senses, definitive of it. Only the rational, modern and mature mind could comprehend that some events "just happen" and that there can be no profit in seeking an explanation of them. In both colonial anthropology and social theory, the accident was produced through modernist discourse as a space, filled by the as-yet inexplicable. In the nineteenth century, nosology – the study of the classification and arrangement of diseases – also produced the accident as a marginal category of misfortune. Medical interest in the sequelae of accidents (the deaths and, later, injuries caused by them) necessitated some attempt to explain the inexplicable, and to impose order on the heterogeneity of misfortunes that are described as "accidents". In so doing, medicine produced the accident as marginal misfortune, a remnant of its embryonic nosology. It also produced a paradoxical category, defined on the one hand as a blameless misfortune and on the other as one surrounded by moral enquiry.

In Britain, the Registrar-General's classification of diseases has, since 1839, formally labelled some injuries as accidents. Although one facet of the nosological categorization of accidents has been the attempt to place accidents in terms of their medical outcomes, and thus to provide a pattern by which these disparate injuries could be understood, a second facet has been the implicit acknowledgement that accidents are essentially a lay category, defined by dimensions other than those of medical outcome. The inclusion of accidents in nosologies was an essential precursor of epidemiological enquiry into accidents, which by definition rejected the "unpredictable" nature of accidents. Through epidemiological mapping accidents reveal underlying patterns, and can thus be brought within a rational discourse of statistical predictability. But in this medical literature on accidents is a tension: accidents are first caught and placed in nosological tables and mapped through epidemiology, yet simultaneously they remain examples of what is unclassifiable, they are the "leftovers" of a rational medical discourse.

Nosology and the accident

Although the misfortunes described in everyday life as "accidents" produce a range of outcomes (a broken cup, a pregnancy, a wet toddler), it is accidents which cause injuries and death that have perhaps attracted the most attention, as these necessitated medical interest. Accidents became a focus of a specifically "professional" epidemiological interest in the middle of the twentieth century, when accident prevention emerged as a public health problem. The rise and implications of accident prevention are examined in the next chapter. Until the 1950s, though, accidents were largely neglected as a discrete subject of study by medicine. As the medical historian Roger Cooter has noted, there were few calls for specialist treatment for accidental injuries before the First World War, and little action until afterwards (Cooter 1993: 80). Another historian, in reconstructing the history of violent death in Philadelphia, complained of accidental injury that "nothing relevant has been written about its history or sociology, and the sources are nearly as brief as the bibliography" (Lane 1979: 35). However, such silence, like the silence of social theorists, created accidents and our knowledge of them as eloquently as any more visible discourse could have done.

First, if medicine has had little interest in the treatment or prevention of accidents until recently, the development of comprehensive mortality statistics did necessitate some interest in their classification as a cause of death. The logic of nosology, and the inclusion of accidents as a separate cause of death in medical statistics, produced accidents as specifically "medical" misfortunes, but ones that did not fit easily into developing classifications of causes of death.

The Registrar-General's classification

In Britain, the cause of death first had to be registered in 1838. Even in restricting their interest to those accidents that caused death, the early medical statisticians were faced with a challenge in imposing order on a seemingly disparate set of causes and outcomes. The first Registrar-General's report listed, for instance, the following causes among the 4,845 deaths that were classified as "Deaths by Violence': choking on blackberries; being struck by lightning; drinking boiling water; bites by a ferret, a lion and a donkey; pit explosions; emphysema following a fall and inflammation following a prick from a thorn.

This heterogeneity was a problem, given the aim of the first Registrar-General to present causes of death as facts as scientific in their arrangement as any other which "admit of numerical analysis" (Registrar-General 1839: 63). To achieve this involved aggregating individual causes of death within larger categories, which, it was hoped, would provide a basis for meaningful deduction. In an appendix, the first statistician to the Registrar-General, William Farr, wrote:

> Medicine, like other natural sciences, is beginning to abandon vague conjecture where facts can be accurately determined by observation; and to substitute numerical expressions for uncertain assertions . . . the physicians of this century will be saved from the fallacies of partial generalization. (ibid.: 64)

Following in the tradition of Graunt and Petty's projects in political arithmetic at the end of the seventeenth century, the 1839 Registrar-General's report commenced with the hope that it "will not disappoint the expectations of those who hope to derive, eventually, from that source, materials of vast improvements to the advancement of the Science of Vital Statistics" (ibid.: 8). In order to provide such material, Farr outlined the classification to be used for arranging deaths by cause (see Fig 4.1). He saw the main division of causes of death as being between external and internal causes:

> two classes, passing into each other, but as distinct as day and night; the first class comprising all that can be referred to external violence, suffocation, poison, lightning, and fire; the second, such as under certain circumstances spring up spontaneously in the organism, and are represented by inflammation, cancer and rheumatism. (Registrar-General 1839: 65)

Farr was concerned that the new rational science of vital statistics should eventually provide an all-embracing explanation, and that as many causes as possible should be brought within the remit of "political arithmetic". Such a project necessitated first attention to the accuracy of recording. Farr noted, for instance, that many of those recorded as simply "Sudden Deaths" may obscure "a certain number of cases of poisoning which escape undetected by the coroners and the juries" (ibid.: 75). It also required appropriate aggregation of those disparate, individual misfortunes that made up the rates, so that the classification system would itself produce the kind of data that were amenable to interrogation for patterns. There should not, claimed Farr, be too much refinement in the

---

Epidemic, endemic and contagious diseases
     (e.g. cholera, dysentery, small pox, plague)
Sporadic diseases
       • of the nervous system
       • of organs of respiration
       • of organs of circulation
       • of organs of digestion
       • of urinary organs
       • of organs of generation
       • of locomotion
       • of the integumentary system
       • of uncertain seat (e.g. gangrene, epitaxis, dropsy, atrophy)
Deaths by violence

Figure 4. 1 Farr's classification of diseases, 1839. *Source*: Registrar-General 1839: 66.

classes used, because if they are too exactly defined "no general principles can be deduced from small numbers; accidental irregularities destroying the results, according to the well known doctrines of probability" (ibid.: 70). The causes of death that were to become classified as accidental were, therefore, like other "external" causes of death, merely grouped together, with no attempt to classify them further.

By the second report, Farr divided external causes into three groups: Intemperance, Starvation and Violent Death. The "Violent Deaths" proved problematic. They were left over from other, more homogenous categories, grouped merely by fact that death was caused by what Farr called "impressive external causes" (Registrar-General 1840: 7), rather than by any biological processes or sites of anatomy. However, Farr noted that the lack of any analysis of the sudden deaths was a shortcoming of his embryonic system:

> The violent deaths are extremely numerous and will perhaps lead to a general enquiry into their causes, – drowning, fires, accidents with machinery, the bursting of steam-boilers, explosions in mines, and poisons, which can be procured of the most destructive and subtle nature, with extraordinary facility. (Registrar-General 1840: 7–8)

In the same vein, Farr also listed particular causes of death from want of food and from cold, noting that these were "in some instances the effect of accident, but more frequently of destitution" (ibid.: 7). Further analysis and classification, he implied, would render even this group of random, individual misfortunes as "scientific facts". Indeed Farr's developing classification for deaths suggested that most were now much more than individual and disparate misfortunes. Like the rates of births and marriages, the distribution of causes of death formed a pattern from which underlying laws and regularities could be deduced. In 1848, one Registrar's introduction to the annual report claimed that "The fluctuation in the marriages of a country expresses the views which the great body of the people take of their prospects in the world" (Registrar-General 1848: ix), and went on to review changes in the marriage rates from 1754 to 1845 by linking them to the changing economic fortunes of the country. The same introduction noted the regular effects of temperature on the death rates, noting that a fall in mean temperature destroyed lives and that a mild season would save them. There was a growing confidence and optimism that the new science of statistics could provide meaning through the examination of such patterns. By 1854 even epidemics, which for Graunt, a century earlier, had been chaotic and unpredictable visitations, found their place in a predictable pattern: "an epidemic is invariably followed by a period of low mortality, which is again accounted for on the supposition that the weakly die of an epidemic, who under ordinary circumstances would die in a year or two years subsequently of some other disease" (Registrar-General 1854: iii).

Even if the precise reasons for these short-term fluctuations attributable to outbreaks of epidemic disease were not yet known, at least they were placed, and thus comprehensible, in the long term. In their heterogeneity, then, violent deaths continued to pose a problem for such analysis. The idea of the "accidental" provided a partial solution, in creating motivation as a primary axis of classification.

Nosology and motivation

Motivation and the moral content of the category of violent deaths was explicitly addressed for the first time in Farr's appendix to the 1854 report. Noting that in England there had been a long tradition of referring deaths "likely to be caused by wilful, careless or accidental violence" (Registrar-General 1854: 129) to the coroner's court, in order to distinguish those deaths for which there was some culpability from others, he went on to suggest:

> Some of the external causes that in too many instances are fatal are wilfully or negligently set in motion by men, and the act is homicide or suicide. This subject deserves to be fully investigated, for the mental states appear to admit to a large extent of moral and physical control. (ibid.: 136)

In the absence of any apparent anatomical or pathological pattern, this moral content of the class of "violent" causes of death provided a possible organizing principle, for now they too could be classified into discrete groups. Accidents did not fit well into the now well-established nosology based on anatomy and function, but they could be ordered around an examination of the intentions of the victim or others. The fatal medical sequelae of accidents were thus classified initially not by the body part affected, or by the extent of disablement of a physical function, but by a moral judgement. In the 16th Report (Registrar-General 1856), following international standardization from the first Statistical Congress in Brussels which intended to institute commonly agreed diagnostic criteria and labels as well as classifications, Farr introduced a new classification that divided deaths into five classes, namely:

(a) Epidemic, endemic and contagious,
(b) Constitutional,
(c) Local,
(d) Developmental, and
(e) Violent.

In the 1862 report, Farr commented on the utility of motivation as an axis for organizing the last class:

> Human agency plays so important a part in this class, that it might be made into the basis for orders. Thus a man may die 1. a glorious death in battle (pro patria mori); he may die 2. by an act of homicide (murder, manslaughter); he may die 3. ignominiously on the scaffold (execution); or 4. abandoning the post where God has placed him, he may take away his own life (suicide); 5. he may die by a surgical operation 6. he may die by accident.
>
> If this grouping be adopted, the mode in which the death is produced by wounds, chemical injuries, poisons, asphyxias, and mechanical forces, would form secondary heads. (Registrar-General 1862: 78)

These distinctions for violent deaths are based purely on the moral meaning of the death: whether glorious or ignominious; whether the victim or an other was culpable. Those with no discernable moral content are the "left-overs", the accidents. The medical sequelae of accidents were now classified by specifying their immediate cause, but their definition mirrored lay terms. An accident was an event for which there was no motivation, but which lay on a boundary between the need for a cause (the coroner's court would be asked to attempt to provide one) and the lack of a "real" cause as defined by the new scientific principles of statistics, which made "accidental irregularities" themselves regular and predictable events through aggregation. From the unrefined category of external causes of death when annual statistics were first published by the Registrar-General in 1839, accidents had become the last order of medical classifications of causes of death: those that have occurred with no known medical cause, or at least none that fits into the rational system of medical knowledge, and have no known motivated cause.

Ordering the disordered

Farr's suggestion in 1840 that a "general enquiry" into the causes of violent deaths would prove fruitful was followed. The analysis of causes of "violent" death became more detailed over time, and accidents became distinguished from other forms of violent death. The class of accidents became more internally differentiated in official statistics. The last order of causes of death has undergone perhaps more revision than any other. The original grouping of external causes of death used by Farr in 1839 included an undifferentiated catalogue of injuries and accidents. The introduction of the first internationally agreed classification (Registrar-General 1856) brought, as we saw above, a division of violent deaths along lines of culpability. From then on, the circumstances surrounding accidental injuries resulting in death were the subject of ever more sophisticated classification techniques, as the location and cause of accidental deaths were recorded and other information followed. The first kinds of accidental death that were separated out in their own table in the Registrar-General's annual reports were those happening in mines and railways, which were distinguished from others from 1863 onwards.

The problems posed by the heterogeneity of the class of accidents continued, however, to be of concern to epidemiologists. In 1941 a report by Greenwood et al. (1941) on deaths by violence cited changes in classification as a deterrent to analyzing trends over time. They noted the increasing numbers of accidents owing to motor vehicles: from two deaths registered in 1896 to 235 in the years between 1931 to 1938. One respondent to the paper noted that

> until recent years violent deaths have been nobody's business in the official sense, apart from industrial accidents and homicide . . . the Registrar-General's analyses of accidental deaths have suffered from obscurities in classification and . . . have failed

to provide much material for those who may have wished to study these deaths in relation to social factors. (Greenwood et al. 1941)

This call for more sophistication in the reporting of accidental deaths was heeded, and throughout the second half of the twentieth century accidental deaths were subject to increasingly detailed analysis.

Detailed cross-tabulations of causes of accidental death were sporadic in the annual reports until the middle of the twentieth century when, in 1948, coroners were required to include information on the death certificate about where the fatal accident had occurred. The tables included in the statistical returns of the Registrar-General illustrate the growing interest in categorizing and counting accidents. In 1950, there are three tables that describe accidental deaths in the annual report; one listing poisonings by place of occurrence, age and sex; one describing deaths from violent causes according to the nature of the injury; and the third describing accidental deaths by external cause. Gradually, other information was reported: in 1958, for instance, a further table was added, to classify deaths from road accidents and from accidental falls. In the 1965 report, deaths from accidents in the home and residential institutions were also included in separate tables. The implications of this growing interest in the causes and outcomes of accidental injury are explored in the next chapter.

Contemporary categories of accidental death

The 9th and 10th revisions of the International Classification of Disease Categories (WHO 1977, 1992) maintained in essence the original distinctions reported by Farr in 1848. In the 9th revision accidents remained in the last category, Order XVII, which, unlike the other orders, was based not on a system of the body or a group of disease-causing agents, but covered a seemingly disparate range of fatalities. Reporting on deaths in this class the Registrar-General still imposed some order by dividing Deaths from Violence along moral lines into deaths caused by others (homicide), deaths caused by the victim (suicide) and deaths from which no fault can be attributed: the accidents.

Up until the 9th revision (WHO 1977) of the Classification of Diseases, Injuries and Causes of Death there were two alternative series of classification codes for Order XVII (WHO 1967). These series of numbers were designated by "N" and "E" prefixes. The series prefixed by N numbers described deaths by the nature of the injury (a fractured spine, a sprained wrist or a burn). Those codes prefixed by E described accidents in terms of their external cause; a fall, a road traffic accident and so on. After the 9th revision, the N-prefix was dropped as this became the main classification and the E-prefixed classification described a subsidiary ordering.

The 9th revision produced a primary classification by nature of injury that was similar to the other orders of the classification in that injuries are described by the area of the body to be affected. Thus, for instance, code numbers 800–804 cover various fractures of the skull and code numbers 805–809 cover fractures of the spine and trunk. This classification in essence described the medical sequelae of accidents, making no attempt to classify accidents as such. The supplementary E–code classification was an attempt to describe the environmental and social contexts of the accident. First, codes were available to describe the place of the accident: E840 is an accident to powered aircraft at take-off or landing, E910 is accidental drowning or submersion. Second, there are codes that refer to the physical environment: E900 is excessive heat and E906 lightning. Codes could specify whether the accident happened at work or in a private dwelling, and could give information about the presence of other people: E886 codes a "fall . . . from collision, pushing or shoving" and E814 codes a "motor vehicle traffic accident involving collision with pedestrian". The fact that a supplementary system of classification was needed is evidence that accidents cannot *just* be defined in terms of their outcomes – they are essentially, as noted earlier, defined by reference to the way in which they were caused and even a nosological attempt to force accidental injuries into anatomical classification has to reflect this. In summary, the primary classification described injuries, while the supplementary classification described accidents. The most recent International Classification of Diseases (WHO 1992) maintains two sets of codings, although those describing external causes (now coded V01 to Y98) are only to be used in addition to another code from the series describing the consequences of external causes (coded S00 to T98).

Within the subsidiary E-number series were three subsets of codes, which attest to the moral nature of the categorization of accidents. A death by submersion was classified not by the external cause in terms of an environment or external agent, but by the motivation of the agent. If the victim was the motivated agent, the death is coded E954: the

Table 4.1 Deaths from selected accidental causes by age group and sex, 1992 (England and Wales).

Cause of death	Gender	≤ 1	1–4	5–14	15–44	45–64	65–74	≥ 75	Total
Motor vehicle	Male	5	29	144	1,674	477	203	316	2,848
traffic accident	Female	3	19	67	432	195	155	339	1,210
Falls	Male	1	9	19	173	218	244	663	1,327
	Female	3	2	3	46	97	197	1,593	1,941
Poisoning	Male	–	5	1	347	122	16	16	507
	Female	–	1	3	113	55	21	34	227
Accidents caused	Male	4	29	14	69	66	31	59	272
by fire or flame	Female	3	18	14	32	37	37	86	227
Suffocation*	Male	13	8	23	96	60	34	45	279
	Female	8	4	2	19	19	41	77	170
Drowning	Male	3	20	11	98	41	8	12	193
	Female	1	9	3	15	12	6	20	66

*Including inhalation and ingestion of food causing obstruction of respiratory tract.
Source: OPCS 1994b, Tables 4 and 7.

classification for "suicide and self-inflicted injury by drowning or submersion". If the motivated agent is another person, the classification became E964 – assault by submersion (drowning). If blame or moral responsibility for the drowning could be attributed, it was coded E910 – accidental drowning or submersion. There was even a code for drowning where the motivation cannot be clearly established – code E948 – so that there was no danger of a motivation being wrongly ascribed. The series of codes E950 to E959 are used to describe suicides and self-inflicted injuries and the codes E960 to E969 are used to describe homicide and injury purposefully inflicted by another person. A third series, E970 to E978, is used to describe deaths and injuries arising from the motivated though perhaps not blameworthy actions of a human agent. These are the codes that describe injuries resulting from legal interventions, including code E978 for legal executions.

Table 4.2 Fatal accidents in children aged 1–14 years in England and Wales by sex and social class (mortality rates per 100,000 population), 1970–72.

	Social class of father					
	I	II	IIIN	IIIM	IV	V
Boys	25.8	39.0	44.5	56.3	66.2	122.0
Girls	18.8	19.0	21.4	24.4	35.1	63.1

From DHSS 1980, Table 6.7. *Source*: OPCS 1978: 175.

For medicine, then, even by the second half of the twentieth century, the accident was not easily caught by a nosology based on either the mapping of disease on to the body or the nature of the specific pathogen (virus, parasite, bacteria or cancer). Accidents can affect any part of the physical body, with no respect for medical framing, and they are caused by an unpredictable and potentially infinite array of agents. They are, as events, not classifiable along biomedical variables, and their medical sequelae are just as diverse. The persistence of an alternative classification, even if a subsidiary one, testifies to their problematic nature. Prior (1989) has suggested that the relegation of E-codes to a supplementary classification in the 9th revision served "to place the active subject(s) in parentheses. They are an associated, but not a primary, causal agent in processes leading to death. And they are certainly not regarded as essential to either the classification of death or to understanding its nature" (Prior 1989: 42).

This elision of the active subject, argued Prior, was part of a wider shift in medical discourse by which "humanistic accounts of death were removed from the medical register and effaced from the certificates" (Prior 1989: 45). However, although modern nosologies have sanitized causal accounts of death from social contexts in general, they have only partially succeeded. Some deaths, it seems, can only be recorded if we examine the moral context: whether the death was willed, and whether any human agent should bear responsibility. The persistence of E-codes, even if only as a supplementary classification, demonstrates this, and no "violent" death in modern Britain is certified before a coroner's court has decided which moral class it belongs to.

Thus, accidents still form a residual category for nosology, based not on anatomy or an analysis of pathogens, but on what is "left over". Accidents cannot be defined purely in terms of their medical outcomes, as classification depends also on analysis of social circumstances and on culpability. Farr laid the basis for conceptualizing some accidents as medical misfortunes, potentially as amenable to statistical analysis as any other cause of death. To a certain extent, this project was successful, in that the disparate causes of "accidental" death are now aggregated, internally classified, tabulated and cross-tabulated in official publications. These tables elide the particular and unique circumstances of each misfortune, recreating it as merely an instance of a type (a road traffic accident, a head injury, a home accident). However, the active subject has not completely disappeared from these sanitized accounts of fatal accidents, in that (unlike for other causes of death) the very designation of "accident" arises from a judgement about a moral context.

Patterns and predictability – the rise in epidemiology

The epidemiology of accidents is now well established. When aggregated, accidents appear not as unique misfortunes, but as statistically predictable events, with identifiable social, environmental, psychological and biological risk factors. An examination of the death rates for accidents (that is those "external causes" not identified as homicide or suicide) reveals certain regularities over time. First, accidents have been the leading cause of death for children over one year old for the last 25 years. In England and Wales in 1992, 563 deaths of children aged between 28 days and 14 years were attributed to accidents, representing 16 per cent of deaths in that age group (OPCS 1994a). Second, as Table 4.1 shows, males are more at risk than females for accidental death at all ages. There are also patterns in the locations and causes of those deaths in different age groups: falls are the largest cause of accidental death for the elderly; the home is the most common location of accidental death for those under five years old.

In addition to the statistics routinely reported by the Office of Population Censuses and Surveys, there has been a considerable amount of epidemiological study of the correlates of increased accident risk. First, a range of social factors has been identified which suggest that some subgroups in the population are more at risk than others. Accidents in the home requiring hospital treatment, for instance, are reported as more common in socially disadvantaged households, those with overcrowded accommodation and those in rented accommodation (Alwash & McCarthy 1988). Data from the 1970s suggest that fatal accidents disproportionately affect those from lower social classes (see Table 4.2): indeed, for children the social class gradient for accidental deaths is greater than that for any other cause of death. For girls aged between 1 and 14 years with a father from social class V, the risk of a fatal accident is three times that of those with a father in social class I. For boys, the risk is five times greater (DHSS 1980: 175).

Other social factors correlated with high accident rates include how often the family has moved house and low maternal age (Stewart-Brown et al. 1986), and the number of stressful life events suffered by a family (Sibert 1975).

Second, biological factors have also been identified which predispose some people to accidents. For instance, lack of development of motor ability and speed judgements make children particularly vulnerable to accidents as pedestrians on the roads (Ampofo-Boateng & Thomson 1991, Sandels 1975). Physical disability contributes to the high proportion of home accidents among the elderly (Graham & Firth 1992) and poor physical co-ordination makes some children more vulnerable than others (Arnheim & Sinclair 1975).

As well as the social and biological factors that have been correlated with accident risk, there are a wealth of psychological factors. A World Health Organization report (WHO 1981) on accidents involving children and adolescents summarizes the research on those psychological and environmental predisposing factors that increase vulnerability to a "risk situation", and various "precipitating factors" that increase its likelihood. Psychological traits such as "unbalanced personality, excessive aggressiveness/passivity [and] over reaction to stimuli" and characteristics of the family, such as size, marital discord and parental substance abuse are mentioned as predisposing factors. Precipitating factors include heightened emotional tension or the social pressure to "perform" in certain ways. There is some evidence that traits like aggression and over-activity are particularly associated with accident rates (Bijur et al. 1986), particularly for boys (Bijur et al. 1988). Whether being "accident-prone" is in itself a psychological trait has also been debated, with some evidence that treatment for an accident is a predictor of future serious accidents (Kendrick 1993). Such evidence has led some to conclude that "accident-proneness" is "a stable personality characteristic that predisposes an individual to have accidents" (Husband 1973). However, it has also been claimed that such arguments are a misinterpretation of statistics. As accidents are relatively rare events, we would not expect the number of accidents an individual has to be randomly distributed: their rates are better modelled with a Poisson distribution, which reflects that some individuals are likely to suffer more than one accident purely by chance (Langley 1982).

Risk factors

Cross-tabulations of these various and diverse risk factors enable dangers to be more and more exactly specified. The risk of accidental drowning, for instance, depends on age and site, with young children most at risk from baths and garden ponds and older children from canals and the open sea (Kemp & Sibert 1992). Psychiatric disorders in mothers interact with social class to increase accident risk in children: Brown and Davidson (1978) found that the children of working class mothers with psychiatric disorders had accident rates of 19.2 per 100, compared with 9.6 per hundred for those with mothers who had no psychiatric disorders and rates of 5.3 and 1.5 per hundred, respectively, for children of middle-class mothers with and without psychiatric disorders. Increased stress has been suggested as the mediating variable, as deprivation may increase stress, so reducing parents' ability to supervise children (Alwash & McCarthy 1987). The development of computer technology has enabled statistical techniques such as logistic regression and factor analysis to be applied to multiple risk factors (see, for instance, Stewart-Brown et al. 1986). The potential for correlating these risk factors seems limitless.

The social production of accident statistics

Medical knowledge about accidents is based on these population statistics, and "risk factors" are calculated from them. Such "knowledge" is routinely presented as uncontroversial "truth" about the causes of accidental death and injury. A nice illustration is one study of British General Practitioners' (GPs') knowledge of accident prevention, which used a questionnaire to "test" their knowledge about the risks for accidental injury in children (Kendrick et al. 1995). The GPs were asked some general questions about childhood accidents and to list which of the following were risk factors for childhood accidental injury: maternal age under 20; single parenthood; previous accidental injury; four or more children in family; socioeconomic deprivation; family stress. Over 80 per cent correctly identified the risk factors. The researchers reported that female GPs, those aged under 45 and those with hospital paediatric experience were more likely to get a higher score on the knowledge part of the questionnaire, and that those with a high score were more likely to have a positive attitude to accident prevention work. To "test" GPs in this way assumes that there is a professional consensus about the causes of accident injury, and that good clinical practice follows from an individual GP's knowledge of that consensus.

There are, however, major problems in assuming that the statistics about accident death and injury from which risk factors are calculated reflect any external "reality" of accidents, even if we set aside for one moment questions about the social construction of accidents themselves. Given what we know about the reliability and validity of the recording of other causes of death – such as suicide and non-accidental injury in children – we can infer similar compromises to the reliability and validity of accident rates.

Reliability

Although there has been little written on the social production of accident statistics, there has of course been considerable sociological interest in another cause of sudden death: suicide. Research on suicide dates from before Durkheim's classic study (Durkheim 1963), but has had perhaps a privileged place in sociological work ever since. Indeed, it has been noted that "suicide" has become almost synonymous with "unnatural death" in sociology (Prior 1989: 52). Suicide rates have provided an enduring motif of the success of positivist research, demonstrating law-like regularity and apparent relationships to social variables such as religion, social status or levels of integration, and a fertile ground for debate around the value of such research. Durkheim demonstrated an inverse relationship between the amount of social cohesion within a group and the rate of suicide within that group: a proof for "scientific" sociology. An apparently unique, individual act was shown to be a "social fact", observable only through statistics and linked at the social level to other measurable social variables. "At each moment in its history", claimed Durkheim, "each society has a definite aptitude for suicide" (Durkheim 1963: 48). Social cohesion provided a prophylactic device against suicide, evidenced in the lower rates among Catholic and Jewish groups than Protestants (who were perceived as having less religious cohesion), lower rates among married than unmarried men and lower rates in times of economic and political stability. The study of accident rates has no such history, but the critical debate around the work on suicide may well provide a model.

The reliability of official statistics for studying suicide rates has been long recognized as a problem, given the different criteria that are used in different recording systems, and the different moral and legal meanings of suicide that might influence those who record deaths (see, for instance, Adelstein & Mardon, quoted in OPCS 1976: vi). As accidental deaths are defined in part by those that are found not to be suicides, this implies similar problems for the reliability of accident mortality rates. There are certainly indications that the reliability of accident morbidity data is widely compromised by systematic biases. Certain kinds of road accidents, for instance, are routinely under-reported. It has been estimated that some 40 per cent of road traffic accidents are never reported to the police and therefore never appear in the statistics. These are likely to include dispro-portionate numbers of injuries of pedal cyclists (DOT 1993) and pedestri-ans (Teanby 1992). Other sources of routine accident statistics, such as the Department of Trade and Industry's Home Accident Surveillance System, only record those injuries that are treated in Accident and Emergency departments (DoT 1980), therefore excluding injuries treated at home or by other parts of the health service.

Although mortality statistics are more comprehensive, there are also likely to be biases operating that systematically exclude certain kinds of accident. Prior (1989: 83), for instance, notes that deaths of the elderly are less likely to come to the attention of a coroner's court, and so less likely to be the subject of the investigation that could define them as "accidental".

If suicide forms one possible alternative verdict to accident, intentional injuries are another. In children, the diagnosis of non-accidental injury has been more readily made in recent years (NSPCC 1976), so there are clearly problems with interpreting trends over time. Given the evidence that non-accidental injuries are identified through a complex process of assessment of social, clinical and environmental clues (see Dingwall et al. 1983), rather than any clear criteria about clinical signs, there are unlikely to be consistent rules about the identification of non-accidental deaths in childhood, and so, by implication, little consistency about how "acciden-tal" injuries and deaths in childhood are identified. Similarly, the diagno-sis of Sudden Infant Death Syndrome (SIDS), now the major cause of death for infants, was only widely identified in Britain from 1971 onwards (OPCS 1982) and only formally recognized as a cause of death in 1977 (WHO 1977). Reconstructing death rates for what is now called SIDS relies on re-interpreting past records of "accidental suffocation" or deaths from unknown cause (OPCS 1982). Given that "accidents" are what is left over when such alternatives as non-accidental injury and SIDS have been taken into account, and that these diagnoses are demonstrably unreliable, it can be inferred that there are considerable problems in using accident rates as a basis of knowledge about the incidence of accidents.

Validity

Moving on to validity, the literature on suicide similarly suggests problems with interpreting accident rates. In his work on suicide, Douglas (1967) claimed that official statistics are not only unreliable but useless for the purpose to which they are put in sociological research, being merely tautological indicators of the subject under study. For instance, "self-sacrifice" was explicitly excluded from much of the European data on suicide, yet there are still attempts to infer rates of "altruistic" suicide from such data. Douglas also cited the example of an American coroner who would only return a suicide verdict if a note was found, clearly excluding many other kinds of suicide from the local statistics. Official definitions of suicide are, Douglas argued, constructed from imputed social motivations, which are then inferred from examining the officially defined rates. He took as an example the issue of demonstrating intention, claiming that Durkheim should have recognized the problems:

> Durkheim himself considered imputations of "intention" to be the most unreliable form of information. Had he simply noted that even the laws specify "intention" as necessary for a legal categorization of suicide as the cause of death, he would have realized that *even his own arguments would necessarily lead one to reject the official statistics on suicide as a most unreliable form of information.* (Douglas 1967: 186, emphasis in original)

Again, similar arguments could be made by inference about the validity of accident statistics. One example from morbidity statistics is the recording of home accidents. Guidance given to hospital clerks who record cases of "accident" for the Home Accident Surveillance System (DoT 1980) advises that they exclude injuries resulting from deliberate attack from the data, but include children under 14 injured while fighting. Suspected drug overdoses should be included as "accidents" if the child is under 12. Like Douglas's example of inferring "intention", such age-related rules make the inference of accident rates at specific ages in childhood rather meaningless. What an "accident" consists of is explicitly defined with reference to social norms about maturity and responsibility, such as "children under twelve do not decide to kill themselves" or "children under fourteen are not responsible for injuries inflicted while fighting".

In an attempt to avoid some of these methodological problems in the study of suicide, Douglas advocated a re-examination of Weberian methodology, employed to uncover patternings in the social meaning of suicide. This could be done, he suggested, through the study of such media as suicide notes, allowing an "empathetic" sociology of suicide that would take the social meanings and motivations of the actors as the subject. Such methods are clearly inappropriate to fatal accident rates that, by definition, are those with no clues as to the motivation of the deceased.

Douglas located the disproportionate interest in suicide in the West's "moral" problem of whether individuals have the right to take their own life, and the nineteenth-century concern with the philosophical problem of free will versus determinism, a debate highlighted distinctly by contrasting psychological studies of suicide as an individual act with sociological (or "moral statistical") studies of suicide rates. In contrast, Atkinson, more recently, has characterized this interest as "fascination at a distance" (Atkinson 1978: 9), claiming that the interest has not been in suicide as such but in demonstrating social laws. Atkinson followed Douglas's criticisms of the positivist tradition to some extent, agreeing that the social facts used to "explain" suicide rates can equally adequately explain different registration rates, but his research question was a very different one. Rather than being interested in suicide *per se*, his aim was to explain how some deaths get characterized as suicides. The answer, "deaths get categorised as suicides in much the same way as anything else gets characterised" (Atkinson 1978: 196), was, he admitted, somewhat disappointing, but his focus on the processes by which officials come to define a death as a suicide is a useful departure, and proves a fruitful one for examining the social production of accident rates.

Coroners, and their officials, who may have a key role in selectively forwarding evidence and opinions to the coroner, were identified as key actors in this process. Their role was identified as particularly important as there was found to be no "official" definition in the guidelines for coroners of what a suicide was. However, even where rules about proper procedure existed, coroners did not necessarily follow them. Atkinson quoted as evidence of a coroner working without reference to the rules a case in which a jury was sent out to decide between verdicts of "accident" or "misadventure': classifications that were no longer distinguished in the official returns (Atkinson 1978: 91). Deaths became labelled as suicides through the interaction of medical and legal professionals, following what Atkinson called "cues" to a case of suicide. Such "cues" included notes, threats, mental state and the mode of death. A hanging, for instance, might less equivocally be taken as a suicide than a road traffic accident or a drowning, where other cues, such as the discovery of a pile of clothes on a river bank, would be needed. Given the wide reporting of coroners' decisions, particularly in the local press and the fact that they rely on common sense rather than professional views, Atkinson claimed that "the role of coroners in maintaining and sometimes changing shared definitions of suicidal situations attains a crucial importance" (Atkinson 1978: 145).

Coroners and the production of fatal accidents

Coroners' courts are perhaps even more central to the production of accidental death, as there are no "official" guidelines at all in the advice to coroners about how to decide whether a death should be recorded as accidental (Jervis 1986, Kavanagh 1985). Even if there is no definition of suicide, these guidelines do at least contain some discussion about the verdict. In contrast, there is none about accidents: presumably the definition is self-evident enough to require no elaboration.

Epidemiological knowledge about risks for accidents is largely based on examination of fatal accident rates. In 1992, 10,449 of the 558,313 deaths registered in England and Wales were classified as accidental or as the result of adverse effects of accidents (OPCS 1994b). Almost all of these accidental deaths came to be defined as such in the coroner's court. During a coroner's inquest into a death, medical and legal experts, and lay witnesses, negotiate the definitions of accidental death through the process of demarcating it from other, more culpable deaths. The coroner thus plays a key role in the production of knowledge about accidents in contemporary Britain. In a study that examined both the formal guidelines provided for coroners and the processes by which actual accidents came to be defined (Green 1992), I argued that the verdict of "accidental death" arises not from any intrinsic characteristics of the death or its manner, but from a moral interrogation of the facts surrounding it. In short, accidents came to be defined as such within the social context in which the death occurred. The coroner has a difficult task in the English legal system: he or she must balance neutral "fact-finding" for the state (such as identifying the medical cause of death) against other functions: providing meaning, solace or catharsis for the bereaved, and "public service" in terms of issuing warnings about hazards in the community.

The Broderick Committee, which was set up to review the coroner's role, concluded that the remaining "moral" functions of the court were an anachronism in contemporary Britain: the coroner's role should be a purely neutral one, concerned only with accurate recording of the facts of death (Broderick Committee 1971). Indeed, the Coroner's Rules advise that coroners should be solely concerned with establishing who the deceased were and how, when and where they came to their death. Rule 36 explicitly states that "Neither the coroner nor the jury shall express any opinion on any other matter" (Kavanagh 1985). However, in a society that has been said to cope poorly with death (see, for instance, Elias 1985), and perhaps particularly poorly with deaths for which no human or divine cause can be found (the "accidents"), the coroner's court provides one of the few arenas for the production of meaning. Such meaning was seen here to emerge from a moral interrogation of the "facts" that produces classification of fatal misfortunes resonating with what could be described as a "lay" classification of accidents: that they are unexpected, unwilled and for which no-one was to blame. It is not, then, surprising that there is a large space for the interplay of commonsense and "official" definitions of the accidental, for it would be impossible for any purely bureaucratic classification system to operate.

There was no discrete category of "accidental" death. Such deaths are produced in the gaps left by other categories in the classification system, which had clearer definitions. There was certainly no formal advice provided for coroners about what an accident is, or how it should be identified. Despite the lack of clear criteria for defining a suicide noted by Atkinson, there are still criteria that have to be fulfilled, however local and arbitrary they are, such as proof of motivation. Accidents are more negatively defined: they are what is left when all other deaths have been accounted for. The grounds of eligibility are purely negative; there must be no motivation, no culpability, no legal responsibility uncovered. Accidents appear publicly to negate implications of responsibility for the fatality, on the part of the deceased or any other actor.

The negotiable accident

Such negations are, clearly, the subject of negotiation, and the coroner's verdict may be merely one point in this process, as the media attention that sometimes surrounds coroners' verdicts of "accidental death" in controversial cases indicates (see, for example, Bergman 1991). Media reports of coroners' accident verdicts are presumably "newsworthy" largely because of the room left for contestation, and reports often include comments by relatives or friends of the deceased who disagree with the official verdict. Thus, after an inquest jury found that his son had died "accidentally" when hit by a police car during a high-speed chase, a father was reported as saying "[the] police and the jury should be ashamed of themselves. We will pursue it" (Myers 1994). Similarly, the mother of a patient who died after being given a drug injection in Broadmoor was reported as being "very disappointed" with the accident verdict given (Guardian, 26 October 1991). Occasionally, relatives may gain leave to appeal to the High Court to overturn coroners' accident verdicts, as did six relatives of those who died in the Hillsborough football stadium disaster (Guardian, 3 November 1993). Far more commonly, however, the coroner's verdict of "accident" is recorded unchallenged, at least in the public arena.

These examples illustrate that the coroner's decision (upon which much epidemiological "knowledge" is founded) is not necessarily the end of point of debate around whether a death was accidental or not. They also suggest, perhaps, that there can be no end point to such a debate, no "final" verdict, on an accidental death. As accidents emerge from the gaps left by other verdicts, their assignation is in a sense always provisional; pending potentially endless moral enquiry.

One hundred and fifty years after Farr attempted to impose order on his heterogenous category of deaths from external causes, the category of "accidental deaths" is still neither discrete nor self-evident. Unlike deaths from suicide, or even homicide, or from particular diseases, they are connected merely by what they are not, rather than by any affinity. In this light, it is perhaps unsurprising that the "moral" functions of the coroner's court persist, despite the Broderick Committee's attempts at "reform" (Broderick Committee 1971). It is precisely those functions that produce fatal accidents.

Although the "ideal" accident is an event for which no-one can be blamed, the coroner's court is an arena of public truth-telling and record-keeping within which moral decisions are made. The random peripheral stuff of accident is not an answer to moral culpability, but the very raw material from which culpability is constructed. The fatal accident is a paradox, in that it is both an inexplicable chance event that cannot be explained at the personal level, but also a tragic misfortune that demands explanation. Such explanation as is provided in the coroner's court has to suffice, though, for both the bereaved and the record keepers of the state. The fatal accident (the individual event upon which epidemiological knowledge is founded) is produced within a morally loaded space over which society can publicly affirm and negotiate the culpable. It appears that there is no such thing as a "pure" accident: deaths can only be classified as accidental after moral scrutiny of the social circumstances of the event excludes responsibility.

Within the nosology of the nineteenth-century medical statisticians, the accident is inevitably marginal, for it is produced through exclusion. Accidents are defined not by what they are, but by what they are not: deaths, or injuries, with no apparent moral meaning. Aggregation and tabulation rendered the accident as meaningful, in that rates could be interrogated for correlates, but still at the margins of epidemiological enquiry. The next chapter explores how the challenge of predicting the unpredictable in the late twentieth century has transformed the "random accident" into the "preventable accident".

Chapter 5

Health promotion and the preventable accident

Introduction

If the accident was relegated to the margins of medicine during the nineteenth and early twentieth centuries, it has in many ways moved centre stage in the second half of the twentieth century. As the last chapter noted, from the middle of the twentieth century there has been a growth in epidemiological knowledge about accidents, based largely on examinations of fatal accident rates. The most striking transformation of our knowledge about accidents has been not its growth, however, but the construction of a very different kind of accident. Accidents have been transformed from random misfortunes, which can only be understood in aggregate, into preventable misfortunes.

Indeed, preventing accidents has become a widespread professional activity in the second half of the twentieth century in Britain, with many public bodies having a legitimate role to play. These include voluntary organizations such as the Royal Society for the Prevention of Accidents (RoSPA) and the Child Accident Prevention Trust (CAPT); health authority public health departments; local authorities and government departments such as the Department of Transport and the Department of Trade and Industry, which collate statistics on traffic and home accidents respectively. On a day-to-day level there are a number of individuals whose remit includes monitoring, and offering advice on the prevention of, accidents. These include health visitors for accidents to young children in the home and trade union health and safety officials at work. In all areas of social life there are professionals who assess accident risks. The activities of these professionals construct individual workers, parents and children as potential accident victims who, by knowledge and vigilance, must engage in constant surveillance of their risk environment.

In *David Copperfield*, Charles Dickens' Mr Micawber could claim that "Accidents will occur in the best regulated families and in families not regulated . . . they may be expected with confidence and borne with philosophy". By 1993, such sanguine acceptance was no longer possible: "Most accidents" claimed Britain's Department of Health, "are preventable" (DOH 1993: 9). Official health policy, both international and national, reflected this focus on accidents as preventable misfortunes, and also prioritized such prevention as a public health problem. The World Health Organization (WHO) policy document *Health for all 2000* (WHO 1985) set out targets for its European region: "By the year 2000, deaths from accidents in the Region should be reduced by at least 25% through an intensified effort to reduce traffic, home and occupational accidents" (WHO 1985: 48).

Given the trend of decreasing death rates from accidental injury, this target was likely to be exceeded in Britain, so new targets for prevention were set in the policy document *The health of the nation*, which identified accidents as a "Key Area", or a national priority for health. The targets were:

> To reduce the death rate for accidents among children under 15 by at least 33% by the year 2005 (from 6.6 per 100 000 in 1990 to no more than 4.4 per 100 000)
>
> To reduce the death rate for accidents among young people aged 15–24 by at least 25% by the year 2005 (from 24 per 100 000 to no more than 18 per 100 000)
>
> To reduce the death rate for accidents among people aged 65 or over by at least 33% by the year 2005 (from 55.8 per 100 000 to no more than 37.4 per 100 000). (DOH 1992: 104)

This chapter traces the transformation of the accident from an unpredictable misfortune into a preventable misfortune, and explores the particular forms that techniques of accident prevention have taken in the second half of the twentieth century.

The emergence of accident prevention

A focus on the prevention of death and injury from accidents has been a relatively recent phenomenon. Until the mid-twentieth century, prevention may have been implicit in the patterns produced by ever more detailed statistics, but was not explicitly addressed as a discrete activity. Indeed, prevention was sometimes seen as a largely improbable enterprise. In 1941, commenting on the increase in aviation accidents, Greenwood et al. were pessimistic about change, even with the sobering influence of the world war:

> Unless the experience through which so much of the world is now passing excites such a passionate hatred of the air that aeroplanes are classed with opium and proscribed – a fantastically improbable exhibition of herd intelligence – civil aviation may well compete seriously with motoring as a cause of death. (Greenwood et al. 1941)

There may have been a growing awareness of accidents as a cause of death and disability, but until the second half of the twentieth century, there was little public concern with preventing these events. Turner (1978), in his analysis of disasters discussed in Chapter 2, noted that social scientists had neglected the causes of disasters as a legitimate arena for research in the first decades of the twentieth century: "In retrospect, it seems rather strange that there could have been such an extensive, yet tacit, agreement that there was no point in devoting time and resources to the examination of the factors which led to the production of the disasters" (Turner 1978: 39).

The same point could be made about accidents more generally, and the neglect was not confined to social scientists. Policy makers and the medical profession had little interest in studying the causes of accidents or how they could be prevented. After the First World War the British Ministry of Reconstruction noted, for instance, that health legislation was conventionally concerned with epidemic disease, and that there was also a "heavy burden cast upon [public] funds by incapacity to work due to 'debility' and similar conditions of ill health" which they believed should be addressed (Ministry of Reconstruction 1919). No mention was made, however, about accidental injury or its prevention. Even by the end of the Second World War, in 1944, a Ministry of Health document outlining the government's plans for the new National Health Service was concerned with the treatment of injury, and the development of fracture treatment and rehabilitation in particular, but again did not discuss prevention. Accidents, it seems, were primarily a challenge for the rehabilitation services: "the modern aim is total rehabilitation and re-employment . . . The difference between the facilities [of different hospitals] may determine whether or not the patient ultimately makes a full recovery from the effects of his injury" (Ministry of Health 1944: 7).

That accidents would happen was a given: the problem was one of dealing with their outcomes and returning victims to gainful employment as soon as possible.

The definitions of accidents in these reports from the early twentieth century assume a consensus. They are definitions that derive from "common sense" and ones that appeal to a shared public view. These definitions echo the characteristics of accidents outlined in Chapter 1: they are essentially unpredictable and unmotivated events, for which medicine can be expected only to respond, not prevent. So, for example, one report from the United States from 1949 defined accidents as including "any suddenly occurring unintentional event which causes injury or property damage" (National Safety Council 1949) and the World Health Organization defined an accident as "an unpremeditated event resulting in a recognisable injury" (WHO 1957). This view of accidents as being essentially one shared by the public was reflected in legislation. The 1946 National Insurance (Industrial Injuries) Act set out the basis for claiming compensation for loss through industrial injury that occurred by accident. Injury was defined as "physiological injury or change for the worse" and an accident was "an unlooked-for mishap or untoward event which is not expected or designed".

The professionalization of accident prevention

This assumption of shared public and professional definitions of accidents disappears in the middle of the twentieth century, when a self-consciously professional approach emerged. This professional voice situates itself as explicitly opposed to lay beliefs about accidents, which stress their unpredictable and therefore unpreventable nature. A key turning point is perhaps Gordon's (1964) paper on the epidemiology of accidents, first published in 1949. Gordon argued that wartime experiences suggested that the incidence of trench foot, originally thought to be caused by cold, and therefore not amenable to medical research and intervention, was affected by foot hygiene, which could be improved with careful investigation as to which men became diseased, and what factors contributed. In peacetime, he argued, accidents posed a similar challenge. Although they might appear as inevitable features of the natural world (much like cold), a careful analysis of the interactions between hosts, agents and vectors would reveal regular patterns. Like many endemic diseases, certain accident rates (such as those for home accidents) appeared remarkably regular from year to year. Others (such as road traffic accidents) mimicked the seasonal incidence rates of other diseases. "Accidents", argued Gordon, "evidently follow as distinctive movements in time as do diseases" (Gordon 1964: 20). As such, they could be brought within the realm of public health medicine, with their epidemiology mapped and interventions devised to reduce their incidence.

By the 1960s, accidental injuries had become a major public health concern in Britain and the United States, with the medical profession concurring with Gordon's assessment that accidental injury was a "disease" like any other. One report, which described accidents as the "neglected epidemic of modern society. . . the nation's most important environmental health problem" (National Research Council 1966), castigated the public for their apathy, suggesting this could be countered by utilizing education methods developed for public information about polio and other epidemics. A British report (Royal College of Surgeons c. 1963) echoed this tone of crisis, claiming of accidents that: "this disease is endemic and universal, continuous and increasing". More significantly it concluded that few accidents were "unpreventable", given that those attributable to unpredictable natural forces were rare.

Accounts of the rise of accident prevention

The relatively recent concern with accidental injury and its prevention is explained in the epidemiological literature as a consequence of the increased relative mortality rate of accidents compared with other causes of death, once infectious diseases had declined in importance as a cause of death in the West. Accidents became the leading cause of death in childhood from the 1940s. As Table 5.1 shows, fatal accident rates have declined steadily since the middle of the twentieth century in England and Wales, as they have in other industrialized countries (NAHA/RoSPA 1990) but they remain the third leading cause of death and a major cause

Table 5.1 Deaths per million population from accidents and adverse effects.

Year	Accidents & adverse effects	Suicide	Homicide
1945	425	92	6
1950	342	102	5
1955	366	113	4
1960	388	112	5
1965	375	109	6
1970	355	81	7
1975	309	75	10
1980	283	87	8
1985	250	89	7
1990	232	78	5

Source: OPCS 1992b, Table 9.

of disability (WHO 1985). However, the relative increase of accidental deaths as a proportion of all deaths since the middle of the twentieth century does not convincingly explain the rising interest. Farr, the first statistician to the Registrar-General for England and Wales, noted as long ago as 1839 that the rate of "violent death" (which included accidental deaths) equalled that from typhus in the year under review and that these deaths were, moreover, of particular concern as they were of those "in the meridian of life; and in a political sense [whose] lives are of the highest value" (Registrar-General 1839: 75).

The comparative neglect of accidental injury in public health until the middle of the twentieth century is also sometimes attributed to difficulties in conceptualizing accidents within a medical model of disease: "we recognise that many factors are involved in the causation of accidents, whereas certain diseases are caused by a single germ or agent" (American Public Health Association 1968). Ironically, in the debate about the relative difficulty of claiming compensation for industrial disease, ill health caused by accident is perceived as resulting from an immediate and single cause as opposed to disease which has complex casual origins (Stapleton 1986). As was suggested in Chapter 4, it was in part the development of medical nosology in the nineteenth century which classified the accident in moral terms, to organize this disparate range of causal factors. By the middle of the twentieth century, this classification was found wanting, as public health attempted to bring accidents within its remit as an "epidemic" like any other.

Interest in accidents as a professional strategy

Another explanation for the emergent interest in accidental injury as a disease, describable with the same language used for infectious diseases, lies in analyzing it as an intra-professional strategy used by specialists in accident and emergency medicine to develop an autonomous sphere of medical practice and expertise. There is some support for this view. Calnan, for instance, argued that up until the late 1950s in Britain the hospital accident and emergency department (then generally called "casualty") had been a neglected area, exciting little professional interest (Calnan 1982). Examining the position of a casualty department in terms of Freidson's (1970) analysis of the development of professions, Calnan noted that it posed several problems for professional autonomy. First, the work flow is client-controlled: most attenders at casualty departments are self-referred, and come at any time and with almost any medical condition. Second, although situated in the hospital, casualty departments are at the same time part of the less prestigious "community" provision, in that they are basically primary care facilities. Only after the Platt Report of 1962 were district hospital departments developed as centres of specialist trauma treatment, with a change of name from "Casualty" to "Accident and Emergency" to underline their status as specialist centres, rather than walk-in primary care departments. The powerful professional lobbies behind the reorganization of hospital accident and emergency departments were orthopaedic surgeons and the Casualty Surgeons Association, who had perhaps a strategic interest in developing less "client-centred" services. In terms of exclusionary professional tactics, moves to define accidents (by definition the legitimate object of accident and emergency work) as a disease like any other, and one requiring a specialized medical approach, seem functional.

Although a claim for the need for a uniquely expert approach to accidents may well have reinforced professional strategies, there remains a question about why such claims were not made (or at least not met) until the middle of the twentieth century, despite the growing importance of accident cases as a proportion of medical work during the nineteenth century. As Cooter notes, "by the 1880s the accident victim was the archetypal patient in large voluntary hospitals" (Cooter 1993: 8). For Cooter, it was largely economic forces that explain both the emergence of accident medicine as a specialism and the growth in status of orthopaedics as a profession. The management of accidents was neglected as a professional strategy until into the twentieth century in part because they happened to the labouring classes, and (unlike infectious disease) did not threaten the health of the wealthy or influential. Orthopaedics developed in the treatment of crippled children, war-wounded veterans and industrial accidents, who largely excited only "professional indifference" (Cooter 1993: 81) as they provided no potential for lucrative private practice, and remained treated by local general practitioners, poorly skilled hospital out-patient staff or (by the end of the century) volunteers from the St John Ambulance Brigade. Before the 1880s, argues Cooter, there was little medical or surgical interest in the treatment of accidents evidenced in the professional literature, and what little there was tended to focus on those that were likely to affect the middle classes, such as street and railway accidents. It was economic factors that also provided the incentive for the organization of accident services and the specialization of those who provided them. Cooter takes the building of the Manchester Ship Canal as a symbolic pointer to the emergent professionalization of accident treatment at the end of the nineteenth century. Between 1888 and 1893 the Manchester Ship Canal Project employed 10,000 to 20,000 labourers, for whom an integrated accident and medical service was created, consisting of a network of three hospitals and local general practitioners (Cooter 1993: 100–2). This service, argues Cooter, met the short-term economic needs of the company, which had economic incentives to finish building on time, through minimizing the cost of accidents. Such costs included time off work for the injured and also those who had to take them to hospital, together with the growing possibility of employer's liability for accidents in the workplace. A dedicated accident service also epitomized a new approach to efficiency in the management of labour, in which workplace accidents came to be seen not as isolated misfortunes but as a class of events that could be the object of medical concern.

This account of professional interests has, then, perhaps more significance for explaining the emergence of accident medicine as a specialty rather than the development of a preventative approach, for during the period of Cooter's account (1880–1948) the debates were around the proper treatment of accidents and such questions as who should treat them, how they were to be paid for and how the victims were to be transported to hospital. There is no concern here with preventing such events in the first place and with seeing accident causation as well as treatment as an activity properly within the province of medical experts.

The expert voice

What is perhaps of more interest here is the *content* of this new professional voice on accidents. These later reports on accidents overtly situated their approach as counter to a common sense, or lay understanding, of the cause of accidental injury, and this self-proclaimed attempt to correct public misconception continued throughout the second half of the twentieth century.

The focus of the emergent "professional" view of accidents was their predictability and thus preventability. It was suggested in the previous chapter that, by the middle of the twentieth century, epidemiology described accidents as resulting from constellations of risk factors, rather than random and unique events. These constellations rendered the accident as worthy of study, as in them could be found patterns and meaning. In accidents, epidemiology found a new challenge: to predict the apparently random and render it amenable to rational analysis. If random accidents were essentially outcomes of a medical understanding undifferentiated from a lay one, then preventable accidents required a distinctively professional approach.

In Britain, the development of a separate "professional" voice that could speak about these new tabulations of fatal accidents can be traced for example through the changing activities of the Royal Society for the Prevention of Accidents (RoSPA). RoSPA was founded in 1923, originally as the National "Safety First" Association which evolved from a conference concerned with the increased number of traffic accidents during First World War lighting restrictions (RoSPA 1992). Despite the original concern with what could be termed "external" factors (such as dangers in industry and on the roads, exacerbated by wartime restrictions), by the 1930s RoSPA's remit had enlarged to include accidents in the home, and the Home Safety Committee was formed in 1932. One RoSPA poster dating from the Second World War combined warnings about specific wartime dangers with advice on preventing accidents in the home. Headed "Mrs Wiseman on Home Guard", it included the following illustrated couplets:

> Baby is too young to teach –
> So put the teapot out of reach.
> All good HG's hide their rifles away –
> Before young Tommies come out to play.

> Take baby, well wrapped, when you answer the door –
> Or baby may never need bathing no more!
> Tommy was tempted but didn't touch –
> The queer ticking thing near the rabbit hutch. (RoSPA 1992)

Whether at play, at home or at work, the general public were encouraged to abandon their common-sense views on the unpredictability of accidents. Prudent action could not only save lives threatened by the risks of war, such as unexploded bombs or the Home Guard's gun, but also lives endangered by the more mundane risks in every home. Reducing the number of accidents became not merely a matter of reducing dangers in the external environment (of the factory, or dark wartime streets) but also one of assuming personal responsibility for assessing risks in the immediate home environment.

By 1950 a Ministry of Works inquiry into accidents in the home could confidently conclude that "the majority of home accidents can be attributed to personal causes . . . or such factors as ignorance, lack of judgement, carelessness or psychological disorders" (Ministry of Works 1950: 46). A study of factory accidents, despite admitting that "accidents are built into most industrial work", bemoaned the apathy of workers who assumed "that little could be done to avoid accidents" (Powell 1971). On childhood accidents, one writer notes that "It is unfortunate that the word 'accident' tends to imply an event which is unpredictable and therefore unpreventable, but of course accidents are as capable of analysis as any other event" (Jackson 1977: 4). In literature aimed at public health professionals and at potential victims and their carers, the messages that accidents are "by no means random occurrences" (CAPT 1989) and that it is "vital to counter the view that accidents are random events due to bad luck" (Henwood 1992) become ubiquitous.

Surveillance and the proliferation of risks

Chapter 4 described the growth of epidemiological knowledge about accidental injury and death throughout the twentieth century. During the second half of this century, this growth has become an explosion. Reports from the epidemiology and health education, which cover accidents in fields as diverse as skiing (Philipp & Philipp 1988), fishing as an occupation (Rafnsson & Gunnarsdottir 1993) and farms (Cameron et al. 1992,

Cameron and Bishop 1992), attest to the growing sophistication of knowledge about risks of accidents for different occupations, their interactions and possible preventative measures. "Can we help to prevent skiing accidents?" was the, presumably rhetorical, title of one report (Philipp & Philipp 1988). The very act of collating the data necessary for these studies, and of advocating the collection of more data (as almost all do) is in itself seen as a preventative activity. The surveillance of risks is in part a necessary precondition to their management: indeed, surveillance emerges as the key to management.

As Henwood (1992) concludes, "epidemiological evidence makes it clear that the risk of accidents is largely quantifiable in terms of social, environmental, lifestyle and demographic factors" (Henwood 1992). Accidental injury is demonstrably non-random, in that its epidemiology can be mapped. With this mapping, in its ever increasing sophistication, comes the knowledge necessary for prevention. Ultimately, therefore, accidents can be prevented: "RoSPA recommends that all health authorities adopt a positive approach to accident prevention based on the premise that the majority of serious accidents could be avoided or prevented and that the risks of serious injuries can also be reduced" (Henwood 1992). Given the boundless possibilities that exist for monitoring risks and for preventing accidents, it is not surprising, perhaps, that the literature on accidental injury is today largely a literature of prevention, rather than of treatment or rehabilitation. It seems more likely, then, that the emergence of accident prevention cannot be adequately explained merely as an inevitable reaction to the growing relative importance of accidental injury in a time of low overall mortality, or as a professional strategy employed by medical specialists, but rather may be a product of a rather different understanding of rationality and responsibility. Tracing the emergence of accident prevention as a discrete professional activity suggests that it has been made possible within a discourse of risk and its management. Preventing accidents, as well as ameliorating their effects, is entirely justifiable: preventing an accidental injury rather than attempting to manage its medical sequelae is clearly a humane and reasonable goal. Accidental injury causes death, disability and distress; its social cost is incalculable. However, the kind of prevention implied by many of the reports examined above is an example of the kind of "privatized" risk management described by O'Malley (1992) in relation to crime prevention. Rather than accepting the self-evident "social good" of preventing accidents, it may be worth examining why particular strategies are chosen in preference to others, and what implications a "risk management" strategy has for the meaning of accidents as misfortunes.

Preventing accidents: the possible approaches

The major problem for an approach to reducing accident rates that depends primarily on primary prevention is that these "risks" extracted from tabulated data on accidents exist only at the population level. Translating them into individual risks is a rather misleading activity, as it suggests "that there is something about the individuals . . . that would make them more or less prone to 'having an accident'" (Prior 1995: 137). It may be worth, then, looking at how epidemiological data on accident rates in populations and subgroups of those populations have been utilized in the activity of accident prevention.

Like any other health promotion activity, accident prevention can be modelled as operating on one or more of three levels. Tertiary health promotion is an activity concerned with reducing the effects of existing disease (or accident). Such activity would include the improved rehabilitation services proposed by the Ministry of Health noted above, or First Aid training. Secondary health promotion aims to reduce the chance of disease happening in groups from a population who have been identified as "at risk". In terms of accident prevention this involves reducing the chance of injury if an accident does happen by, for instance, wearing seat belts in cars or crash helmets on bicycles. Primary health promotion activity is directed at "keeping healthy", at reducing the chance of disease risk factors developing in the whole population. It is this level (the prevention of the accident happening in the first place) that uniquely characterizes contemporary accident prevention. It is evidenced in a broad range of activities, such as teaching road safety (or "kerb drill") to children and persuading parents to install a vast range of safety equipment in the home and to be endlessly vigilant of the potential risks their children face (see, for instance, RoSPA 1984, Smith & Smith 1991).

At all these levels there are three strategies that are conventionally associated with accident prevention activities, the "3 E s"; namely education, engineering and enforcement (Cliff 1984). Education involves raising awareness of hazards and how to avoid them. Examples might include road safety training for children or leaflets about hazards in the home.

Table 5.2 Accident prevention: examples of possible interventions at three levels.

Level	Example	Strategy
Primary	Posters on hazards in the home	Education
	Minimum safety standards for toys	Enforcement
Secondary	Seat belt legislation	Enforcement
	Replace concrete with safer playground surfaces	Engineering
Tertiary	First-aid training	Education
	Introduce "air ambulances"	Engineering

Engineering involves altering the environment to reduce the chance of an accident happening, or to reduce the damage done if an accident does happen. Examples might include fluorescent stripes on children's outdoor wear to make them more visible to motorized traffic or child-resistant pill bottle tops. Finally, enforcement involves providing formal sanctions against risk-taking behaviour (such as not wearing seat belts or helmets) (see Table 5.2).

The WHO's *Health for all* policy suggested that a combination of engineering and enforcement strategies would be most effective:

> In the prevention of accidents . . . programmes should be developed with a view to determining and then eliminating or reducing hazards . . . and to designing safer goods . . . encouragement should be given to the adoption of internationally agreed vehicle design changes that will improve health and safety. . . Legislation and economic incentive should be established to encourage the design and marketing of safer products. (WHO 1985: 49–50)

The health of the nation (DOH 1992), in outlining possible approaches to achieving the targets noted above also recognized that a multi-agency approach (establishing "healthy alliances") that looked at various strategies should be adopted. Significantly, though, it also noted that: "the government will rely primarily on information and education and will avoid the imposition of unnecessary regulations on businesses and individuals" (DOH 1992: 106).

An adequate explanation for this emphasis, in contrast to the more social programme suggested by the WHO, must lie in part with the economic and ideological concerns of the Conservative government of the time in Britain. A programme such as that advocated by the World Health Organization would incur considerably more costs than one based on education, and Britain, not having signed the *Health for all by the*

Year 2000 declaration, had no obligation to wide-ranging social interventions in order to reduce accidents. In keeping with new Right concerns with "rolling back the state", there was also an evident wish not to appear to impinge on freedom of choice and individual liberty (see DOH 1993). However, this emphasis on education as a primary method cannot be explained solely as a result of economic or narrowly political factors, as it is largely shared by the medical profession. The Royal College of Physicians, for instance, noted that there was scope for environmental and legislative change, but concluded that: "In the end, however, it is changes in attitude and behaviour that will bring accident and injury experience down to acceptable levels" (Royal College of Physicians 1991: 120).

Accounting for the prioritization of education

At first sight this prioritization of education and changing behaviour as the route to accident prevention seems strange, as there is little evidence that it was likely to succeed in terms of an instrumental effect, that is the impact on accident rates. Policy makers had at their disposal some evidence that both engineering and enforcement strategies could reduce the mortality rates from specific hazards. The introduction of legislation to enforce seat belt use for drivers and front seat passengers in Britain in 1983 is one example of an "enforcement" strategy that apparently achieved the aim of reduced mortality. The Department of Transport evaluated the new legislation (DOT 1985) and found first that it was successful in changing behaviour. Whereas education strategies had only raised seat belt wearing to 30 per cent of front seat occupants, the new law raised it to over 95 per cent. Second, this change in behaviour resulted in a reduction of the numbers of drivers and front seat passengers killed or seriously injured. The numbers of drivers killed or seriously injured in road traffic accidents fell by 23 per cent after the law came into effect, and the numbers of front seat passengers killed or seriously injured fell by 30 per cent (DOT 1985).

Engineering approaches have also had some documented successes. The introduction of flameproof material for night dresses and the child-resistant pill bottle tops reduced mortality rates in childhood from burns and poisoning respectively (Sibert et al. 1977), and changes to road layouts to separate pedestrians from motorized traffic have been shown to reduce childhood road traffic accidents (Sutherland 1992).

One notable success from the United States was the "Children can't fly" campaign (Spiegel & Lindaman 1977), which was reported to utilize both engineering and education strategies to reduce the number of falls from windows, which accounted for 12 per cent of all accidental deaths in New York City. The programme involved a media campaign highlighting the dangers of open unguarded windows, door to door visits from an outreach worker who counselled parents on prevention and the distribution of free easy-to-install window guards for families with pre-school children living in the tenements in high risk areas. In two years, the project recorded a 50% drop in all reported falls from windows and a significant reduction in fatal falls. The strategy that seems to have contributed most to the success of this project, though, was the engineering one: no falls at all were reported from windows where guards had been installed.

Evaluating success

Others, most eloquently Adams (1995), have argued that these engineering and enforcement strategies are also inherently limited because they do not take into account the way in which human behaviour changes in response to reduced risk. Adams refers to the idea of a "risk thermostat': a psychological mechanism that sets the level of risk with which an individual feels comfortable (Adams 1995: 20). If the environment is made safer (by, for example, providing soft safety surfaces on playgrounds, or by enforcing seat belt use) then individuals increase the amount of risk they face by, for instance, jumping from a higher rung of the climbing frame, or by driving faster. Adams argues that this "risk compensation" undermines efforts to reduce accidents: making environments safer is likely to lead to more risky behaviour. In addition, risk may be redistributed to the most vulnerable members of society. Thus if car drivers (secure in the knowledge that they are protected by air bags, seat belts and a crash-resistant car chassis) drive faster, they endanger pedestrians and cyclists. Although seat belt use might reduce fatal injuries to drivers, it may increase those to other, less well-protected, road users. The implications of Adams's argument for accident prevention are interesting. If making cars safer means drivers drive less carefully, then making cars more dangerous would lead to more careful driving. His most radical suggestion is for the "driving column spike" (Adams 1995: 155) to replace the air bag, which would undoubtedly increase the care taken by most drivers. Adams's arguments are convincing, and his reanalysis of the "successes" of accident prevention certainly undermine any faith in engineering or enforcement strategies as routes to reducing accident rates. However, Adams admits that his arguments have been peripheral to the planning process and have had little impact on public health policy. In terms of the research consensus, and the information available to health promotion experts in the early 1990s, there remains a question about why education was prioritized as a strategy despite the apparent strengths of other approaches.

The "success" of any accident prevention programmes is of course extremely difficult to evaluate. Any individual accident event is "caused" by many environmental, cultural and personal factors, and age-specific mortality rates for particular causes are usually too small to gauge significant change. This is what Adams refers to as the problem of "not enough accidental deaths" (Adams 1995: 69). Even when reduced mortality rates can be observed, they are not in themselves evidence of unqualified success, even in terms of health gain, as Roberts (1993) has highlighted in his analysis of the decreasing number of pedestrian deaths in road traffic accidents. In England and Wales between 1968 and 1987 pedestrian deaths fell by 67 per cent for those under four years old, and by 39 per cent for five- to fourteen-year-olds. This represents, argues Roberts, neither the success of road safety campaigns nor improved road designs, but rather the reduced exposure of children over this period to traffic, as they are no longer able to play in the streets or walk to school safely. This may have had the effect of reducing childhood mortality, but possibly at substantial social cost. Car-driving has become more common, making roads increasingly hazardous for those children who are using them. In 1961, for instance, 80 per cent of children walked to school. By 1981, 80 per cent of children were being driven to school (Sutherland 1992). This decrease in the pedestrian activity of children clearly has implications for their physical health, as opportunities for outdoor play and walking are diminished, but also has implications for psychological health. Mayall (1993) has documented the importance for children of a domain outside the adult-controlled worlds of home and school, in which they can develop their own sense of responsibility and rule-making. This domain is potentially eroded by increasing reliance on parents for transport and the perceived hazards of "outdoors", leading to increasing amounts of children's leisure time being spent in the home. Others have pointed to the decreasing sense of "community" in streets where heavy traffic has made avoiding traffic accidents a priority (Hillman et al. 1990). Roberts (1993) also points out that even with increasing car ownership, one-third of families in Britain do not own a car, and so have no choice about escorting their children by car to school. These are the families whose children may also have fewer alternatives to the now-dangerous streets in which to play. Overall, then, pedestrian deaths may have decreased, but the social class profile of mortality is likely to be sharpened.

There are, then, no absolute ways to measure the "success" of accident prevention, as gains in reducing accident rates may be offset by losses in other prioritized areas of health (such as heart disease, or emotional well-being), but there is some evidence that engineering and enforcement strategies can have a demonstrable impact on mortality rates for specific causes of death. As reductions in the mortality rate from accidental injury, and not social justice or improved psychological health, are the explicit aims of current public policy, these strategies are perhaps the obvious target for further research and activity. National health policy in Britain has, however, emphasized education as the key strategy, and education targeted at primary or secondary prevention. There is also evidence that the largest number of initiatives actually undertaken are based on education rather than engineering or enforcement strategies. One review of accident prevention interventions notes that the majority were designed to raise awareness of safety issues or increase knowledge of risks (Popay & Young 1993). Initially, this bias seems perverse as there is little evidence of success so far, and many reasons to be pessimistic about future success.

The limitations of education as a strategy

One initial problem with developing education strategies as the major way of preventing accidents is the logical one that has already been suggested. Risk factors for accidental injury are based on statistical data from populations, and refer to specific population risks based on social and demographic factors such as social class, gender, age and occupation. To develop educational strategies is to imply that these risks can be somehow personalized, and that individuals can alter their chance of having an accident. Statistical correlations alone disclose little about cause, and it has proved difficult to translate "risk factors" into educational advice for prevention.

In addition, most accidents are multifactorial in cause, and identifying the significant action that would have prevented the disastrous combination of factors may only be possible with hindsight. As Bytheway notes in a discussion of statistics on accidents to the elderly:

> Statistics on accidents . . . can beguile one into thinking that the "problem" is simpler than it really is . . . It is not too difficult to think up the "obvious causes" of the typical accident and conclude that if only the old person had looked in all directions before crossing the road (or whatever) the accident could have been prevented. (Bytheway 1978)

After the event it may be possible to identify causes, but prediction, with so many possible factors to consider, is more problematic.

There is little evidence that education has had any impact at all on accident rates (Croft & Sibert 1992). One intervention that was evaluated was the "Play it safe!" campaign, which consisted in part of television programmes aimed at increasing parental knowledge of household risks. No demonstrable effect on associated accident rates was found (Williams & Sibert 1983; Naidoo 1986). Ironically, though, much of the very literature that demonstrates the relative ineffectiveness of education as a strategy also advocates more education as the solution. One study of accidents to children (Carter & Jones 1993) found, for instance, no significant differences in either knowledge about safety or in ownership of safety equipment between parents of children who had had accidents and those who had not, but still concluded that what was needed was more education, opportunistically at the child health surveillance clinic and during home visits. Indeed, there seems to be little evidence for even preventative actions such as those recommended by health promoters having much direct impact at all. Melia et al. (1989) studied the homes of children who had reported an accident to hospital and a group of matched controls. Although they found that those who had had accidents were more likely to have fathers who were unemployed and have had "a major upset" at home over the last twelve months, there was no significant difference in the number of safety hazards spotted by health visitors in the homes of the two groups of children. Hazards were the unsafe practices that are the target of much health promotion aimed at parents: absence of fire guards, loose flexes, access to matches, windows openable by children, and loose stair carpets.

It seems, then, that even if education does change behaviour (itself a rather dubious assumption), the changed behaviour (taking recommended preventative actions) will not necessarily prevent accidents. Education about accident risks was still, however, the most commonly mentioned recommendation in epidemiological reports, even where the complex factors involved in accident causation are noted. For instance, one paper on accidents among elderly people concluded that: "We had difficulty attributing an event to any one factor. Most resulted from an interaction of environmental hazards, physical disability, and carelessness or excessive risk taking" (Graham & Firth 1992).

Despite this cautious conclusion, the authors still went on to suggest that the "key" question for accident prevention was "whether an education programme for the whole population or specific targeting of selected patients would be more effective in reducing home accidents?" To educate, this implies, is a virtue in itself.

This conflict in the literature begs the question, why persist in educational strategies when there is little apparent incentive for doing so? The answer implied by the "professional" voice in epidemiology is that health promotion fails because the public are either ignorant of risks, miscalculate risks or persist with erroneous lay beliefs in the random, and therefore unpredictable, nature of accidents. Education has failed so far because the messages have not been understood – so more may help. The epidemiological evidence suggests that – at its most extreme – "Nearly all 'accidents' contain an element of neglect by exposure to risk, except those accidents which are true acts of God. Some would argue that these too can be avoided by appropriate action" (Polnay 1992).

But in the health education literature, the public are seen to be resistant, clinging on to anachronistic views about accident causation: "Accidents are not totally random events striking innocent victims like bolts from the blue, although they are often described in this way. Accidents have a natural history in which predisposing factors converge to produce an accidental event . . ." (Stone 1991).

Accident prevention has, then, been largely concerned with educating the public about the risks they face and how to reduce them, and has been specifically concerned to counter supposed "lay" views in the random occurrence of accidents. This concern has been in line with official policy aiming to reduce fatal accident rates, although there is little evidence that education has much impact on those rates or (given the similar claims about "lay" beliefs in reports both from the 1950s and the 1990s) on what are thought to be popular conceptions of accident causation. Education based on individual action elides the multi-factorial aetiology of most accidents: including factors over which the individual has little or no control. Exhorting the public to be vigilant about single risks (whether they are unguarded fires or cars without seat belts) is hardly consistent with the findings of either major accident investigations or epidemiological evidence, which stress the constellation of risks involved. Despite such logical limitations and the unsurprising lack of success to date, accident prevention has, however, continued to focus on education.

A divided professional voice

Conflicts between moral and epidemiological accounts of accident causation

The resilience of supposed lay theories of accident causation has been widely cited as a hindrance to the development of more sophisticated prevention strategies, in that they have been seen as infecting the purity of a more professional approach. One professional response has been to attempt a sanitation exercise, and adopt a uniquely professional vocabulary untainted by lay concerns. Robertson (1983), for instance, noted that the study of accidents is surrounded by issues of blame attribution, which do not occur in other health problems: we do not, he argued, seek to attribute blame or seek compensation for the transfer of infectious disease. To avoid these contaminating issues, he advocated a study of "injury control" rather than accident prevention (Robertson 1983: 2) that would focus on injuries as the result of a transfer of energy. This would enable an "epidemiological model of human damage" (Robertson 1983: 23) involving a study of hosts, agents and vectors.

Indeed, there has been a persistent, if muted, voice in epidemiology that has argued for the abandonment of accident as a useful category in medicine. Evans argued that:

> "Accident" conveys a sense that the losses incurred are due to fate and are therefore devoid of rational explanation or predictability. Yet the motivation to study subjects like traffic safety is to discover factors that influence the likelihood of occurrence of, and resulting harm from, "crashes", the preferred term. (Evans 1993)

Evans's objections to the term "accident" are again that it is somehow contaminated by lay associations of an unwilled and unknowable process; it "suggest[s] in addition a general explanation of why it occurred without any evidence to support such an explanation . . . the word accident [should be replaced] by a more objective and crisp word" (Evans 1993). In the same vein, Doege (1978) argued that it was "time for medicine to dispose of the 'accident' and 'accidental injury'", given that it is an "ambivalent, misleading anachronism" (Doege 1978). There have been some successes in abandoning the word "accident" with all its connotations. In Britain, one has been the retitling of the OPCS series that reports on deaths from ICD causes 800–999 (DH4). Until 1991, it was titled *Accidents and violence* (OPCS 1991). In 1992, it was renamed *Injury and poisoning* (OPCS 1992a). These attempts to substitute a more "objective" word that does not carry "lay" connotations of chance and luck are, however, undermined in two ways that reflect the paradoxical nature of accidents in the late twentieth century.

First, if epidemiology has been increasingly concerned to make accidents predictable and preventable, somehow sanitized of their moral lay connotations, it has paradoxically magnified both the uniqueness of the individual accident and the moral dimensions of that event. The space in which "real" accidents (events for which no explanation can be provided and for which no-one can be blamed) occur may have been diminished by increasing the domain of the known and patterned. What remains, however, are still the remnants of a medical classification system: random, individual misfortunes that are not amenable to the statistical explanations of epidemiology. Epidemiology attempts to map accidental events, but inevitably such mapping is incomplete, and there is still a marginal category not yet accounted for. A leftover category of "mere accident" is still created by exclusion from other objects of medical enquiry, such as non-accidental injuries for the casualty doctor, Sudden Infant Death Syndrome, or possible homicide for the forensic pathologist. It is not just "lay" beliefs that contaminate the epidemiological accident, but those generated by the very logic of the nosology that created "accidents" as a marginal category of disease. This residual category is fluid: it contains that for which there is no explanation *as yet*. Accidents occupy a liminal space temporally as well as conceptually.

The logic of nosological classification provides a second source of resistance for the claims for an "objective" definition of accidents, in that these injuries are difficult to classify if divorced from their original (and social, rather than medical) causes. All head injuries are not the same, even if the eventual medical sequelae are. As a textbook on forensic medicine notes, the wounds sustained by accident are quite unlike those from homicide or suicide, which: "follow certain traditional rules . . . accident is something unforeseen. It is not planned and does not, therefore, develop along orthodox lines" (Simpson & Knight 1985: 68).

It is not just that accidents were constructed through what was left over after other, more patterned causes of death were accounted for, but that this exclusion was originally organized around moral enquiry. Even Doege, in his call to abandon the term "accident", noted "a basic need to distinguish between intentional and unintentional injury" (Doege 1978), although he provided no clinical rationale for such a need. It seems impossible adequately to describe accidents, even in a medical discourse about injury, without appeal to the moral discourse that creates them. As an example, one study of farm accidents (Cameron et al. 1992) mentions the following contributing causes in addition to the purely "epidemiological": trespass, inadequate supervision, smoking in a barn, lack of prosecution of farmers who allow children to ride on or drive tractors and lack of legislation prohibiting the use of all-terrain vehicles without crash helmets. Any account that includes individual misfortunes can, it seems, only adequately describe accidents by reference to the moral, and often legal, factors that surround them. The creation of accidents as a nosological category was predicated on a moral classification, with which new classifications based on risk and its assessment come into perhaps inevitable conflict.

The problem of case definition

To develop a purely clinical discourse of accidents as injuries, stripped of these social and moral connotations, requires perhaps some consensus about the proper object of that discourse: what is to count as a "proper" accidental injury. Achieving a consensus about what does constitute an accident has proved, however, problematic. Even restricting attention to events with physical injuries as outcomes leaves several, overlapping, sets of events as contenders, including minor injuries, those requiring hospital admission or treatment and those resulting in death or long-term disability. Fatal accidents are very rare occurrences, but accidents for which medical attention is sought are far more common. Estimates are that each year one child in five visits an Accident and Emergency department

(Sibert et al. 1981) and similar proportions seek medical care from their general practitioner (Agass et al. 1990, Carter & Jones 1993). Around 10,000 children each year are permanently disabled through accidental injury (CAPT 1989). Almost all of us have considerable experience of events we would describe as "minor" accidents to the body: cuts, bruises, stubbed toes or scalds.

These events, although they may all be caused by "accidental" injuries, have rather different aetiologies as well as outcomes. They are, in short, the products of quite different maps of risk factors. Stewart-Brown et al. (1986), for instance, noted that these varying case definitions affect the risk factors that emerge as relevant. They found that large family size and loss or replacement of a natural parent were only risk factors if accidents to children were defined as those resulting in hospital admission, not for accidents with other outcomes. Environmental risk profiles also differ depending on case definition: most non-fatal accidents happen at home, whereas the road is the site of most fatal accidents (Walsh & Jarvis 1992). Poisoning accounts for few deaths in those under 15, but for a high proportion of hospital admissions (Woodroffe et al. 1993). Epidemiology may, then, be clear that an accident is not what the public think it is, but there seems to be as yet no consensus about any clinical definition that would produce a suitable object for a purely clinical discourse.

Sociological explanations for the failure of education

If ignorance and the resilience of lay ideas have been offered by epidemiologists as both explanation for the failure of health education policies so far and as rationale for their continuation, sociologists have concentrated on the structural barriers to the adoption of accident prevention strategies by individuals. In their work on safety on a Glasgow housing estate, Roberts and her co-workers offer a comprehensive structural critique of accident prevention policy (Roberts et al. 1992, 1993). They found that although professionals adopted a model that held accidents to be caused by negligence and believed that more education was needed, parents were actually well aware of risks, in fact more aware of specific local dangers (such as unguarded holes in the pavement) than professionals. They took considerable steps, both individually and as campaigners, to keep their children safe, and of course managed to do so almost all of the time.

Education aimed at increasing awareness of dangers merely increased maternal anxiety as hazards were often environmental ones that little could be done about by individual carers: sockets with no on/off switches, balcony railings that toddlers could crawl under and unguarded holes left by workers. The cost of safety equipment, such as stair gates, fireguards and cooker guards, was prohibitive, and again a source of guilt: parents may recognize a need for such equipment, but not be able to afford it. Parents were not ignorant or irrational, argued Roberts et al.: they shared to a large extent the concerns of the professionals to prevent accidents.

Structural critiques imply one explanation for the persistence of the educational emphasis in accident prevention, despite the lack of documented success for these strategies. That is, they function to channel attention away from the structural inequalities that pattern accident rates and instead utilize what Crawford (1986) has called a "victim blaming" ideology. This explanation has received some attention, from Tombs (1989, 1991) for instance, who has argued in his analyses of accidents in the chemical industry that an ideology of "accident-proneness" which blames the victim for the accident is functional for industry, given that protective strategies such as thorough testing of new technologies and products for their safety stand as an obstacle to the pursuit of profit. The portrayal of workers, claims Tombs, is contradictory: on the one hand accident prevention relies on the control of worker behaviour, which produces an ideology of passive recipients of safety messages who can have nothing to contribute to the process of safety. On the other hand the workers should, through their actions, pre-empt and prevent accidents. Safety messages for workers focus almost exclusively on their duties to avoid accidents (not drinking alcohol, wearing protective equipment and clothing, knowing the position of fire extinguishers), but the views of individual workers or the trade unions that represent them are often not legitimate, as they encroach on the management's right to manage. In a similar vein, Nichols and Armstrong (1973) argued that the pressure to keep up production in factories meant that safety regulations would routinely be circumvented, regardless of how much safety training or knowledge the workers and foremen received. Improving training (or even increasing sanctions for breaking health and safety regulations) would, they argued, merely increase the incentives workers and foremen had to hide the accidents that did inevitably occur.

Naidoo (1986: 25–6), in an account of the "Play it safe!" campaign, which aimed to reduce childhood accidents, also argued that educational strategies are underpinned by an ideology of individualism, in which the environmental and structural factors that constrain safety are ignored. Such a focus, she argued, inhibits the development of collective action to achieve change (such as campaigning to improve play facilities) and reinforces not only individualism but, in this case, the construction of parents as having sole responsibility for the safety of their children.

A second explanation: preventative action as talisman

Such structural critiques offer a convincing political account of why education appears to have priority over other possible strategies. They also offer some insight into why epidemiology persists in constructing a "lay" view as a foil for its more rational expert account; that is, that the construction of "lay" views as irrational necessitates further attempts to correct them. However, for such strategies to permeate with so little opposition, in such a range of fields, suggests there may be other possibilities, or at least explanations of why education strategies of accident prevention can gain such legitimacy. One further explanation for the endurance of accident prevention that is based on education could also be suggested.

If the preventative actions recommended have no proven utility in preventing accidents, they may have more value as talismans: as rituals appealing not to a rational modernist control of direct causes and their effects, but to a rather different rationality, that of risk and its management. "Taking precautions" does not appeal, perhaps, to a deterministic model in which certain actions (or inactions) pose a specific danger that can be avoided, but to a more contemporary model of fate and risk. Education strategies persist because they construct individuals as responsible for the surveillance and management of their own risk environment. Such responsibility is seductive: few would resist by arguing that they were incapable of assessing and managing risks for themselves. Although preventative actions may not directly prevent accidents, they demonstrate an adherence to the calculability of risk, and so perhaps reduce uncertainty at a cognitive level. By reducing the dangers in our environments we construct ourselves as competent risk managers.

The transformation of accidents, from unpredictable misfortune to preventable outcome, is not only a facet of shifting perceptions of "dangers" and "risks". It represents perhaps a rather more widespread cultural shift in the late twentieth century, in how we construct security, causality and misfortune. The next chapter will explore the wider implications of a focus on "risk" to locate the accident as a significant marker of changing social formations.

Chapter 6

Risk and high modernity

Introduction

It has been suggested that a focus on risk might help locate the shifting place of accidents in our classification of misfortune. From being marginal misfortunes at the boundary of rational classificatory systems, accidents have become the paradigmatic outcomes of risk; they are at the centre of late twentieth-century concerns. That an accident has happened demonstrates that risks have been inadequately managed, and the epidemiological study of these outcomes thus provides a key arena for demonstrating the effectiveness of risk technologies. The accident can no longer be taken for granted, invisible unless missing as it was in the 1930s; it becomes visible as the marker of the success of risk management techniques. A key arena in which the accident has become visible is public health. Targets of reductions in accident rates justify ever more sophisticated techniques of risk assessment, and also, in O'Malley's (1992) phrase, "privatize" risk management. Managing accidents becomes the concern not of the state or the health service, through the provision of improved trauma treatment or more stringent traffic speed legislation, but primarily of the individual who potentially suffers them. The implications for the victim of a discourse in which the accident should not happen are perhaps even bleaker than those of modernist rationality. Rationality could provide no solace, or opportunities for revenge for such misfortunes, but it implied (at least ideally) no blame either. Victims of the failure of risk management may not be seen as malicious, but they are in a sense culpable, in their ignorance. Installing stair gates to prevent childhood falls, wearing cycle helmets to reduce the effects of head injuries, or fitting window guards may have a negligible effect on the amount of "safety" in the universe. Such actions do, however, demonstrate perhaps a belief in the possibility of managing risks, and signify responsibility, as a parent, a cyclist or a householder. As one book, aimed at educating the parents of small children about preventing accidents, notes, accident prevention is largely about good parenting and: "As a new Mum you should already be feeling that surge of responsibility that comes with bringing a new life into the world" (Smith & Smith 1991: 16).

This might suggest that a discourse of risk is irresistible; that we are all engaged in constant surveillance of our risk environments, and management of those risks through "talismatic" prevention. To do otherwise would be to marginalize oneself not only as irresponsibly fatalistic, but also, in the example above, as an inadequate parent. However, it has also been noted that there are limitations to the epidemiological constructions of accidents as outcomes of risk constellations in, for instance, the continuing references to accidents as a marginal nosological category, as well as a central one.

How can we make sense of the emergence of the preventable accident, and its seeming irresistibility? In Chapter 3 it was suggested that "common sense" about accidents in the early part of the twentieth century (that they were random coincidences that only the irrational would try to understand at the local level) was possible because rationality itself was relatively unproblematic. Once the consensus around rationality had been fractured, the tension between the accident as necessary to rational explanation but also despised by it becomes more apparent. In the last decades of the twentieth century there are signs that the accident as a kind of misfortune occupies a rather different space to that natural and obvious category of the 1930s: the accident, like rationality, becomes somewhat problematic. This chapter locates the discursive shifts that have produced a different kind of accident in the late twentieth century.

Accidental cause as anachronistic explanation

The first indication that accidents occupy a rather different location in late twentieth-century classifications of misfortune is the finding that a belief in accidents, rather than indicating a specifically modern mentality is constructed in some arenas as, on the contrary, rather anachronistic. Those individuals who adhere to explanations of events that involve fate, luck or chance ("accidental" causes) have been characterized as not modern, but on the contrary as somewhat irrational. Two examples, the psychology of cause attribution and a report from a mountain rescue organization, illustrate this contemporary unease about the accidental as a legitimate explanation for misfortune.

The psychology of cause and blame attribution

The psychology of cause attribution is concerned with how people adapt to misfortune; the relationship between attributions of cause, responsibility and blame; and whether an attribution of blame (whether self-blame or blaming another agent) is adaptive for the individual. Empirical evidence from psychological studies suggests that blaming others for "accidental" misfortunes leads to poor adjustment, but there is less consistency about the impact of self-blame on psychological health (Tennen & Affleck 1990). Shaver and Drown (1986) suggest that one source of uncertainty arises from the difficulty in talking about "blame" in asking respondents about their reactions to accidents. Accidents are, they claim, still a particular kind of misfortune in which the concept of "blame" is missing by definition. There is perhaps a limit to the explanatory power of such empirical studies to look at blame attribution for accidents, if "accidents" themselves are defined in practice as any event for which blame is not apportioned. The argument becomes rather tautological.

What is perhaps more interesting is the place accidents have had in this literature as explanations of misfortune, rather than instances of it. One of the most influential works in the field of the psychology of cause attribution, at least in terms of citation (see Rotter 1982: 145), has been the development of the internal–external locus of control construct, which was designed to identify through responses to a questionnaire whether ideas of fate and chance were more important to individuals than belief in self-determination and the ability to control one's own destiny. Rotter characterized belief in accidental explanations of events as an instance of "external" factors; forces outside the individual. Respondents with a strong "external locus of control" attributed more salience to accidents, fate and chance as explanation for events in their lives than to factors within their own control.

Although Rotter claimed explicitly that the external pole of his continuum was not by definition the negative one (Rotter 1982: 272), and that extreme scores on either end of the continuum indicated "pathological" beliefs, the implication of much of his writing was that the external pole was the least desirable one. The definition of an external locus of control is a belief in the power of "luck, fate, chance or powerful others" to control the outcome of behaviour. In his original article, Rotter quotes Veblen on a belief in luck being characteristic of "primitive" societies and claims that behaviour based on "accidental" reinforcements will lead the subject to "learn the wrong things and develop a pattern of behaviour that Skinner has referred to as 'superstitious'" (Rotter 1966). Such an evaluation is difficult to reconcile with a claim that the external locus was not interpreted to indicate pathological beliefs. Even with later revisions such as the Interpersonal Trust Scale, which differentiated those who react to a belief in external control with passivity from those who use the belief defensively, Rotter's work has in practice been used to define individuals with a strong internal locus of control as the "positive" end of a sample.

One obvious application of these models has been in the field of health promotion. Although recent theory in health promotion is somewhat more sophisticated, citing its agenda as "empowerment" rather than a more paternalistic "education", much of the research on lay views of health has implicitly used this notion of an "internal locus of control" to identify individuals who are most likely to react "rationally" in the field of health behaviours. People who consider that internal factors (such as their health maintenance behaviour) have the most salience for whether they stay healthy are most likely to be receptive to messages about how to alter their behaviour in a healthy way. Those who see health as a matter of chance or accident are less likely to be receptive. Specific Health Locus of Control scales have been developed (see, for example, Wallston et al. 1978), which have identified three dimensions: Internality, Powerful Others and Chance. One questionnaire item that contributes to a high score on the "chance" dimension is "Most things that affect my health happen to me by accident" (Wallston et al. 1978).

People who score high on Chance and low on other scores have, for instance, been hypothesized as being "fatalistic; [with] poor use of all services" (Bradley et al. 1990) and as being more likely to delay seeking help and abandon medications (Wallston et al. 1978). The likely impact of health promotion messages will, in this model, differ in terms of how fatalistic the target population is. This "fatalism" has been linked to both lower social class (as indicated by education and home ownership) (Pill & Stott 1982) and ethnicity (Laungani 1989), although more recent work suggests that "fatalistic" beliefs are as prevalent among the middle classes (Davison et al. 1991). To risk overstating the case, the extensive use of Rotter's scale has meant that beliefs in fate and the "accidental" causes of ill health have only been studied as irrational lay beliefs; anachronistic and dysfunctional within the modern rational corpus of belief.

To argue that the attribution of "accidental" cause to "non-accidental" misfortunes such as ill health is constructed as anachronistic is not, of course, the same as arguing that there are no events that are still seen purely as "accidents", for which no responsibility or blame could be legitimately attributed. One category of misfortunes that are commonly referred to as accidents is injuries and deaths that occur when mountain climbing. It might be worth, then, turning to how the cause and responsibility of these are attributed. One contribution to the social knowledge of mountain accidents comes from the reports of Mountain Rescue Associations.

Mountain accidents

In an annual report from the Lake District Search and Mountain Rescue Association (LDSAMRA *c.* 1992) lies an illustration of how one specific set of misfortunes labelled as accidents – those that happen on mountains – are created by one voluntary organization. In these statistics there are several clues to a rather different construction of the accident to the one made possible by developments in probability in the seventeenth century. First, any belief in bad luck or fate as the cause of injury is constructed as negligently irrational or ill-informed. The LDSAMRA's annual report on incidents from 1991 describes 255 "mountain accidents", which cover injuries sustained while walking and climbing as well as rescues of people who have fallen ill on mountains. Examples include falls while walking and climbing and rescues of those suffering from hypothermia after

Table 6.1 Mountain accident incident reports, 1991.

No.	Type	Date and call out time involved	Age	Home town	Weather and ground conditions	Clothing, equipment, footwear – helmet	Known experience	Cause of accident	Location of accident	Injury detail
40	Fell walking	28th 19.15 Man	47	Blackpool	Light wind, sub-zero temperatures	OK	Some	Exhausted, over-exertion, benighted	Great Gable area	Mild hypothermia (found after 5 hours)
41	Fell walking	28th 10.34 Man	70	Gravesend, Kent	Warm, clear, dry ground, OK	Town clothes, trainers	Not known	Bird-watching, slipped and fell down river bank	Elterwater, Gt Langdale	Fractured ankle
		March								
43	Fell walking ATC group exercise	3rd 15.28 2 Girls 1 Youth	15 15 16	Norfolk	Gales, cold, wet snow on the tops	Reasonable	None	Became exhausted on walk in the bad conditions	Mart Crag Moor, Gt Langdale	All exhaustion exposure
44	Ice/ snow climbing	3rd 14.00 6 Climbers	NR	Whitehaven	Low cloud, new snow	Satisfactory; crampons/ice axes	Not reported	Party of 6 avalanched out of gully	Central Gully, Great End	5 light injuries 1 broken back and pelvis
45	Fell walking	13th 15.25 Youth	13	Milton Keynes	Hazy sunshine, mild, dry, damp ground	Good	Limited	Running down slope slipped on rock	Winder, Howgill Fells, near Sedbergh	Fractured right clavicle
46	Fell walking	15th 20.15 Man	43	Guisborough North Yorks	Dense, low hill fog, snow patches fresh wind 7°C	Moderate, running shoes no sac, map or compass	Doubtful (poor navigation)	Became lost in mist	East of Knock Fell Pennies NY 740-303	Mild hypothermia (13-hour incident)
47	Walking	16th 13.00 Man	52	Cambridge	Showery	Poor footwear, ordinary day clothes	Not recorded	Slipped whilst jumped over boggy patch	Crummock area	Left ankle fractured
48	Hunting	16th 11.25 Man	NR	NR	NR	Hunt-following gear	NR	Blacked out on fell	Hall's Fell Ridge	Leg injuries
49	Fell walking	16th 13.04 Man	54	Huddersfield	Clear, cool, ground wet in	Good	Not known	Slipped on footpath	Mitchell Knott	Lower leg fractured

becoming lost or benighted. They range from the tragic to the trivial. Each case is listed with details of the type of incident, time of the call-out, demographic details of victims, the weather conditions, the clothing and equipment of victims, their experience and the immediate cause, location and outcome of the accident. Table 6.1 reproduces cases from one page of the report.

The implication of these data is that there are two levels of cause for each of these misfortunes. First is the immediate cause; for instance slipping on a wet path or tripping over a rock. But prior to these are the conditions that made such an immediate cause more likely to occur: the environmental and other factors that can be used to predict "an accident waiting to happen". Thus the inadequacy of walkers' clothing is noted, or their lack of experience. Victims miscalculate risks by underestimating the weather; they flout risks by wearing inadequate shoes and clothing; they display ignorance of risks in their lack of experience. Significantly, the appeal is clearly to an epidemiological model of risk calculation, where the attribution of responsibility for specific accidents does not rely on any direct causal link between the actual risk that has apparently been miscalculated and the injury sustained in the individual event. The "original causes" (weather, clothing, skills) are merely correlates (in the sense that in taking such risks, it is implied, one has a statistically greater chance of suffering an accident), yet the listing of them (irrespective of the actual injury sustained) constructs a field of responsibilities for preventing the accident. The predictive power of these correlations would be difficult to demonstrate empirically, given that the number of people who take risks (such as wearing inadequate clothing) but who escape accidental injury is not calculated. The data consist only of actual misfortunes, and the relevant "facts" about them.

In one case, for instance, a man suffered spinal injuries and a fractured scapula in an accident that clearly did not result directly from his carelessness or miscalculation of any calculable risks. The event is described thus: "On walk from car park to pose for a photograph, [he] fell backwards over a boulder" (LDSAMRA *c.* 1992: 43). However, it is still noted that his clothing consisted of "canvas shoes, town clothes" and that his experience was "doubtful". Boulders in car parks perhaps provide a yet to be calculated risk, but the victim here has already demonstrated his "deservedness" of accidental injury through his inability (or unwillingness) to calculate the chances of mountain accidents. The actual causes seem not to be an issue. The important point, it is implied, is that those using mountains for leisure should calculate all possible risks. Failure to do so implies a certain culpability. Although such an accident might be constructed as being caused merely by "bad luck" in private accounts, in this public account it is implied to be a statistically predictable outcome of a set of risk factors.

In the report itself, luck does have a part to play, but not as a contributor to the causes of accidents. Luck is mentioned only in the context of the extent of injury sustained. In one case (LDSAMRA c.1992: 6), for instance, a man who was solo-climbing fell 500 ft and sustained a sprained neck and lacerations to scalp and nose. The outcome was described as "very lucky" in parenthesis. To fall so far and escape with only minor injuries is perhaps "very lucky", but there is no suggestion that to fall at all (be it over a car park boulder or into a ravine) is unlucky.

The message that luck has little part to play is reiterated at the end of this report, in the public information intended for those who use the mountains and surrounding countryside for recreation. Like the rest of the work of Mountain Rescue Associations, this advice is based on many years of experience in saving lives and helping the public to use the countryside more safely: it is not intended here to belittle such advice, which is at one level "common sense" about the precautions one ought to take when climbing or walking. What is interesting, however, is how this "common sense" constructs responsibility. The information for walkers and climbers (see Fig. 6.1) explicitly holds the victim responsible: "British mountains can be killers" it notes, "if proper care is not taken" (LDSAMRA c.1992: 66). Proper care is a daunting prospect involving predicting not only the weather and the physical environment but also protecting against what the recommendations call "plain damned carelessness". Accidents, even in such high-risk recreations such as rock-climbing or long-distance hiking, should not happen. They only do so if the public fail to take due care to calculate known or knowable risks.

Risk and expertise

It is not only the general public who potentially miscalculate the risks of mountaineering. *The Times* on 21 August 1995 carried two obituaries of British climbers, after the tragic deaths of Alison Hargreaves, killed in a storm while descending from the summit of K2, and Paul Nunn, who died in an avalanche on a previously unclimbed peak in the Karakoram range in Pakistan. Both were experienced and respected climbers: Hargreaves,

Figure 6.1 Advice to walkers and climbers.

Live a little longer

British mountains can be killers if proper care is not taken. The following notes cover the *minimum* precautions if you want to avoid getting hurt or lost, and so inconveniencing or endangering others as well as yourselves.

Clothing

This should be colourful, warm, windproof and waterproof. Wear boots with nails or moulded rubber soles *not* shoes, plimsols or gum-boots. Take a woollen cap and a spare jersey; it is always colder on the tops.

Food

In addition to the usual sandwiches, take chocolate, dates, mint cake or similar sweet things which restore energy quickly. If you don't need them, someone else may.

Equipment

This *must* include map, compass, and at least one reliable watch in the party. A whistle, torch and spare batteries and bulbs (six blasts or flashes repeated at minute intervals signal an emergency), and, in winter conditions, an ice-axe and survival bag are *essential*. Climbers are all urged to wear helmets.

Company

Don't go alone, and make sure party leaders are experienced. Take special care of the youngest and weakest in dangerous places.

Emergencies

Don't press on if conditions are against you – turn back even if it upsets your plan. Learn first aid, and keep injured or exhausted people warm until help reaches you. Get a message to the Police for help as soon as possible, and report changes of route or timetable to them if someone is expecting you. The Police will do the rest.

Dangers which can always be avoided

and should be until you know how to cope with them:

Precipices, slopes of ice, or steep snow, or very steep grass (especially frozen), or unstable boulders.

Gullies and stream beds. Streams in spate. Snow cornices on ridges or gully tops. Over-ambition. Plain damned carelessness.

Dangers which may surprise you

and should be guarded against:

Weather changes – mist, gale, rain or snow. **Get forecasts, and watch the sky in all quarters.**

Ice on paths. **Carry an ice-axe and crampons – *know how to use them.***

Excessive cold or heat. **Dress sensibly, and take a spare jersey.**

Incipient exhaustion. **Know the signs; rest and keep warm.**

Accident or illness. **Don't panic. If you send for help, make sure that the rescuers know exactly where to come.**

Flight of time. **Learn your own pace. Plan your walk. Allow double time in winter conditions.**

It is no disgrace to turn back if you are not certain. A party must be governed by the capabilities of the weakest member.

Reproduced from LDSMRA *c.*1992.

the first woman to climb Everest solo without oxygen, is described as having "an international reputation as a superlative mountaineer", and Nunn, president of the British Mountaineering Council, as having a "distinguished" career marked by the pioneering of several new routes. Both climbers are quoted in these obituaries on their acceptance of the inevitable risks that accompany mountaineering at this level; in Hargreaves' words that "there is no gain without risk" and in Nunn's concern that "the soul of climbing is being contested, threatened, by. . . organized recreations, unquiet minds". Those that have beyond doubt demonstrated an ability to calculate and manage risk have, perhaps, a legitimated authority to risk an accident. These tragic deaths are at one level heroic: accidents that were not unexpected misfortunes, but instead ones whose risks were exactly known, understood and courted.

However, even Alison Hargreaves, whose climbing skill and experience were without question, was the subject of debate around the adequacy of risk management. The obituary noted the views of "those who accused her of selfishly putting her career as a climber before her duties as a mother", and, despite quoting Hargreaves' robust defence of her career choice, refers to her role as a mother no fewer than six times, including a mention of her job as chairman (sic) of a local playgroup. Nunn was also survived by a partner and two children, although there are no references to his role as father or husband. It is, perhaps, unsurprising that discourses of risk are not gender-neutral, and can be used to construct appropriately gendered roles, such as "responsible mother". It is more surprising that even Hargreaves, one of the most celebrated climbers of her generation, has apparently limited legitimacy to "risk" an accident.

Rationality and risk

There are suggestions here that the rationality outlined in Chapter 3 as being a precondition for accidents to emerge may now have somewhat different contours. A belief that some events are "just" accidents now appears decidedly irrational. The rationality that emerged from the late seventeenth century involved deterministic notions of direct cause and effect: a wound festers, in Evans-Pritchard's example, because it gets dirty. The toe is cut because the boy was clumsy enough to bump into a tree stump. All else is mere coincidence and there is nothing to be gained in trying to account for the tree stump being in the same place at the same time as the toe. Accidents were what was left over when such explanations reached their limit, the random misfortunes distributed by laws of probability. These statistics on mountain accidents imply, however, that accidents happen not when deterministic laws are inapplicable but when individuals fail to demonstrate adherence to other laws; those of statistical probability. Weather conditions, inadequate clothing and lack of experience constitute a field of knowable and calculable risks. Accidents happen not when combinations of these factors come together in an unpredictable way, but when they are miscalculated or ignored. In 1931 Evans-Pritchard's young friend was merely unlucky. If his misfortune had disabled him on a modern English mountain, he might expect facts about his experience, clothing and footwear to be interrogated and listed. Although not held officially culpable for tripping on a tree stump, the statistics to which his accident contributed would generate a map of responsibility; a field of risks that he should have adequately negotiated.

There are, then, signs that the belief that some events are "just accidents" has a more ambivalent status in contemporary Britain. As the review of medical classifications of accidents in Chapter 4 suggested, the epidemiology of accidents has become increasingly more detailed. By the middle of the twentieth century there was a growth of production of knowledge about accidents and how their occurrence is patterned, which produced not a disparate group of random misfortunes but a set of events correlated with social, environmental and psychological risk factors. Far from demonstrating an unproblematically "modern" outlook, a belief in coincidence or luck begins to demonstrate an anachronistic "lay" view of accidents, compared with that of professionals in accident prevention and risk assessment. Lévy-Bruhl's modern mentality attributed a certain category of events (those attributable to the random play of chance in an otherwise determined universe) to the accidental. Today it appears, at first sight, that only the primitive persists in a belief in the random accident. It is as if in the late twentieth century the remainder of the universe has been made calculable, if not precisely known. Through epidemiological mapping even chance events have been made predictable, and the accident no longer has a legitimate place. There are here some suggestions that contemporary discourses of risk and its management have produced a rather different accident as a type of event and a rather different status for the accidental as causal explanation. In short, beliefs in accidental cause have shifted from being definitive of a modern cosmology to being anachronistic.

129

The example of the recording of mountain accidents furnishes some clues to an understanding of the role of accidents in contemporary discourses about misfortune. It seems that accidents are no longer merely left overs of our classification system but have been (or are being) transformed into the outcomes of predictable (at least in theory) risk factors. Rationality, as it has been characterized so far, is no longer an adequate explanatory system in which to situate the accident, for the accident no longer results from the inevitable boundaries of that system. First, then, it may be pertinent to revisit some of the debates about rationality noted in Chapter 3, to explore whether the rationality that was seen to characterize cosmology between the late seventeenth and early twentieth centuries has been replaced by some other discourse about what constitutes reasonable behaviour and belief.

Second, the notion of risk appears to be a key one. To describe a "risk" suggests an individualized statistical prediction, in which the population statistics that emerged in the West from the late seventeenth century have been translated into individual "chances" of a misfortune occurring. It has already been noted that by the middle of the twentieth century rationality had been contested as both a normative ideal and as an adequate description of contemporary explanatory systems. It may be useful to examine more closely the fracturing of this consensus around rationality to attempt a characterization of late twentieth-century explanatory models, and the space occupied in them by accidents.

The demise of rationality?

Foucault is one writer who has rejected any easy equation of modernity with "rationality", if rationality is taken to be a description of the dominant discourse following the Renaissance developments in science. Examining the domains of natural science, political economy and grammar, he claimed:

> This new configuration may, I suppose, be called "rationalism'; one might say, if one's mind was filled with ready made concepts, that the seventeenth century marks the disappearance of the old superstitious or magical beliefs and the entry of nature, at long last, into the scientific order. (Foucault 1989: 54)

Even the "slightly more perceptive" (Foucault 1989: 56) who typify this rationalism as containing "contrary forces" have, argued Foucault, an inadequate analysis. A more convincing characterization of the modern age (or the classical age in Foucault's account, from the mid-seventeenth century to the end of the eighteenth) is that of an *episteme* of knowledge based on order and on difference, as distinct from the Renaissance, when knowledge was configured around essential similarities. To describe such a knowledge as "rational", he argued, implies that it emerged from the failures of pre-classical thought. Such a description assumes that rationality was essentially predicated on the attempt to make nature calculable with *mathesis*, the "universal science of measurement and order" (ibid.: 56). Thus in the conventional formulation the classical project is an empirical and quantifying one, concerned to reduce all of nature to quantifiable relations, and the "more perceptive" formulation merely adds that some aspects of life (perhaps the "human" qualities) are irreducible. This formulation is, says Foucault, still inadequate. Instead he describes the fundamental characteristic of knowledge in the classical period as being about the link with *mathesis*, which was primarily one of order, and only secondarily of measurement: calculability is not the central issue (Foucault 1989: 57). The characteristic tool of classical knowledge was *analysis*, which replaces the interpretation of the Renaissance period. Analysis is of *signs*, which can be ordered (potentially exhaustively) within a table (the archetypal form of classical knowledge). A table quantifies signs, but more significantly, in Foucault's account, it demonstrates the relationships between them (Foucault 1989: 74). Like Hacking (1975), Foucault describes signs as having changed their nature after the seventeenth century, having lost their Renaissance connection with the signified; they cease to be "a form of the world, bound to what [they] mark by solid and secret bonds of resemblance or affinity" (Foucault 1989: 58). The sign is thus divorced from the "teeming world . . . and lodged henceforth within the confines of representation . . . in that narrow space in which they interact with themselves in a perpetual state of decomposition and recomposition" (Foucault 1989: 67). For Foucault, this classical *episteme* was supplanted at the end of the eighteenth century by a new knowledge, now based on analogies and organic structures (Foucault 1989: 227), in which the sign signified invisible structures, or "great hidden forces developed on the basis of their primitive and inaccessible nucleus, origin, causality and history" (ibid.: 251). The "problem of Man" occurs within this new age; and the human sciences are one facet of this.

The classical project was a comprehensive one, with a *mathesis* as a unifying foundation that could potentially include all branches of knowledge. The new *episteme*, however, was fractured at its beginning: there was no single or comprehensive rationality, only what Hacking (1987) has referred to as "styles of rationality".

In terms of describing the place of the accident, Foucault's criticism of a characterization of modernity (his classical period) as "rational" is pertinent. The tables of the Registrar-General reviewed in Chapter 4 are perhaps an example of the kind of analysis he argues is characteristic of the *episteme*. In them, the accident is not merely quantified, but placed in relation to other "signs" (of infectious disease, of suicide) and then subdivided into internal classes (railway accidents, home accidents, road accidents) that are tabulated against signs of social states (age, gender, occupation). Foucault's argument warns of the dangers of assuming that contemporary analysis (the ever more sophisticated cross-tabulations of the risk factors of accidents, for instance) are a progression from this; merely a more refined version. Instead, we might find a radical discontinuity, with accidents as the product of some quite different discourse.

However, despite Foucault's critique, it seems useful to retain the notion of "rationality" to describe the emergent consensus of the late seventeenth century, which lasted, in certain fields of knowledge at least, until the middle of the twentieth century. A precise periodization may not be possible, but there are some grounds for looking for a shift in explanatory discourses in the middle of the twentieth century. When Sharpe was translating the medieval coroners' rolls in 1913 and Evans-Pritchard was describing the "irrational" Azande in 1937, they could still appeal to an ideological consensus that accidents were a given, indisputable feature of a "rational" universe.

How, then, are we to characterize the late twentieth century in order to differentiate it from this period of "rational" consensus? Giddens (1991) uses the term "high modernity". High modernity is characterized by "a widespread scepticism about providential reason, coupled with the recognition that science and technology are double-edged" (Giddens 1991: 27). Giddens claims that such scepticism is not merely the province of intellectuals and that an "existential anxiety" is typical of wider society, whose members have constantly to negotiate risk and uncertain futures. In 1919, Weber could characterize the rationality of modernity as one in which all things were in principle calculable: as individuals we may not know how a particular technology (the motor car, the pharmacological action of medicine) works, but we assume that someone (an expert) does know, and that "there are no mysterious forces, incalculable forces that come into play . . . one can, in principle, master all things by calculation" (Weber 1948: 139 (first published 1919)).

The "expert" in the late twentieth century

It is the status of this "expert" who does know that has shifted in high modernity, whose infallibility is no longer trusted. Science and technology are, it is argued, no longer the province of accepted experts with automatic credibility. Freudenburg (1993) has coined the term "recreancy" to describe this loss of faith in individuals and institutions in whom (it is implied) we would have trusted in former times. "Recreancy" implies a failure to fulfil either the social obligations expected or to warrant trust. Freudenburg uses the term to denote any behaviour that falls short of these obligations, whether intentional or not. This is significant for this discussion, given that the modern "accident" (in the nosological accounts of the nineteenth century and anthropological ones of the early twentieth century) was constructed in terms of motivation. In this light, the concept of "recreancy" recalls Figlio's (1985) argument that an accident could only happen when negligence (which was essentially unmotivated) entered employer–employee relations in contract law. However, "recreancy" is perhaps rather more diffuse: any expert individual or organization can fail in their social obligations, whether a contractual relationship existed or not.

In looking at how people perceive risk, Freudenburg claims that the strength of belief in "recreancy" (for instance of government departments) is more significant than the traditional factors of risk perception analysis, such as technical assessments of the actual risk posed, or the socio-demographic characteristics of the risk perceiver. An analysis of beliefs in recreancy, he argues, may be more productive than sterile debates about whether perceptions of risk are rational or not. In empirical studies they are a better predictor of attitudes to specific risks than gender, political ideology or measures of self-interest. The key to understanding whether risks (in his example, those of the management of nuclear waste) are seen as reasonable or not is an analysis of views in the fallibility of experts and public bodies. Freudenburg notes that the value of this approach is likely to be greatest in domains in which an "accident" is likely to happen. The definition he chooses of an accident is also significant for this discussion: "an occasion in which a miscalculation leads to the break-down of customary order" (Molotch 1970, quoted by Freudenburg 1993: 928). Accidents are here explicitly attributed not to luck or fate but, like the mountain accidents in the example above, to miscalculation. Neither are they the inevitable misfortunes of the 1930s, which any rational actor should expect as, at times, inevitable.

Risk perceptions

If accidents are produced and understood not through the interplay of de-terministic and statistical laws, but through the calculation (or miscalcula-tion) of risks, perhaps the crucial question is that of understanding what constitutes a "risk" in the late twentieth century. Like rationality, the term "risk" has been utilized in a wide range of discourses in which it serves rather different purposes. Douglas (1986) has reviewed some of these in her study of *Risk acceptability according to the social sciences*, from seventeenth- and eighteenth-century theorizing about the "risks" of gambling, through nineteenth-century "utility theory" to the sub-discipline of "risk assess-ment", which she dates as beginning in the middle of the twentieth cen-tury, when the relative benefits and dangers of an emerging nuclear energy industry were first debated in the public arena. She argued that, although risk perception has received considerable attention from psy-chologists, economists and organizational theorists, there has been little study of the cultural influences on risk perception. How risks are selected as significant, and how people, in modern society, come to take certain risks and not others, has been a problem of psychology rather than one of cultural theory, with a consequent focus on risk perceptions as pathologi-cal or irrational. Freudenburg (1993) makes a similar point; that sociologi-cal attention to risk has largely been directed at the characteristics of individual risk perceivers.

The growth of cultural analyses of risk

There has been, however, a considerable body of more recent work on how risk perceptions are situated in particular cultural forms. Some of this work takes an earlier study by Douglas (1973) as a starting point.

Here, Douglas suggested an anthropological approach to "risk assessment", which would focus on how the organization of society can structure the perceptions of individuals within it of where dangers lie. Her analysis rested on the relative strengths of two organizing principles, called "grid" and "group". Grid referred to the "scope and coherent articulation of a system" (Douglas 1973: 82). Thus a strong grid indicated a system in which there was a high degree of shared agreement about classification and meaning. Group referred to the amount of control an individual could exercise within the system: a strong group was one in which there was a high degree of control over action (Douglas 1973: 84). The articulation of grid and group within a society (or sub-culture) helped to determine how such misfortunes as accidents were perceived by that cultural system. Where both grid and group are strong, that is, a cultural system that was both strongly externally bounded and with a high degree of consensus about internal norms, then "Disease and accident are either attributed to moral failures or invested with nobility in a general metaphysical scheme which embraces suffering as part of the order of being" (Douglas 1973: 136).

In contrast, where there are strong external boundaries but weak internal classification, misfortunes such as accidents may, she argues, be attributed to witchcraft. Thus the degree of individual freedom to act and the strength of consensus about cultural norms structure the attribution of misfortunes, and how they are classified.

This analysis has been used by Bellaby (1990) to examine risk perceptions within groups in contemporary Western society. He explored why different people may have radically different conceptions of the risks that they face in a study of different groups of workers in a pottery factory. Here, perception of the risks of the various work settings within the factory were seen in terms of the relationships these settings had to the factory as a whole. Those workers who worked in the extremes of physical conditions (such as the kiln workers, who worked in extremes of heat, or those in the cold and wet of the sliphouse) considered themselves "hardened" to risks. Hardship strengthened immunity to risk. Others in more marginal work places (those decorating the pots), on the other hand, considered themselves vulnerable to physical risks. This was not, claimed Bellaby, merely a case of irrational attitudes to the physical environment. Instead, Douglas's (1973) analysis of "grid" and "group" as organizing principles offered a way of conceptualizing the stances of these workers. Cultural perceptions of risk could thus be seen as being patterned by the relative strengths of grid and group. Thus, the kiln and sliphouse workers had strong "group" boundaries (they worked, for instance, in an area to which other groups of workers were not admitted) but had weak "grid" boundaries: the workers were not internally differentiated. These workers saw themselves as "risk-immune", as being strong enough to cope with the rigours of their tasks without danger. In contrast, both shop stewards and family directors, who share strong grid and group positions are described as "complacent" about risks, whereas process workers (with strong grid, but weak group) were vulnerable to the risks of the working conditions, such as the dampness of the environment.

Another example of what could be called a "cultural" analysis of risk perceptions is Carter's (1994) study of risk perceptions within a nuclear power station. Carter examined gender as one cultural division that structures risk perceptions, and accounted for how these beliefs were held within discourses of power and of the calculability of risks. The relations of power within the station were essentially gendered, and it emerged that discourses of risk were too. Nuclear radiation, for instance, was constructed as a calculable risk: knowable, manageable and scientific. Safety messages and working practices for workers at the power station emphasized the "safe" levels of radiation in the plant, which could be measured and monitored. These were compared (in, for instance, the safety training videos shown to workers) with the threats of unknown radiation from the "natural" environment. The home was referred to as the most dangerous place, as it was unregulated, in contrast to the ordered and managed environment of the plant. Safety training pointed to the dangers of the home, compared with the managed safety of the power plant. These discourses of managed scientific risk compared with the dangers of unregulated "natural" or domestic risks were constructed, argued Carter, within gendered dichotomies: male, science and ordered opposed to female, nature and unregulated. Danger, he argued, did not so much reside in the natural or female spheres as arise from the possibilities of transgression: from flows of radiation from one sphere to the other. The relations of gendered power were intricately tied to the construction of "risks" within the work place, as evidenced in the discomfort of some workers with female managers: those who had transgressed expected gender roles.

The work of Bellaby and Carter, and many others who have explored the cultural construction of risk in other domains (see, for instance, Davison et al. 1991 on heart disease risks; Warwick et al. 1988 on young people's beliefs about AIDS; Plant & Plant 1993 on adolescents' risk-taking behaviour; Roberts et al. 1993 on accidents; Rogers & Pilgrim

1995 on childhood immunizations), suggests that analyzing individual risk beliefs as deriving from cultural rather than psychological factors has been, in recent years, a rich field of enquiry. In this body of research, perceptions of risk are taken as rational, when situated in their cultural context, rather than as irrational, or pathological. Risk-taking behaviour is presented as reasonable behaviour, in terms of the internal logic of a cultural system. Risks are therefore not purely external or objective dangers, but are produced, negotiated and manipulated within social interaction. This body of work (largely from the 1980s and 1990s) has constructed risk in a particular way, in terms of the motivations people (as members of cultural groups, rather than as psychologized individuals) have for engaging in "risky" activity.

Some assumptions of a cultural theory of risk

A "cultural" theory of risk and risk-taking produces a particular knowledge about what risks are and how we manage them. The first set of assumptions problematize any direct relationship between knowledge and behaviour. Knowledge about the distribution of risks and how to manage them does not imply that action will be taken to reduce them, for several reasons. First, action taken to reduce one risk may increase vulnerability to another. Taking a risk (and so risking an accident) may be the result of a rational calculation of the possible benefits of a particular action – or indeed the symbolic meaning of the act itself. Luker (1975), for example, in her study of why women may risk an unwanted pregnancy (often described as an "accident"), analyzed some of the "costs" that may be involved in not taking that risk. Although such behaviour as having unprotected heterosexual penetrative sex when not trying to get pregnant may be seen as either ignorant or irrational, there are, she argued, some very "rational" reasons why that risk may be taken. Not "being careful" indicates trust, which may be a highly prized commodity in relationships. Taking precautions will mean having to address explicitly the fact of having sex, which may be difficult to do. As Luker noted, the chance of getting pregnant if having unprotected heterosexual sex for one year may be 80%, but the *risk* for each woman on each occasion is either one or nought.

Second, there are situations in which deliberately taking risks is socially legitimated within particular sub-cultures: children's "dares" or parachute jumping for charity. In this light, specific risks can also take on different meanings at different points in the life cycle. Backett (1992), for instance, noted how respondents in her study of middle-class health beliefs often described certain behaviours as being "healthy" for young adults but reckless for those with family responsibilities. Men in particular cited such activities as rugby or drinking excessively as a healthy part of early adulthood, but as being inappropriate for their current situation as parents. Taking risks is clearly at times not only a rational but also a prudent option. Backett's respondents saw dangers in the excessive avoidance of risk, as this could lead to fanaticism about health and an inability to keep life in balance.

As Kickbusch (1988) has noted, taking certain risks may be essential to building up particular social identities. Bunton & Burrows (1995) point to the importance of interpreting "risk behaviours" in the light of consumption practices. Drug use, for instance, may increase "cultural capital" while cigarette smoking plays an "important cultural function . . . [and is] used in ritualistic and expressive ways that have little to do with any consideration of the health risks" (Bunton & Burrows 1995: 216). In this context, the amount of risk taken (for instance the number smoked) is of less interest than the "style" of the risk taken, as evidenced by the cigarette brand preferences of different occupational groups or genders.

There are also cultural contexts in which the intrinsic pleasure of a recognizably accident-prone activity outweighs the negative possibilities of the risk. Thus, the explanation of why Air Force pilots volunteer for such a high-risk profession lies in "the amount of pure joy the flier derives from flying . . . the extent to which the flier's defenses have been challenged by circumstance" (Jones 1986). For such activities, like dangerous sports, the risk may contribute directly to its attraction despite controversy about the level of risk that is socially acceptable. As one climber put it: "You put handrails up Everest, you'll get an ice pick in your back" (Engel 1994).

Adolescence has also been described as a period in which taking certain risks is (at least to an extent) socially legitimated. Plant and Plant (1993) argued that some of the psychological features of adolescence as it is constructed in Western society encourage risk-taking. One feature of adolescence is the so-called myth of "invulnerability" whereby "young people, often at their physical peaks, typically view themselves as invulnerable" (Plant & Plant 1993: 113). Using illegal drugs, experimenting with sex and riding motorbikes are the kinds of risk-taking behaviours viewed here as "normal" in that they are engaged in by a large proportion of adolescents. Taking some risks is seen, then, as a legitimate stage of adolescence, pathological only when taken to excess. Defining "excess" is of course problematic. Accidents such as a motorbike crash or a drug overdose are one sign, perhaps, that excess has been reached. Even where a certain amount of risk-taking is legitimated, the accident serves to mark the boundary of reasonable risk: the accident is the ultimate indicator that a risk "taken" has been miscalculated.

The first set of assumptions created by a cultural theory, as opposed to a psychological theory, of risk relate, then, to the disruption of causal relationships between knowledge (measured by the extent of agreement between the potential risk taker and the "expert") and behaviour. "Expert" accounts of risks in these accounts are as much social constructions as lay accounts, and the interest is in elucidating the internal logics of each and their relationship to each other, rather than problematizing "lay" beliefs as irrational. The second set of assumptions of cultural theories of risk relate to the field of potential risks which, given that it is socially constructed, is potentially infinite. However sophisticated knowledge about risk factors and the correlations between them becomes, it is not possible to map all of the risks we face, or even to develop agreed criteria upon which recognized risks can be assessed. We cannot know whether we face an ever increasing range of risks or a diminishing one, as risk assessment is a political enterprise, with risks judged "acceptable" or not in terms of the values and beliefs by which they are assessed. If there can be no consensus about the prioritization of a specific set of risks, there is clearly scope for accidents to happen that are held to be miscalculations by one group, but reasonable risks by others. In such cultural accounts, then, the apparently non-utilitarian action is not the pathological belief examined by psychologists in order to ascertain barriers to rational choice: it is rather seen as one possible rational choice; even if a problematic one in terms of an apparently risk-aware culture.

Accounting for sociological interest: the "risk society"

This recent literature seems, then, to address the gap Douglas identified in the social sciences for a cultural analysis of risk perceptions (Douglas 1986). However, Douglas had suggested that "as the neglect of culture is so systematic", addressing questions about the cultural determinants of individual risk perceptions would need "nothing less than a large upheaval in the social sciences" (Douglas 1986: 1). How did it become possible not only to address cultural questions about risk, but for such questions to become central to the sociology of health and other areas?

One answer is that the "upheaval" Douglas considered as a prerequisite for a cultural analysis of risk seems to have happened, and may go some way towards understanding the new location of accidents in our classifications of misfortune, as it is perhaps a more general upheaval than one just of the social sciences. In a later work, Douglas suggests that the word "risk" itself has come to signify something new; specifically that "the word 'risk' has come to serve the forensic needs of the new global culture" (Douglas 1992: 22). By this she means that it organizes many of our debates about blame and responsibility. Risk is no longer a neutral term for the calculation of probability, it signifies "danger" specifically. There are, Douglas argues, a fixed number of possible causes we can attribute to misfortune. We moderns, she argues, no longer look to ancestors, or witches, but see danger and the analysis of misfortune in terms of vulnerability to risk. The delineation of precisely what "risk" does now signify has been the subject of considerable sociological enquiry in recent years. As risks have been identified as key to the production of contemporary accidents, it is perhaps worth examining some of these arguments.

Douglas's comment that "risk" has come to signify "danger" specifically is less convincing from the vantage point of a decade of work on risk. In his introduction to *Risk*, Adams (1995) argues that debate about risk assessment permeates all areas of human interest. In evidence he reviews the stories carried by one day's newspapers, and claims that reports about sport, politics, health and motoring are essentially about assessing and managing risks. Risk is what defines news, he argues, and "Even the gardening pages were dominated by the problems of decision making in the face of uncertainty" (Adams 1995: 2). Indeed, risk has become a key issue for discussing not only accidents but living in general in the late twentieth century. Beck (1992), for instance, has suggested that it is the distribution of risks through which modern industrialized society is divided, rather than differential access to the production of wealth. The traditional divisions of industrial society, such as class or gender, are dissolved, claims Beck, within the individualizing process of late modernity in which the individual's biography becomes more salient than their class allegiance in forming identity. However, systematic inequalities still exist. New social movements are not, however, formed along class or gender lines but

emerge to "react to the increasing risks and the growing risk consciousness and risk conflicts" (Beck 1992: 90). When Beck discusses "risk" he
refers not to abstract calculations of benefits and dangers, but to concrete
misfortunes with every-day implications for the whole population: radio-
activity, children with chronic breathing problems caused by sulphur
dioxide emissions, poisoned foodstuffs. All societies have had to face danger: what distinguishes "risk" in late modernity is, for Beck, both the global implications of the risks we face (pollution does not just affect those in
the factory, it affects the entire food chain and could potentially destroy
the planet) and the reflexive role of science and technology in their generation. We can no longer look to the rationality of scientific progress for
the solutions to technical problems, because those problems are themselves the result of scientific progress: science and its critics compete for
rational legitimacy.

The accident in the risk society

Such fracturing of consensus around how risks are to be managed is perhaps also typical of the social construction of risk in the last decades of the
twentieth century. If both the scientific establishment and new social
movements are internally divided over how to manage risks – of, for
instance, genetically engineered food products – then the population is
faced with myriad competing claims to "solutions" and no clear method
of evaluating them. Giddens suggests the day-to-day implications of this
fragmentation: "To live in the universe of high modernity is to live in an
environment of chance and risk . . . Fate and destiny have no part to play
in such a system" (Giddens 1991: 109).

"Fate" and "destiny" have had, however, no legitimate part to play for
the last two hundred years. What is perhaps different about "high modernity" is that, as Hacking (1987) puts it, "chance has been tamed". Accidents, like any other misfortune, can no longer "just happen", but have
become predictable in terms of probability, chance and risk. They are the
paradigmatic marker of a failure of risk management.

If we can take Giddens' statement as a workable summary of aspects of
contemporary discourse, or at least the cluster of beliefs that relate to causality and legitimate ways of imputing it, the accident, as it emerges from
rational thought, has no place. In a world that is made knowable through

141

probabilistic reasoning where deterministic law does not suffice, chance itself is calculable. Several writers have argued that the "accident", as it has been understood in rational modern cosmologies, has (or will) disappear in high modernity. Ewald (1991), for instance, notes that accidents are essentially individual misfortunes, unique happenings that concern only the victim and the protagonist, if any. The rise of insurance, and with it the notion of risk, dissolves the individual subject of the accident, for we all share risks. They belong to the population, and our individual share of that risk is merely an average. Insurance, he argues, is the "practice of a type of rationality potentially capable of transforming the life of individuals and that of a population". Insurance displaces modernist notions of fault and blame. The "accident victim" no longer has to prove the culpability of another agent to receive redress: he or she merely insures against the known risk of suffering from an accident. The "loss" suffered is recompensed as a financial sum, and victims have only themselves to blame if their particular misfortune was inadequately insured.

Castel (1991) further argues that a discourse of risks forms a new mode of surveillance, in which the entire population is subject to continual assessment for risk factors. Preventative strategies, he argues, become possible when there are the techniques to calculate the statistical correlations of risk factors. Again, the individual subject is dissolved in this new mode of control, for in preventative strategies the individual relationship (for instance between doctor and patient) becomes secondary to the construction of the patient as a constellation of risks. The multiplication of possibilities for intervention is potentially infinite, for we can never know all risk factors. For Castel, this new mode of surveillance is "a grandiose technocratic rationalizing dream of absolute control of the accidental" (Castel 1991: 289). The myth is one in which all the risks (for psychiatric disorder, or for having an accident) can be precisely enough calculated for their prevention.

The concept of a "risk society" serves to characterize not only a contemporary orientation to chance and misfortune, but also a contemporary style of power. Following Foucault's delineation of the concept of "disciplinary power" (Foucault 1979), in which the individual is constituted as an object of knowledge, to be reformed or "normalized" through disciplinary means, O'Malley (1992, 1993) has characterized risk as a new strategy, in which the individual is of little concern. Risk techniques operate not by normalizing individuals through altering their behaviour, but by statistical manipulation of the facts about aggregated individuals. It is a technique of accommodation, through increasingly sophisticated knowledge of the risks of sub-groups of the population: "whereas disciplines evolved in the early part of the modern era, as defensive strategies for managing the 'dangerous classes' by coercion, exclusion and correction, the risk-based tactics and categories are more incorporative and meliorating" (O'Malley 1993: 6).

One corollary of the development of risk-based techniques, argues O'Malley, is the reduction in opportunities for resistance. The statistical risk categories produced to describe populations do not correspond to the ways in which individuals see themselves, and they are consequently not obvious centres of group mobilization. O'Malley's example of the development of risk technologies is that of crime prevention, which he argues has become more individualized: it is individual citizens who are encouraged to reduce risks through a range of preventative strategies such as adequately securing cars and houses or not walking alone at night. Such an approach is prudential and situational, constructing crime primarily as an outcome of individual failure to prevent it rather than of criminal biographies. There are clearly some parallels here with the management of accident risks, which were examined in the last chapter. Here, the importance of these arguments about risk and its management as a strategy of power is significant because they produce the accident as a paradigmatic outcome of miscalculation. The logical outcome of risk calculations, as Castel suggests, is that they produce a preventable accident.

Of course, such a possibility is a myth in that techniques of calculation based on statistical probabilities can never predict specific individual events. The myth is a powerful one, however, which makes possible the statistics on mountain accidents that fix the accident within a web of risk factors, rather than as an individual misfortune. Accidents no longer demonstrate the proper limits of rational explanatory systems, but rather individual failure. Contained in this myth of preventability is a paradox, as Prior (1995) has pointed out. The mapping of risk factors for accidents can only produce a rate (for instance for road traffic accidents) that describes a population. It cannot be legitimately used to describe an individual's risk of having an accident; only the risk of particular sub-groups of that population (women, children, oil rig workers) having an accident.

In practice, however, accidents happen not to groups or to populations but to individuals, who must account for their personal misfortune. A tension thus emerges, between the myth of preventability and the occurrence of what ought to have been prevented. The accident as an event still occupies an essential place within the taxonomy of misfortunes, but in the "risk society" of high modernity it has radically shifted. A new dimension has emerged as a key factor in the analysis of misfortune: that of calculability. As explanation, the accidental is redundant, and the gap left for explaining personal misfortune has grown.

Periodization

It is suggested, then, that this implies a periodization of European thought involving three dominant discourses, which could perhaps be crudely summarized as "fate", "determinism" and "risk".

In the first, before the second half of the seventeenth century, events in a life occur as part of a personal destiny. The accident, a chance happening that was not willed, has no place, as all events fit into a pattern.

By the end of the seventeenth century, fate and destiny are replaced by a discourse of determinism, and accidents emerge as the leftovers of that explanatory system. They are an essential category of misfortune, and a belief in accidents becomes definitional of modernity by the 1930s, when "rationality" could unproblematically describe Western cosmologies. Accidents are inevitable features of the universe, given the vagaries of nature at the local level, to be expected from time to time but not worthy of serious investigation.

This consensus around rationality was fractured in the second half of the twentieth century, heralding what some have characterized as a "postmodern" age in which no hegemony can be assumed about science, reason or rationality. One aspect of this late twentieth-century phase is a discourse of risk and its management. If misfortunes such as accidents arise from knowable and calculable risks, they are transformed into potentially preventable events. If the risks are as yet imperfectly understood, then at least their consequences are preventable. Misfortunes such as accidents are calculable and if not avoidable, then potentially so. At what point did the transformation of the accident from a marginal and unremarkable misfortune to a central one produced through sets of risk factors amenable to management take place?

In Chapter 3 it was argued that the "modernist" accident became possible through an interplay of the logics of determinism and probabilism. The erosion of determinism by the extension of probabilism to a growing range of human activity has been well documented. Porter (1986), for instance, argues that the crucial shift in the application of statistics was the move from using error theory to control for variation to that of using it to examine variation. Throughout the nineteenth century, the Gaussian distribution (originally applied to such problems as controlling minor errors in the observation in astronomy) was increasingly used in the social sciences: by Adolphe Quetelet to produce his calculation of the "average man" in 1844 or by Durkheim at the end of the century to examine suicide rates to uncover social laws. Others have documented the cultural facets of the emergence of probability as a legitimate organizing principle. Bork (1980) argues that a probabilistic understanding of the world has possibly filtered out from scientific knowledge of such things as kinetic theory in thermodynamics or the role of randomness in evolutionary theory. In culture, Bork suggests, it manifests itself in cultural forms as diverse as the musical compositions of John Cage, the art of Jackson Pollock or even the decreasing use of "order" in layout, such as the right justified margin.

The decline of determinism

A key precondition of conceptualizing misfortune as an outcome primarily of risk is perhaps, then, the decline of explanations based on deterministic causes and their effects, and a rise on those based on relationships between statistical probabilities. Between 1800 and 1930, claims Hacking (1987), "chance is tamed": determinism is eroded and probability emerges as the dominant discourse. Indeed in his view "the taming of chance and the erosion of determinism constitute one of the most revolutionary changes in the history of the human mind" (Hacking 1987: 54). Determinism, or the view that "the world was . . . governed by stern necessity and universal laws" (ibid.: 45) was eroded as chance became manageable. Hacking describes this as a four-stage process.

First, from 1820 to 1840 there was an exponential increase in availability of printed numbers. From these it became possible to perceive regularities in facts about human behaviour. Between 1835 and 1875 there was a growing faith in the regularity of numbers. Adolphe Quetelet, the Belgian astronomer and statistician who led the First International Statistical Congress, proposed the idea of *l'homme moyen*, the average man. Social and even moral characteristics, he proposed, were distributed like any other natural phenomena, and could be studied using Gaussian laws of error. From 1875 onwards was the third phase, in which statistical laws became autonomous: correlations did not have to be reduced to underlying causes. Finally, between 1892 and 1930, determinism was finally laid to rest, and "it became virtually certain that at bottom our world is run at best by laws of chance" (Hacking 1987: 45).

Hacking provides a convincing account that chance has been "tamed", and it is possible that the growing importance of probabilistic reasoning and a corresponding diminishing space for deterministic reasoning at the beginning of the twentieth century opened the space for a discourse of the accident, even if it was at first restricted to those domains in which it was absent. However, Hacking's account also raises perhaps the question of why this happened by the beginning of the twentieth century. Daston (1987), moving away from the analysis of pure discourse, suggests some environmental and structural reasons for this shift, in her examination of changing nature of insurance in the light of mathematical laws of chance. Although the rise of insurance started in the eighteenth century, these early attempts were, she argues "less prudential than reckless" (Daston 1987: 235). Today gambling is perceived as the taking of unnecessary risks for a possible gain, and insurance as the attempt to avoid unnecessary risk, but, argues Daston, there was little to distinguish them until relatively recently in European history. Maritime insurance, for instance, was based solely on the experience of the underwriters. Their assessment of risks relied on their knowledge of issues such as the skill of the captain, the likely weather conditions and the condition of the ship and upon the prevailing market forces of competing underwriters rather than any statistical analysis of the risks involved in a voyage. There was no distinction between gambling and insurance: in fact life assurance was illegal in much of Europe until the nineteenth century. Paying for insurance was a gamble: in the eighteenth century one could buy insurance against cuckoldry, lying or even losing in the London lottery. Such schemes were not, argues Daston, based on the calculation of probable risks but on experience and the market. Those offering fire insurance did not, she notes, even collect statistics on fires.

The increase in understanding of statistics was one precondition for the development of a prudential system of insurance. Only when mortality tables were, for instance, based on observed death rates rather than on assumed equi-probable chances of dying, could insurance be anything other than a gamble. That it is no longer seen as "merely" a gamble is perhaps illustrated by reactions to the losses incurred by the Lloyds

"Names" on the insurance markets in the late 1980s and early 1990s in Britain. One agency chairperson was quoted as saying "Reinsurance is high risk, but it isn't meant to be a casino" (Springett 1994). Daston suggests some external factors that made insurance little more than a gamble before the nineteenth century:

> [maritime insurance] was not just astatistical it was antistatistical. Given the highly volatile conditions of sea traffic and health in centuries notorious for warfare, pirates, plagues, and other unpredictable misfortunes, I am not persuaded that this was an unreasonable approach. (Daston 1987: 240)

This comment suggests that a "probabilistic revolution" was not possible before the end of the nineteenth century because the world was simply too unpredictable: accident and misfortune did occur randomly, so there could be no development of laws that relied on patterns. It is not possible to predict the unpredictable. This is not wholly convincing, as it merely begs the question of why the risks of the seventeenth or eighteenth century (plagues or warfare) were seen as random manifestations of God or of the precariousness of the world, whereas the risks of today (heart attacks, industrial pollution) are conceptualized as "knowable". It does, however, offer the possibility of grounding the analysis of discourse in historical conditions. Social mores provide an additional incentive to the utilization of probabilistic theory. By the nineteenth century there was a growing salaried middle class, who had no independent means and the purchase of a sound policy would insure their families against destitution in the event of their death. A heightened sense of familial responsibility, of economic responsibility and an aversion to risk, meant that these were the ideal buyers of insurance that was based not on arbitrary risk but on prudential foresight.

Is uncertainty decreasing or increasing?

Daston's suggestion that the advent of risk calculation was only possible after the environment became less unpredictable raises the question of how certain risks, and not others, are selected as knowable or calculable. It is difficult to accept her implication that the world actually contains fewer risks now. As Douglas and Wildavsky note:

For anyone disposed to worry about the unknown, science has actually expanded the universe about which we can speak with confidence. In one direction, parsecs and megaparsecs enable people to consider huge magnitudes otherwise too difficult to manage, and in the other direction technological advance allows discussion of minute quantities, measured in parts per million . . . The same ability to detect causes and connections or parts per trillion can leave more unexplained than was left by cruder measuring instruments. (Douglas & Wildavsky 1983: 49)

Beck's work of course also suggests a universe of increasing rather than decreasing risk and danger. The difference now, he suggests, is that the risks we face are internal: they are produced by the very scientific advances that were to control dangers. The risks of maritime trade in the seventeenth century were external: from nature, God and enemies. Science today, claims Beck, is reflexive (1992: 155–63), in that it now confronts its own products: science both produces problems (such as pollution) but also has the potential for solutions. Science no longer operates on nature and its dangers as "givens" but as creations of itself. In the "risk society" science no longer has privileged claims to rationality and truth: scientific scepticism is directed internally as well, criticizing its own foundations. Thus critiques of science come not just from outside (from marginal groups) but from within the established disciplines. With an exponential growth in scientific findings science has lost its monopoly as a producer of knowledge, for this over-production carries with it a demystification and uncertainty (Beck 1992: 157). One outcome of this is that:

There occurs, so to speak, an over-production of risks, which sometimes relativize, sometimes supplement and sometimes outdo each other. One hazardous product might be defended by dramatizing the risks of the others (for example, the dramatization of climatic consequences "minimizes" the risk of nuclear energy). (Beck 1992: 31)

Beck describes not a society comfortable with a more predictable environment, but a society beset by risks and their management.

It is not perhaps possible to judge whether there are fewer risks in the late twentieth century or more. Rather, there has been a radical shift in the ways in which dangers are conceptualized. Risk has become a key concept around which our concerns are organized. As we can calculate with finer and finer precision the probability of a certain event given particular sets of circumstances, we can perceive many misfortunes as the outcomes of the inadequate handling of the risks for those events. Accidents have an apparent dual role in such calculations. They are first the archetypal outcome of a risk miscalculation. An accident happens when risks have been inadequately assessed, or incompetently managed. At the same time though, they are in themselves the object of much risk assessment.

The experience of accidents in a risk society

It has been argued, then, that risk is a key concept for understanding cosmologies of misfortune in contemporary culture, and that the risk society has produced a myth that accidents should not happen. However, the calculation of risk factors cannot provide a prediction of individual misfortunes: it can only recreate them as belonging to a population rate. Those who suffer an accident still have to make sense of the event in a meaningful way, including an account of why it happened to them specifically. It has been suggested that contemporary life is characterized both by our decreasing ability to cope with uncertainty and risk (see, for instance, Fox 1980) and by our willingness to lay blame on others for accidents: if they result from the miscalculation or mismanagement of risk, we should be able to identify who was responsible for the miscalculation or mismanagement. Douglas & Wildavsky noted that we demand: "commissions of enquiry into every accident and post-mortems for every death . . . we have enlarged the scope for making someone pay for each misfortune we undergo" (Douglas & Wildavsky 1983: 33).

One aspect of this need to attribute responsibility is the rise of medical litigation in the United States: insurance costs for medical practitioners have sharply risen as they are held legally responsible for an increasing range of outcomes of medical practice. In parts of North California, for instance, doctors can be held responsible for manslaughter if their patient dies after a house call is refused (Douglas & Wildavsky 1983: 34). Although there have been claims that Britain is following this American trend of increasing litigiousness, there is evidence that British accident victims have traditionally been less enthusiastic in holding others legally responsible for their injuries (see Genn & Burman 1977, Blaxter 1976:

192). However, there have been more recent cases of media interest in those individuals who do seek to attribute responsibility for "accidents". One that caused considerable debate was a man who slipped from the Cobb, a well-known part of Lyme Regis shore, and successfully sued the local authority for damages on the grounds they had not signposted the danger.

Douglas & Wildavsky suggested that there is a curious parallel here between primitive mentalities, which hold all deaths to have a cause, and modern ones. If belief in a natural death was a modern development, they suggested, then we are in danger of losing it: "[primitives] demand an autopsy for every death; the day that we do that, the essential difference between our mentality and theirs will be abolished" (Douglas and Wildavsky 1983: 32).

Fate and high modernity

There are, however, considerable limitations in merely equating late twentieth-century beliefs with those that were characterized as "primitive" in the 1930s. We may seek to make the universe calculable, if not exactly knowable, but the accidental is now perceived as an anachronistic explanation of the miscalculated, not a non-existent explanation. We may seek to attribute responsibility for all misfortunes, but this does not directly equate with laying moral blame. Those who see misfortunes as "merely" accidental are seen as uninformed about risk and its proper management. This may suggest that beliefs and behaviours that may appear anachronistic (in that they belong to an earlier age of fate and chance) seem to persist into high modernity, as a minor strand within a dominant discourse of risk calculation. Not only is a belief in the accidental as an explanatory factor constructed as anachronistic, but accidents themselves are explained as the result of fatalistic beliefs. People should not suffer from the unexpected if they are well versed enough in the risks that predict it. However, the "fate" appealed to by those in contemporary culture may have very different meanings to that defined by rationalist discourse of the post-seventeenth century. In their ethnographic account of lay epidemiology, Davison et al. (1992) suggest why ideas that look like "fatalism" coexist with ideas about lifestyle and the management of risks for coronary heart disease. About 40 per cent of their respondents used notions of fate, luck or randomness when talking about coronary heart disease. This did not, argue Davison et al., conflict with the notion that one could also take precautions, as these ideas about risks concerned the distribution of disease, rather than the causes. As a category of modern misfortune, heart attacks have many parallels with accidents. The concept of "risk factors" for heart disease constituted the "candidate" for a heart attack: someone likely to have one. At one level, this made heart disease predictable and knowable, in both lay and professional discourses. However, such risk factors often failed to explain the actual distribution of disease, as those with no known risk factors were known to suffer, whereas others with many (such as overweight smokers) lived to a healthy old age. Davison et al. suggest that, ironically, the very prioritization of prevention in health promotion has emphasized "fatalistic" beliefs. There are, quite simply, no other explanations for those deaths that cannot be accounted for by an examination of risk factors. The victims of accidents are faced with a similar problem in accounting for their misfortune as resulting from the miscalculation of risk: some accidents are seen to "just happen", however careful one is, whereas other people take what seem to be reckless risks yet survive unscathed.

It seems, then, hardly adequate to characterize this contemporary fatalistic attitude to accidents as merely anachronistic. In contemporary culture such beliefs are held within a specific discourse of risk and calculability. The fields in which the products of this discourse are visible are diverse and pervasive: crime prevention, health, leisure activities. These products do not appear only in academic discourse: they appear in leaflets listing the risk factors that women should be aware of if they walk alone at night, they appear in posters at the doctor's surgery on heart disease and they appear in magazine articles on how to avoid injury on the ski slope. Any cultural analysis of contemporary beliefs in fate must account for their relationship to this ubiquitous discourse of risk factors and their management.

Although discourses of risk in high modernity produce an accident as a failure of risk calculation, there is a gap left by explanatory frameworks. The "probabilistic revolution" has mapped the contours of risks and their calculation, through which we come to understand that others do not have accidents, but fail to calculate accurately the risks they face. Given the logical problems with translating population rates into an individual risk for accidents, it is not surprising that this does not wholly satisfy at the level of subjective meaning. In explaining the old question "why me, why now?" the discourses of high modernity provide little comfort: they explain only the general, not the particular. This was also, it was suggested in the last chapter, seen to be true of rational modern discourse, which came to be seen as failing at the level of meaning. What is perhaps new is that rational discourses did not attempt to provide meaning for the individual. The accident was an inevitable happening; unpredictable at the local level, and for which no one could be blamed. A discourse of risk may provide no solace for the victim of an "accident" either – but such events are not constructed as morally neutral. As "chance has been tamed", the occurrence and distribution of accidents is knowable, and the risk factors for them calculable. Ideally, victims should never have suffered in the first place. Even if not legally (or even morally) blameworthy, they are in part held responsible for their own misfortune.

It may be possible to argue that appeals to chance and fate are in some way evidence of resistance to a discourse in which risk is universally and comprehensively calculable. Certainly there are signs of scepticism, for instance on the front cover of the *Sunday Times* (January 1992), which contained only a heading, "1991: a year of glorious follies"; a caption that noted that "The Transport and Road Research Laboratory has devised a formula to enable you to calculate your mathematical chance of having a road accident next year. The formula you have to apply is this:

$$A_c = 0.00633 \exp \{s + g\}$$
$$(1 + 1.6_{pd})$$
$$(_{pb} + 0.65_{pr} + 0.88p_m)$$
$$M^{0.279}$$
$$\exp \{b_1/Ag + b_2/(X + 2.6)\}"$$

The "folly", it is implied, is that such calculation taken to its logical conclusions clearly becomes ridiculous, at least for the individual road user. Even where risks can theoretically be known and calculated, they have little practical value in the avoidance of particular accidents.

Equating contemporary explanatory frameworks with those of other (past) cultures would rely on understanding such examples as evidence of the persistence of anachronistic ideas about accidents, or as resistance to more "modern" cosmologies. If the myth of the risk society is that accidents should no longer happen, accidents have perversely remained a key concept for analyzing misfortune – but they do necessarily occupy the same position as accidents in a rationalist cosmology. In a risk society, our failures to calculate correctly may be attributed to "chance", but it is no longer a chance that operates outside the bounds of rational calculation. Rather, the play of chance itself is precisely calculated.

The centrality of accidents to a discourse of risk

Armstrong (1986), in his analysis of infant mortality, illustrated the tension between what was inexplicable within the explanatory frameworks of the first half of the twentieth century and those in the second. Sudden Infant Deaths (cot deaths) are those with no known cause: inexplicable deaths in infancy. Before 1971, the International Classification of Diseases had no specific category of Sudden Infant Deaths (OPCS 1982). They were, till then, classified as "sudden death – cause unknown" or "hidden" in one of the accidental death categories. A rationalist nosology consigned them to a leftover category. Rather like accidents, they "fell outside the analytical framework", a marginal category that marked the limits of a causal analysis of mortality. Around 1950, argued Armstrong, these deaths moved centre-stage. The very fact that they came with no known cause meant that they were ideal candidates for the new analytical processes of risk calculation, as a challenge with which to demonstrate the universality of emergent techniques of risk calculation. More significantly, they were actually produced by the new framework. A retrospective reading enables such deaths to be extracted from mortality data before 1950 but, as Armstrong argued, they only crossed the threshold of public visibility through new attempts to outline the exact risks of death, and thus explain them.

Cot deaths were, then, until recently very much seen as accidental deaths of infants: random, inexplicable and for which no blame could be imputed. New analytical techniques (those of the "risk society") appeared to provide an explanation (risk factors) for the previously inexplicable and, in doing so, created a new category. This is not of course to argue that infants did not die of the same causes before, but rather that unexplained infant deaths were not visible as a discrete category. The new analytical frameworks were manifested through an examination of patterns in the data. The Registrar-General noted in the Commentary for the 1954–6 Statistical Review (Registrar-General 1957: 168) that there was "no obvious explanation if these deaths were accidental" of the excess male mortality of "accidental mechanical suffocation" and that "there are grounds for believing that a substantial proportion of these deaths may be due not to accident but to obscure natural causes" (ibid.: 4). Once regularities had been discovered, this group of deaths could be promoted to the main body of the medical classification. A growing body of research produced regularities to replace the random occurrence of earlier infant deaths: they are for instance correlated with factors such as the sex of baby, socio-economic class and co-existing respiratory infection (OPCS 1982). Ironically, this stress on the "non-accidental" nature of Sudden Infant Death in the new regime implies that there are "real" accidental deaths: events that are really random and attributable to chance.

In a similar way accidents are no longer the inevitable and necessarily marginal remnants of a cosmology, but have been brought to the very centre, for the accident is a paradigmatic event of risk. In this way the dual nature of accidents in contemporary discourse is, to some extent, unified. For if accidents are the archetypal outcome of the miscalculation of risk, they are the paradigmatic event with which to demonstrate the possibilities of risk calculation. In a rational discourse the accident as an event demonstrated the failures of the dominant cosmology, for it reminded the victim of the unpredictable nature of the real world set against the predictable nature of the theorized world. As an event, the accident today demonstrates only personal failure: the inability of individuals to negotiate an all-encompassing risk environment, in which the accident should not happen. As explanation, the accidental was a despised but necessary part of a rationalist discourse, for it demonstrated a belief in the potential for scientific explanation and the left-over category of "coincidence" for what could not be explained. As explanation, the accidental is now merely despised. Ideally, in the new order, accidents should not happen.

It would, of course, be rash to argue that "risk" now completely dominates common-sense knowledge of what accidents are. There is still evidence of appeals to a rather more modernist notion of the accidental, for instance in the reclassification of some infant deaths as "non-accidental" (with the implication that some remain "accidents"), and the resistance to an all-encompassing model of risk assessment suggested by the *Sunday Times* front cover. Accidents are still ambiguous misfortunes, utilized in contradictory ways in the late twentieth century.

What is perhaps missing from an account of accidents as a product of a discourse of risk, management and prevention is an understanding of how accidents, as misfortunes, are perceived and constructed by individual social actors. These products of risk technologies (advice to parents on children's safety, epidemiological research, reports on mountain accidents) have been examined so far as being autonomous discursive practices, divorced from the social interactions that produce them. The next chapter explores how such interactions contribute to the production of knowledge about accidents, and also explores the extent to which the accident is understood as an outcome of risk management in the late twentieth century by those who suffer them. It examines the private arena of everyday accidents, which are constructed through interaction between friends, family and colleagues in day-to-day conversation and action. Through such daily social interaction, accidents come to be suffered, managed and understood and it is at this level that it may be possible to examine the extent to which accidents have been articulated as an outcome of the management of risk.

Chapter 7

The social construction
of accidents

Introduction

The last chapter situated accidents as a facet of the "risk society". The understanding and management of misfortune in the late twentieth century is, it was argued, predicated on our ability to monitor and manage risks in an ever widening range of arenas. With the fracturing of any consensus about what constitutes "expert" opinion, the responsibility for this risk assessment is individualized. We are all engaged in a seemingly irresistible strategy of constant risk management. Accidents are central to this management in two ways. First, that accidents happen demonstrates that risks have been inadequately managed and, further, that increased vigilance about risks is therefore necessary. Second, accidents constitute the ultimate test of risk management as a strategy: to predict and manage the unpredictable and apparently random. This chapter explores how risk management is achieved at the level of everyday interaction: how we construct ourselves as competent risk assessors through everyday accident prevention activities and talk about them.

There are two initial questions raised by the theoretical literature discussed in the previous chapter. First, to what extent are reported subjective experiences of accidents shaped by appeal to discourses of risk and its calculability? Or is there on the contrary (as much health promotion literature suggests) a set of specifically "lay" beliefs about accidents that stress fatalism and unpredictability? Second, how are "accidents", as a particular category of misfortune, classified in everyday social interaction? A third question arises from the debate around the implications of the risk society for self-identity: how do we construct ourselves as competent social actors in an uncertain world of risk and misfortune?

To explore these questions, this chapter draws on data from two studies that were based on interviews and focus groups with adults and children on the subject of accidents. Although details of the methodologies used can be found in reports of these two studies (see Green 1995, Green & Hart 1996; for a general account of focus groups see Basch 1987), the methodological strategies themselves raised two issues that have direct relevance for the questions above. These were: the difficulties in finding a "lay" sample to explore how non-professionals conceptualize accidents, and the limitations of interviewing as a methodological strategy for accessing people's everyday knowledge about accidents.

The elusiveness of a "lay" sample

In Chapter 5, the emergence of a "professional" approach to accident prevention was examined. This professional approach situated itself as self-consciously opposed to lay, or everyday, understanding of accidents. An initial problem with addressing the question of whether there are specifically "lay" beliefs about accidents is that a sample of lay people proves rather difficult to find. Some of the participants in the first study (Green 1995) were initially chosen for their expertise on some aspect of accidents. "Expertise" was defined as any specialized body of knowledge that might contribute to a public discourse on accidents. This was not necessarily a professional expertise: one interviewee was a mountain climber who had gained his knowledge through a leisure pursuit. Neither was expertise defined as being necessarily consistent with legitimate knowledge about accidents: another was an astrologer, for instance, who had a body of knowledge that was in many respects constructed explicitly in opposition to dominant contemporary beliefs about misfortune. However, if many people claimed some formal, if not professional, knowledge of accidents and their management, then selecting people with no specific expertise, the "lay" public of the accident prevention literature, proved more problematic. Indeed, it became clear that it would be difficult to find a specifically "lay" sample of people to interview, as so many people in contemporary Britain have formal knowledge about accidents. Three mothers, for instance, chosen initially to represent a non-professional view of accidents, did in fact draw on several bodies of professional knowledge during discussion. Two were registered child-minders and had worked in nursery schools, and were thus "professionally" informed about practical and legal aspects of preventing accidents to children. The other was completing a course of study in law that had included study of health and safety legislation. The children in the two studies were perhaps the only interviewees who were identifiable in any obvious way as "lay" people.

Some problems with interviewing as a technique for accessing knowledge about accidents

The qualitative interview is a standard technique for producing knowledge about "lay" health beliefs in medical sociology. There is a considerable body of literature illustrating its usefulness as a methodological strategy for accessing lay conceptions of health and illness generally (Cornwell 1984b, Blaxter 1983); of chronic illness (Gerhardt 1990) and even arenas in which risk assessments are the focus of interviews (see, for instance, Rogers & Pilgrim 1995, Roberts et al. 1993). The qualitative interview would appear, then, to be the strategy of choice for examining lay beliefs about accidents. However, transcripts of in-depth one-to-one interviews on accidents initially seem rather problematic as "data" to be analyzed.

First, respondents made apparently contradictory statements about accidents: for instance claiming at one point that "they just happened" and that nothing could be done to prevent them, and then claiming a short time later that all accidents could be prevented if care was taken. Additionally, interview transcripts often contained many pages of material that seemed to have little relevance for a study of accidents. Stories recounted about accidents were used as springboards to discuss a wide range of other issues: personal philosophies about luck and fate, personal problems relating to social relationships or work, accounts of professional bodies of knowledge that were not related to accidents and, particularly for the children, accounts of risk behaviour in other areas, such as drug use or talking to "strangers". More fundamentally, given that the main strength of using in-depth interviews is to access "naturalistic" narratives, the stories in transcripts rarely had the style of "accident stories" one might encounter in everyday conversation. The very act of consciously reflecting on accidents meant that they almost disappeared. It was as if direct questioning about accidents dissolved them: respondents would begin a story, then claim that "it wasn't really an accident".

Why should beliefs about accidents prove more resistant to uncovering through interviewing than other sets of beliefs? One possible explanation is that the interview, however informal, cannot recreate the social contexts of everyday talk about accidents. Accidents appear in everyday social intercourse in a number of ways. They appear primarily as stories: events recounted for entertainment and to facilitate moral debate. It is possible that such stories function in a psychological way to help relieve the stress of such an event, and perhaps in a social way to construct consensual understandings within social groups about the proper responsibilities one should take. Whatever the motivations for and covert "functions" of telling and listening to accident stories, they are a crucial way in which knowledge about accidents is produced. This knowledge is thus embedded in everyday conversation, and attempts to isolate it as the "theme" of an interview wrench it from the very material from which it is constructed.

A second manifestation of the accident in everyday conversation is as a "bargaining tool". Appeals to the accidental appear during negotiations about apportioning moral responsibility. This example of an interchange between myself and my seven-year-old daughter is perhaps typical:

JG: Can you move that cup or it's going to get knocked over.

Rebecca: No it's not – I'm being careful.

JG: Well, if it does get knocked over, I'll be cross.

Rebecca: You can't get cross if I knock it over accidentally.

To claim that a misfortune was (or would be) caused accidentally is to make an appeal against punitive action. Both of these situations – stories and moral bargaining – are rather difficult to recreate in an interview setting. The invitation to tell the story of the "last accident that you experienced" is somewhat artificial: the interviewer is not an impressive audience, and the act of reflecting on why you have chosen it as "an accident story" is enough to destroy any narrative drive. The contrast between transcripts of the focus-group interviews and one-to-one interviews illustrates this. Both adults and children interviewed in groups produced definitions of accidents in the interaction between themselves, and told stories about accidents that were recognizably similar to ones encountered in everyday social intercourse. There was, in short, a "proper" audience; other participants, who would contradict, encourage and respond to the events as narrated. As an interviewer in a one-to-one interview the role of audience is rather difficult to play without entering into a "normal" conversation and leaving aside even the minimal conventions of interviewing. Those with some expertise on accidents (that is, most of the adult respondents) provided what, in Cornwell's terms (Cornwell 1984a, 1984b) might be called "public" accounts of accidents: what they believed a professional account of accidents ought to consist of. One-to-one interviews, however well the interviewer was known and trusted by the interviewee, can perhaps only ever produce these public accounts. However, the focus-group interviews did provide an opportunity for more "natural" story telling, eliciting less stilted accounts. As Kitzinger (1994) has noted, focus groups may be a particularly useful technique for studying how shared meanings are negotiated and contested in social interaction. Given that accidents derive their meaning only from such interaction, it is not perhaps surprising that focus groups proved a more productive method than interviews for accessing social knowledge.

What is an accident?

The concept of an accident was a meaningful one for all of those who participated in the two studies. They could all, whether "lay" people (like the children) or "professionals" (like an actuary whose work perhaps epitomizes the modern mapping of risk) identify the kind of event that they would label an accident. Accidents first of all described a type of event, usually injuries of some sort:

I fell off my bike a few times. (Anja, aged 8)

I scalded my hand on the kettle. (Jason, aged 8)

Anything that would cause harm to a child. (Health Visitor)

When I banged my knee and it was bleeding. (Adam, aged 6)

However, the label "accident" was also used to explain something about the way in which such outcomes happened. As Anja points out, not all injuries are necessarily accidents:

Anja: Once I did something on purpose on my bike. I fell off my bike because everybody was helping Maria on her new bike. I got jealous that everyone was looking after her, so on purpose I just made myself fall off my bike and then I really hurt myself.

JG: So that wasn't an accident?

Anja: No, 'cause it was on purpose.

Indeed, for many of the children, it was lack of motivation that defined the accidental:

I think an accident is an injury not done on purpose. (Ade, aged 8)

At some point, most of those interviewed provided definitions that appeared to coincide with the "lay view" that emerged from the accident prevention literature; that is, they emphasized either the unpredictability, luck or lack of motivation involved in the causation of the event.

Things like electrocuting yourself by accident . . . you can't predict that. (Actuary)

It's a coincidence, like. Some people get accidents and some don't. (Leroy, aged 11)

Something that happens that's out of your control, that you can't prevent. (Cathy, mother)

It's unintentional. (Pat, mother)

Some definitions provided by these interviewees combined the sense of an accident as the outcome of the event (damage or injury) and the cause of the event.

An accident for me is a bodily mishap that happens to people without any intention of hurt, either on the part of the sufferer or the agent. (Astrologer)

162

It's people falling down the stairs, breaking plates in the sink . . .
half the time when you ask a question how they done it, they've
just tripped for no apparent reason (Home Accident Clerk)

It's something fairly bad for you that's not intentional. (Mountain
Climber)

An accident is something that goes wrong . . . by accident that
actually hurts you. (Amelia, aged 6)

In summary, all of those interviewed could provide an abstract definition of an accident that stressed the unpredictability or the blamelessness
of the act, as well as the kind of outcomes they produced. However, it soon
becomes clear that these initial working definitions – which were usually
provided early on in interviews, and following a direct prompt for a definition – only serve for ideal or hypothetical cases. When people began to
talk about actual events that they had experienced, accidents were rarely
described as either unambiguously unpredictable or unambiguously morally neutral. Indeed, few accounts of accidents from the interviewees' own
experiences matched their own initial abstract definitions.

Predictability

In accounts of accident experiences the principle of unpredictability was
compromised in several ways. The first depended on aggregation. The
actuary, for instance, talked about accidents first as specific events, which
could not be predicted "that would come out as a sort of blit" in the statistics. But in this respect they were like any of the other uncertainties that he
dealt with, and would be averaged out in the process of calculating risks
for sections of the population:

they [life assurance firms] might look at the stats on accidental
death and say "are they significant?" If . . . they were getting a significant number of accidental deaths they would have to [load the
premiums] but typically it's the case that things even themselves
out. (Actuary)

Mapping the rates of events (be they accidents or any other misfortune)

163

did nothing to help predict any individual event. Although a sophisticated knowledge of risks reduced the uncertainty enough for insurance companies to offer profitable Life Assurance products to their customers, they could not help in predicting individual misfortune:

> This guy might look as healthy as can be, a good risk, and then he just pops his clogs for no reason . . . You can get the actual production of these statistics down to a fine art . . . but it will still . . . be an estimate . . . You're dealing with uncertainties and no matter what you base it on, it's basically an estimate. (Actuary)

This contrast between the predictable and unpredictable is presented in epidemiological terms by this professional: the argument that population statistics are not very useful for predicting what is going to happen to a particular individual but that, in general, accidents were predictable outcomes.

Although other respondents did not reduce unpredictability through aggregation, there were other ways of constructing individual accidents as, at least in part, predictable. One important distinction made, explicitly or implicitly, by many people was between accidents that "just happen" and nothing can be done about to prevent, and those that should, by the actions of the victim or others, have been prevented and were therefore predictable. As Amelia put it: "some of them are going to happen anyway".

Two respondents who had considerable experience of dealing with accidents were Home Accident Clerks, responsible for collecting data in hospital Accident and Emergency Departments for the Department of Trade's Home Accident Surveillance System. They also distinguished accidents that "just happen" from those that were more predictable. One thought that accidents could be divided into two kinds, those that could be prevented and those that nothing could be done about:

> Some, as I say, I suppose what I call the sensible accidents can be helped. But as I say the children falling from swings, you'll never stop will you? (Home Accident Clerk)

However, even the latter, which she later defined as the "careless" accidents, were not completely unpreventable.

I mean most of it is carelessness, but if people could be made more aware perhaps they would you know, like they've got curly flexes for kettles and so on. (Home Accident Clerk)

Her colleague likewise initially attributed half of the accidents she saw to "stupidity really, carelessness, which half of the accidents come from" and the other half as "proper" accidents: "They just happen" (Home Accident Clerk).

Even these remaining "ideal" accidents that nothing could be done about, were not, however, purely random occurrences. The idea of the "accident-prone" individual was one factor that reduced unpredictability. Many of the respondents viewed certain individuals as being more likely to suffer accidents than others. Two of the respondents, for instance, described their children as accident-prone; children who are more likely to have accidents than others, regardless of the environmental risks that surround them:

I mean when he started to walk it was always "Oh, my God, there, he's over again!" Every other second he was over, crashing into doors, bruising all over him, it was just an utter nightmare, quite frankly. Yet some children, like Thomas I had to look after, when he got up and walked he waited till he was safe. You know, you weren't every second behind him. He just walked. (Cathy, mother)

My eldest one is always falling down the stairs, always rushing about. I bet she falls down the stairs once a week, honestly. 'Cause she's erratic mainly. There's nothing wrong with the stair carpet, it doesn't matter whether she's got boots or slippers on . . . (Home Accident Clerk)

A large number of factors were seen to put people at risk of accident-proneness, especially for children. Among those mentioned at various points by the respondents were: clumsiness, infections that affect balance, poor eyesight, living in large families, pride, over-eagerness, precocity, being easily distracted or absent-minded, having a butterfly mind, just having had a growing spurt, having a poltergeist and having a "wild" personality. Although this range suggests that "accident-proneness" is an attribute that could be used to describe almost anyone (and certainly any child), there was in practice a consensus about who was accident-prone.

When one of the mothers in a focus group mentioned her child as an example of someone who was accident-prone, she elicited laughs and murmurs of agreement from others who knew the child. Similarly, the groups of children often agreed on which of their peers were "accident-prone", and described them in unflattering terms:

Callum: Tommy Stanton has an accident nearly every day.

Adam: He's a nut case –

Lauren: Yeah, a nutter.

Being accident-prone was seen as a character attribute that was an obvious one, visible to anyone who knew the person, and one that could be used to make accidents in any area of that person's life, to a certain extent, predictable:

JG: . . . do you think pilots have this perception that some of their colleagues are more likely to have accidents than others?

RAF doctor: Oh yeah. But that's the same in any walk of life. You know the accident-prone people . . . there's people you're not at all surprised that they've crunched the car again.

Other people were just as self-evidently not accident-prone. However, not being accident-prone was more likely to be described as the result of "luck" than in terms of the kinds of risk factors that contributed to accident-proneness. Leroy, for example, was seen by his friends as well as himself as someone who could take risks without suffering injuries:

JG: So are there some people who have more accidents than others?

Leroy: Like I've never had an accident before and I reckon that's a coincidence.

Matthew: But he was sitting on the chair right . . . with two legs up like that – and he could have fallen back and broken his leg!

Leroy: Right, so it's coincidence, like. Some people get accidents and some don't.

Similarly, the actuary ascribed the fact that he had experienced few serious accidents to luck:

I haven't had any near misses where I've gone "phew! I was lucky!" I suppose you could say I've never come close to electrocuting myself, or being run over . . . I'm certainly not exceptionally unlucky in that things happen to me. (Actuary)

The only person to attribute not being accident-prone to her own skills or attributes rather than luck was, perhaps surprisingly, the astrologer, although even she "touched wood" with a smile after this comment:

The reason I say that I don't easily have accidents is that I'm so careful. I'm sure-footed and in control. I'm very unlikely to sort of dash or not think. I'm very careful, I plan. (Astrologer)

Even she later noted that such attributes were "typical" of earth signs such as her own. Accident-proneness may result from an identifiable set of risk factors, but invulnerability to accidents results largely from luck.

Moral neutrality

The accident in practice is not, then, unambiguously unpredictable, even as an individual event. Neither, in these accounts, was it an unambiguous statement about moral neutrality. An accident is both a category of outcome and a category of causation, and sometimes accident outcomes were explicitly explained in terms of non-accidental causes:

Sarah [daughter] had an accident last year. Well, call it an accident – I mean I think it was deliberately done by another child, when it happened. That's why I felt so angry about it. (Cathy, mother)

Even where there was no overt questioning of the label "accident" to describe the causation, accounts of accidental events were surrounded by attributions of responsibility and blame:

JG: What was the last accident you had?

Mountain climber: The car! Driving into the central reservation at top speed on the motorway [laughs].

JG: How did that happen?

Mountain climber: It was the other guy's fault and not mine . . . [describes the accident].

JG: So you'd describe it as an accident even though you thought it was his fault?

Mountain climber: It was the other driver's fault in the sense that nobody was, you know, one driver wasn't looking where he was going . . . but it wasn't intentional on their part.

The accident, in accounts like this, arises from actions that were negligent, but not maliciously intended by another agent. Designating an event as accidental does not absolve actors of blame, it merely places the event within an arena of moral negotiation, in which responsibility is attributed. The most common attribution of blame was self-blame:

Sarah [daughter] winged off the top of the work surface in her bouncy chair . . . and you're always told categorically never to put bouncy chairs on work surfaces . . . so the guilt was huge . . . Isn't that awful! (Cathy)

Indeed, in the focus groups held with children, instances of others being held responsible for accidents were rare. The children were quick to accept responsibility for their own safety, and to feel responsible when this had been mismanaged:

Well, if you're riding a bike and if you had an accident, well it must be your fault, 'cause you're riding it. (Femi, aged 10)

The notion of "responsibility" was sometimes reported as a more generalized sense that more care could have been taken, particularly for the mothers interviewed:

When [daughter] caught her finger in the train door, I thought "why did we sit in that part of the carriage" – the door slammed and that was her finger . . . you do feel quite guilty and that – I really thought it was my fault I'd sat her there. (Home Accident Clerk)

Pat: When she fell down stairs at my friend's house – she split her head open – I felt awful. I felt very guilty about that.

JG: Why did you feel guilty?

Pat: Well, I don't know. Maybe I felt I should have been supervising her coming down stairs.

Ellen: But on the other hand you can't actually shadow her the whole time.

Although one might refer to such events as "accidents", they are not purely blameless events, and victims (or their carer) attribute responsibility to themselves, even in cases where negligence is not directly implicated in the causal chain of events. Only accidents in general and those that "just happen" could be described as "no-one's fault". Most specific instances could be traced to particular causes, with blame potentially attaching either to the victim or an other for negligence. The actuary, for instance, suggested Acts of God as classic accidents but, when asked to think of instances, could only identify being struck by lightning:

being hit by lightning or something like that, or being drowned at sea would count – or it might do . . . but it wouldn't be an act of God, it would be an act of negligence on the part of the ship's captain. (Actuary)

Similarly, he thought, most traffic accidents would involve some human agency:

[they happen because] they're a crap driver [or] if their brakes fail, it's the fault of the mechanic who serviced their car. (Actuary)

Adults were more willing than children to attribute blame to other agents, and in the transcripts a wide range of people and institutions were mentioned as being responsible for accidents. For accidents to children these included other carers such as fathers, school teachers and meals supervisors; other children and agencies that were seen to have some specific responsibility for safety, such as local authorities and schools. Here, for instance, Pat describes how she apportioned blame for an accident in which her daughter's foot had been injured when it was caught under a boat on a fairground ride:

169

At first I was angry with Dan [husband] because he was in sole charge of them [the children] at that point, and then I was angry with the ride people because I felt it was a gentle ride, it wasn't a ride that was scary or frightening or had any amount of risk in it . . . I felt it shouldn't have happened, I think there were certain safety measures they could have taken. (Pat)

It is apparent that there are no events that are unambiguously accidental in terms of the definitions first suggested – the term "accident" emerges as a provisional category only, and one that is open to negotiation. Indeed, it seems that stories about accidents serve specifically to organize and debate ideas about moral responsibility, as these three examples illustrate:

Maria: We was sliding down the stairs and I was on her lap and then suddenly I fell down and she fell on top of me.

Anja: And I bumped my head and it really hurt!

JG: And was that an accident?

Maria: Well it was an accident 'cause we were never told that it would hurt us.

Anthony: . . . and I saw my friends ride down these steps . . . and I thought I would be able to do it . . . so I tried it, and I fell over, so that was a silly thing to do.

JG: So what do you think caused the accident?

Anthony: Me being silly, 'cause I shouldn't have been watching other people, what they do, 'cause they might have been cleverer than me!

Leroy: Tell her about that accident when you fell off the roof . . .

Jason: One time, we was playing up on the shed roof, he got up, and I wanted to and we had a fight up there and I fell down . . .

JG: So if you get hurt in a fight, could that be an accident?

Leroy: No, 'cause you shouldn't be being naughty.

For these children, the analysis of accident experiences (which may only be labelled as such provisionally, as Leroy's last comment indicates) involved the identification and apportioning of various responsibilities, such as obeying adults, copying one's friends, accepting dares or knowing your own physical limits.

Accident stories

The "accident story" seems to be a commonly used narrative device for producing this arena of moral negotiation, in which responsibility for the accident is apportioned. Accounts of accidents suffered are often introduced overtly as "stories":

Tell her the whole story, from the beginning, Mel! (Jessica, aged 6)

I haven't told you my story yet . . . (Gavin, aged 10)

And mountain climbers tell great yarns about near misses . . . (Mountain Climber)

Several kinds of accident story were told in these interviews. The first could be called the "accident horror story", lacking in much circumstantial detail and often merely one line long.

I knew a child who grabbed the bars of an electric fire. (Ellen, mother)

Remember that boy who hung himself by his rucksack in the toilet? (Cathy, mother)

This friend of my mum's friend was driving on the motorway . . . and this lorry stopped for no reason, and this friend of my mum's friend just carried on driving, and she went through the window into the back of another car. (Curtis, aged 9)

Such "horror stories" are typically about other (unknown) people or about worst possible scenarios, rather than about personal experiences. They provoke strong reactions in the audience of blame for whoever was seen as responsible, pity for the victim, or merely shocked gasps, but often little in the way of debate or analysis. Many of the children's "horror

171

stories" were almost urban myths, in that they happened to "a boy in the other class" or "a friend of my friend's". They included a story about the boy whose finger fell off after he left an elastic band wound around it and someone who put a whole apple in his mouth and had to have it cut out.

The second kind of story is the personal experience account: the story of a specific event that happened to the narrator (or someone in their care). These stories are much more complex and consist commonly of a brief comment about the setting, a dramatic account of the events leading up to the injury (or other outcome), sometimes a "worst possible scenario" as a hypothetical alternative outcome, and finally an attribution (or attributions) of responsibility. For the fairground accident that Pat refers to above, the "worst possible scenario" was a broken foot. Cathy's "worst possible scenario" in a story about her daughter's hand being hurt in a pump was that "the top of her finger had been taken off". Here is a typical personal-accident experience story, again from Pat, describing a playground incident, in which she holds the school responsible:

> Well, there was that accident with Lizzie at school, which I felt was totally preventable. I felt that was lack of supervision at Downlands [school]. In the playground they were playing that bulldog game, which is a notoriously dangerous game and Lizzie, well she sort of bashed her teeth and lost her tooth through it . . . she said she banged her mouth falling on a drain, so she obviously caught the drain in the wall . . . I think schools, especially dinner ladies and teachers and that, have to be very aware. (Pat)

This one is from the mountain climber, which he perceives as his responsibility:

> I went climbing in Wales with four other people . . . the chap I was climbing with went up first on the first leg of the climb and tied off at the top. I climbed up after him and the theory was that I climbed up the next length. So I got almost to the top of that length and that's where I slipped . . . about three feet before the next ledge, where I could make myself permanently secure, I slipped. And so I fell about twenty foot, after twenty foot the temporary anchors I had been making all the way up took up the slack and I started dangling from that point . . . the actual fall did no damage whatsoever. The circumstances as I fell off having

managed to get my foot wedged in a good crack in the rock so as I
fell off the foot didn't come free very easily and when it was
wrenched out it was twisted quite considerably... with hindsight
it could have been avoided . . . there were several mistakes made.
(Mountain climber)

Unlike the "horror story", these stories provide a vehicle for exploring
various possibilities for apportioning responsibility, and of various different potential outcomes from the same set of circumstances. However, the
accident story is rarely told as straightforwardly as in the examples above
(indeed perhaps only in relatively formal situations such as interviews).
Even in these interview settings, different elements of the stories were contributed or openly contested by members of the audience. This audience
involvement produced the third kind of story, which was a more collaborative account, clearly part of a shared experience. The dramatic account
of the actual course of events is then considerably shortened, often to the
point at which an outsider cannot follow what happened. In this account
of an accident, for instance, it is impossible for many of the audience to
follow what happened (although several of the audience ask for clarifica-
tion), and only the other participant who was involved in the incident described (Katy's mother, Pat) does seem to follow the narrative:

Katy: Because one day at play group like someone was throwing
things and he like ran away before he could hit it –

Sue: What was that?

Ellen: What it? The child?

Katy: Me! I was throwing things and one of them – no, that one I
made, that long thing, started throwing those things

Pat: Oh yes –

Katy: Because they were plastic

Pat: But that's why we tell you to pick them up, so you don't fall over.

Such accounts, condensed to the point at which those who did not
share the experience cannot understand them, suggest that the story has
been told many times, and only a few reminders are needed to elicit
the main message: here, that the "things" should be picked up to prevent

173

accidents. One such story, told by two separate groups of children from the same school, was clearly in this category: it had been told many times and had the status of a playground myth, somewhere perhaps between a "horror story" and a collaborative story. Children contested details such as who the main character was, what his injuries were and whether he went to hospital. Jessica and Amelia's account of the event was the most lucid, and is clearly a collaborative one:

Jessica: Can I tell you something? Once someone tripped when they were high up on the pole and –

Amelia: Yeah, and they broke their nose and they –

Jessica: – and they had to go to hospital and their mother didn't know which hospital they went to.

Amelia: It was that boy, wasn't it?

Jessica: I've forgot.

Amelia: I know who it was – Omar.

Jessica: It wasn't Omar.

Amelia: Uh, uh. He was on the pole.

Jessica: It wasn't Omar.

Amelia: Yeah, people go round that pole sometimes and lots of people climb up and he climbed the pole.

Jessica: It wasn't Omar.

Amelia: And he slipped, um, but I wouldn't really say that was an accident.

Jessica: It wasn't.

JG: You wouldn't? Why not?

Amelia: Well, I don't think it was his actual fault because someone had done it before I think, and told him to do it – said like "I dare you". I don't think it was his fault, but –

Jessica: He shouldn't have done it.

Amelia: He shouldn't have done it, anyway.

This exchange is initiated by Jessica's request to tell a story: "Can I tell you something?", although Amelia then provides most of the details. Although these children are in dispute about who the victim of the accident was, this seems largely irrelevant. What does matter to the successful telling of the story is that they come to an agreement about where responsibility lies. The injured boy cannot be held completely to blame, as this is an activity others have tried (presumably without ending up in hospital) and the possible "dare" legitimated his attempt. However, for these girls, accepting dares does not apparently absolve the victim of any responsibility: Amelia echoes Jessica's "he shouldn't have done it anyway".

Attributing responsibility

There is, then, a gap between the complete lack of blame implied by calling something an accident and the actual amount of responsibility victims and others are apportioned in the account of the accident. In practice, the actions (or inactions) of many people may contribute to an accident, and identifying where responsibility lies can be difficult. Such ambiguity about accidents can be used deliberately to avoid blame, as Anja admits:

I hit Zara once, but I said "it was an accident" (Anja, aged 8)

The ambiguity of such claims to the accidental was also used for humorous effect. Gavin, for instance, was one of a group of boys who were busy squashing ants with their fists on the table as we talked:

Like that was an accident – I just tried to stop Leroy killing one, and then my hand accidentally went "crash"! (Gavin)

When the ambiguity was genuine, for instance when an "accidental" outcome resulted from an act for which clear responsibilities had not been apportioned, adults could be frustratingly unable to accept that it was genuine:

Jessica: Once Hanifa [teacher] was chatting with Yesim [school friend] because she had hurt her hand, it was cut right there [demonstrates] and she [Hanifa] was saying "was it an accident or was it on purpose?" and Yesim said "I don't know" and Hanifa said "You

175

> must know if it was an accident or on purpose" and Yesim said "I don't know" and Hanifa said "just tell me" . . .

JG: Do you think you always know whether –

Amelia and Jessica: No, no!

Jessica: No, but Hanifa thought you must. She said "you must [know]".

The accident in practice, then, is the result of rather more ambiguous responsibilities than the ideal definition first suggests. Sometimes the conflict between abstract definitions and the definition of accidents in practice was followed through to its logical conclusion, and respondents could not think of any events that could ultimately be described as accidents. An RAF doctor, asked what kind of accidents might happen in training, could not think of any that would be "just" accidents, as pilots should predict most uncertain outcomes through their awareness of their causes, such as cloud cover or lightning:

> Let me think of a case. You fly into a hill in cloud, which is always down to pilot error really because he didn't recognize the weather was bad and abort early enough and get up to a higher level . . . (RAF doctor)

> You could have lightning strike. Certainly. But then the question is obviously if there was a risk, lightning risk warning, why was the pilot flying? (RAF doctor)

He explained that any "accidents" resulting from such situations would be investigated officially by a board.

JG: Does the board ever find it was an accident? Do accidents ever happen?

RAF Doctor: I mean basically it can be a mechanical error or a pilot error. There's only two things that can go wrong really, I suppose. The aeroplane or the pilot.

As he comments, "the system doesn't like a pure accident". We might suppose that even if such an event had to be officially attributed with a "cause", it would still be described unofficially, in everyday social interaction, as a tragic accident. However, the doctor went on to describe a mess room ritual that would happen in the event of a pilot dying in such a crash, which suggests that even informally such events would be attributed with a non-accidental cause. This ritual involves, among other things, a ritualistic rubbishing of the dead pilot's professional reputation:

> People start talking about memories of him, and the memories tend to be, "oh well, he always did take risks", you know, "you know what he was like, he always pushed it". (RAF doctor)

The pilot's propensity to take undue risks (to be "accident-prone") perhaps serves to reduce the uncertainty about the tragedy. The notion that an accident could happen to anyone in mid-air is perhaps too much for anyone expected to get into a plane every day and fly to cope with. Even such misfortunes as being hit by lightning have to be explained as predictable – and therefore potentially controllable – events.

Preventing accidents

For many of the respondents, then, there were two kinds of accidents, preventable ones and those that, in theory at least, "just happen" and that nothing could be done about to prevent. The children who participated in the studies were particularly adamant that all accidents could in theory be prevented, and would challenge their peers who claimed otherwise, as these three 11-year-old girls illustrate:

Florence: Accidents are accidents – they'll happen just like an accident.

Emma: But you can prevent them.

Tunde: Yeah, like the knife one [previously related] – if the handle hadn't been sticking over, she wouldn't have got cut.

When the children were asked how accidents could be prevented, they could repeat safety advice they had learnt at school, such as road-crossing drills. Such reports took the form of lists that had clearly been heard many times, or well-rehearsed choruses repeated like mantras:

> And my dad, and he tells me not to pick up any buggy things or
> don't touch dogs without asking the owner and don't take any-
> thing. If a stranger says, "d'you want my sweets?" say NO – if it's
> one of your friends you can say yes. (Jason, aged 7)

JG: Some of you had some ideas about how you could stop accidents
  happening . . .

All [six boys in chorus]: Look, listen, learn . . .

JG: So how do you stop accidents happening?

Amelia: Be very, very, careful!

Adults also provided general advice consistent with this notion of taking more care:

> With tiny children [safety] has to be your first priority – you can't
> be too careful. (Health Visitor)

JG: So can you prevent accidents happening?

Accident Clerk: Yes, by being more careful . . .

Accidents, for these respondents, could be prevented if risks were known
and care was taken to reduce those risks. However, like the abstract definitions, this advice was given in a general sense, and often individual accidents were seen as rather more complex in their causation – or at least the
risk calculation involved in preventing them was seen as being rather less
obvious than the safety advice suggested, as these boys point out:

Anthony: When I was drying up . . . trying to dry it too fast, and the
  plate slipped out of my hand, and I got grounded for a week. And I
  didn't think that was fair.

Matthew: Yeah, and Darren said . . . "well you should have been holding it with two hands!"

Simon: Well, if I'd been holding it in two hands I wouldn't have been
  able to dry up, so Darren's a bit wrong!

Again, the idea that some people clearly took risks and didn't suffer accidents while others were more risk-averse yet did suffer them, undermined any simple faith in "care taking" as prevention. Cathy describes, for instance, a mother who she felt often took "an enormous risk with her child's safety", but whose child never suffered a serious injury:

Cathy: . . . And how that child is alive today is an absolute miracle, but she is . . .

Ellen: And these things happen and there's a certain lack of logic in it. I can remember . . . there was a woman who had a young toddler, and she kept an eye on this child the whole time and was very strict about keeping an eye on it. And then one day she was on the phone, left the door open, child went wandering out, fell down a storm drain and drowned. In this much [demonstrates one inch] water.

All: Oh, oh no.

Cathy: These things do happen.

For these "pure" accidents, those that just happen, the very idea of prevention was a source of humour if the accident did not have such a tragic outcome. Ellen, for instance, recounts the story of an accident that happened to her son while on holiday. He had run headlong into a stone sink, jutting out from the cottage wall and had been briefly concussed. Asked if that could have been prevented, her comments provoke laughter in her audience:

No, because I think you can over-compensate. I suppose the owner of the cottage could have said "beware of outcrops of granite!" (Ellen)

When pushed to describe how individual accidents could be avoided, children also soon saw that there was a limit to how far the preventative logic could be taken, as Amelia's argument with Jessica and her final, sarcastic, response to my question indicate:

Jessica: [You could prevent] falling off your bike, because someone could be there to catch you.

Amelia: I know, but someone might not be there! [In this case] I was just riding along and I knew I was going too fast and I just pulled on

179

my front brake and the back wheel went [makes noise] and I went flying over.

JG: So whose fault was that?

Amelia: I don't think it was anyone's fault, do you? The people who put the tarmac there!

The notion that all accidents could be prevented was seen as flawed, simply because some "just happen". However many risks were taken into account, there were always some that could not be foreseen:

All you can do, I feel, is have control over the things that you know you can control, like holding hands when you cross the road. I mean there are always unforeseen dangers like a bus mounting a pavement [which] can mow you all down or whatever. (Cathy)

You reach for a good handhold and it turns out it's actually a loose rock and not a good handhold – that's luck. Obviously if you didn't go climbing it wouldn't happen. You are taking a risk doing it, you know it's possible . . . you can reduce risks . . . but you can never counter everything that could go wrong. (Mountain climber)

Responsibilities for risk assessment

This is not to suggest that these respondents were "fatalistic" about accidents, or did not take specific actions (as opposed to more general "taking more care") to prevent them. On the contrary, like the respondents interviewed by Roberts et al. (1993), most took considerable steps to keep themselves and others safe. When asked what could be done to prevent accidents to children, the first responses of the mothers interviewed all referred to personal action they could take to reduce accidents in their homes, including installing a range of safety equipment and educating their children about safety consciousness:

Ellen: I mean I think there are for me certain fundamental things, like stair gates are an obvious one. Everyone gets stair gates.

Sue: We never had a stair gate . . .

Ellen: Well, that's terrible parenting!

All: [laugh]

> . . . and I said "don't eat anything that you find in the garden,
> don't eat any berries at all". I thought that was the simplest thing.
> (Cathy)

For mothers, avoiding accidents in the home was seen to be a combination of "common sense" about the hazards that existed and a detailed knowledge of the particular risks to which their children were most vulnerable. Particular children were reported as more likely to, for instance, poke things into electric sockets or run into sharp door catches. Other agencies were also seen to have a responsibility for preventing accidents to children, including schools and other carers who were expected to act *in loco parentis*, and take the same care about hazards that parents did. In addition, parents also made many suggestions that involved "engineering" or "enforcement" strategies, such as advocating that children's bicycles should not be sold without helmets, or writing to the school to suggest that school trips should only use buses with fitted seat belts.

For these mothers, the greatest threats to safety were other people. Danger resided particularly in two groups; those with no "common sense" about how to avoid accidents and those whose particular vulnerabilities to risks were unknown. This latter group consisted mainly of other children:

> I make my home as safe as possible. I mean, I knew where the
> dangers were and my children knew basic dangers, but other children don't foresee those dangers. And they experiment in different ways to your children. So you might be used to watching out
> for your children in certain areas . . . and then another child
> comes in . . . and you've got to watch them all the time. (Pat)

Those with no "common sense" included those with no personal experience of children, and those who had been observed taking what were seen to be undue risks:

Cathy: Some people are very lax, they let go of children's hands. I
mean one teacher let go of a child's hand on that crossing! I mean,
I thought "I don't believe it" . . . When I worked at the nursery, I

mean there were some people there who were very lax.

Ellen: Did they have kids themselves?

Pat: Some people just don't have that common sense, they just don't have that kind of thinking to prevent –

Cathy: No, to me it's just common sense.

For these mothers (who all had primary responsibility in their households for child care), the group of people with no "common sense" about accident prevention also included men generally, and their male partners in particular. Cathy relates the tale of her husband asking her, after seeing a programme on television about scalds from hot water, whether she ran the cold water in the bath first:

Cathy: . . . and he actually said to me [laughs] because he's not very safety-conscious, he said "you do run the cold in first, don't you?"

All: [laugh]

Cathy: After all these years, you know! It had never occurred to him before, so it was educational, that he watched that programme!

Pat: Actually I do notice that men are not nearly so safety-conscious as women –

Ellen: No, they're not!

Pat: I can't go to the park with Dan [husband] because he scares the living daylights out of me . . .

Ellen: Yes, mine's just the same.

The "dangers" here, for these mothers, are perhaps those of inadequate mapping of risks. Other people (men, certain teachers) demonstrate an insufficient understanding of risks, and other children pose unknown vulnerability to risks. It was not just parents who saw danger residing in risks that were unknown, and particularly in "other people's" uncertain knowledge of those risks. The mountain climber, for instance, talked about preventing mountain accidents in terms of knowing the risks one faced when hill walking or mountain climbing. Accidents may happen because known risks were taken:

. . . say. . . walking, continuing to try and do a walk when the light is fading, it's mid-winter and you don't know where you are. If you are lost, trying to continue upwards rather than like head south to the road or something – that would be a stupid risk. (Mountain climber)

However, there was a sense in which such dangers were, like his example of reaching for a handhold that turned out to be a loose rock, known and knowingly risked. More dangerous was unknown risk that arose from ignorance:

I suppose there are those people who would go mountain climbing who have no experience and therefore no knowledge that they are taking those risks, which is fairly careless in the sense that beforehand perhaps you should put some effort into trying to find out more about what you are doing. (Mountain climber)

Such "careless" risks, from inadequate knowledge of the possible dangers one faced, were rather different from those that "just happen" and cannot be prevented. As an analogy the mountain climber contrasts novices who might injure themselves trying to mend a television with the expert:

. . . if you have no knowledge of electronics then it's pretty stupid to open up your television and start sticking a screwdriver into it . . . if you were a qualified electrician you can still have an accident doing that. (Mountain climber)

Danger resides not so much in the external world (the television, mountains) and its hazards (electricity, loose handholds) but in the inadequate mapping of those hazards. Those whose maps are most sophisticated (mothers, experienced hill walkers) may know they are as vulnerable to accidents as the novices, but they report their vulnerability as having known, and therefore safer, boundaries.

Balancing risks

This last comment by the mountain climber, and the one above claiming that "luck" played a part in whether the handhold turned out to be a loose stone, suggests that rather than simple fatalism, what is at work here is a balancing of risks – of known, but remote, possibilities of danger against known pleasures. The only way to prevent the accidents that "just happen" is not to take part in the activity at all:

> It's preventable in the sense that you could say that they were stupid going out in that weather . . . but they have made an assessment of that risk. But you could prevent it, you could prevent them all by sitting at home doing nothing. (Mountain climber)

The risk of boredom is likewise contrasted with the risk of playground injury by Katy, in response to her mother's comments that her father would let her use playground equipment she felt was unacceptably dangerous (as there was only concrete beneath):

> He used to take us there because it was the only bit with seesaws and swings and fun stuff really. Or we had to run around this wooden thing which was boring. (Katy)

Similarly, for the mothers and for the health visitor, taking certain risks was seen as the outcome of avoiding others; in this case those of over-protection:

> Well part of you says you know, they've got to go out, they've got to do things on their own and I can't mollycoddle them the whole of their life . . . and you're torn between that and going completely overboard the other way . . . I've got a feeling that by over-warning children you make them less safe people. (Ellen)

> . . . there are parents who won't allow their children to go on slides or swings, there is that sort of fear I think – when do you let your children out on to the road? Yes, there needs to be some sort of balance [but] I don't think you can be over-cautious with tiny little children. (Health Visitor)

Although these respondents talked about certain accidents "just happening", there was a sense in which the space in which they happened was still calculable through an assessment of knowable risks. Real danger inhabited spaces in which risks could not be known (such as with other children) or when "other" people had no apparent commitment to calculating risks. Even the astrologer, whose knowledge one might suppose belonged to an older age of pure fatalism, pointed out that "modern" astrology was not tied to the fatalism of classical astrology. Unlike any of the other respondents, she commented that accidents were often "meant" to happen, but in the sense that the event had some meaning or purpose, rather than merely that it was inevitable:

> If something happens to you, like . . . you accidentally bump into someone, there's a sense of synchronicity. . . I remember my friend who was knocked over by a motorbike, she said afterwards "I needed it to happen". (Astrologer)

In explaining why accidents might happen at a particular time to a particular person, she explained:

> Well, I can only talk astrologically. Lots of people carry Mars in their seventh house, Mars being the planet of aggression. In the physical, real accidents; fire, explosions, violence . . . now if you're suppressing your Mars energy, more likely it's in the seventh house, which is the house of others, so in a sense it's you living out your aggression through others. (Astrologer)

In classical astrology, she explains, the kind of accident one is likely to suffer is determined by a combination of dangerous signs in the stars; asphyxiation is associated with Mercury and Uranus, burns with Mars, whereas drowning is associated with Pluto and Neptune. The kind of accident is therefore not accidental:

> It is in your chart – you have that propensity, Martian people will usually get hurt in explosions, things catching fire, while others will be more prone to suffocation or drowning. (Astrologer)

However, modern astrology, she notes, which is influenced by the ideas of Jung, appears to view the determinations of classical astrology as merely yet another risk factor to be taken into account:

> It's not used to predict. You can use it to see a propensity – to watch out for that energy within you. Old astrology might have said, you know "beware when on the 14th of March, Uranus passes over Mars – you musn't touch anything electrical". But I would just point out the propensity. (Astrologer)

Fatalism, in short, is not what it was.

Constructing the accident in everyday life

Those interviewed in these studies were not a systematically selected sample, and are unlikely to be representative of the population of contemporary Britain. The adults interviewed were largely from the professional social classes, in terms of their own or their partner's occupation, and they were all of working age. An older or less socially advantaged sample may have very different views. In contrast to some of the findings here, Roberts et al. (1993) report, for instance, that for their working-class respondents accidents were seen as largely caused by environmental hazards, and their prevention was a matter of material improvement to that environment. However, those interviewed did provide a range of possible views, and their accounts of accidents, what they are and how they coped with them provide some interesting clues to the status of the accident as a category of misfortune in contemporary Britain.

Both professional and lay people describe particular events as "accidents" and utilize a working definition of accidents which suggests that they are random misfortunes that result from unmotivated actions. At the same time, however, describing an event as an accident situates it as a morally negotiable event. Our designations of accidents are first tenuous – they serve as provisional explanations, pending more detailed investigation. This is clear in these everyday stories of accidents described above, in which events are analyzed for precipitating factors and possible culpability. Like the fatal accidents produced in the coroner's court, the accidents described by these respondents emerge from a moral investigation of an event. Stories about accidents are vehicles for reaching a consensus about proper responsibilities and the apportioning of blame. It may be that this consensus is contingent and local (as evidenced in the differing accounts of Roberts et al. (1993)), but it is reached through shared accounts of accident stories and the exchange of opinions about culpability and what constitutes negligence.

Risk and social identity

It was noted above that children, particularly, were reluctant to hold others responsible for accidents. Although they could list various agents who had a general responsibility for their safety (such as car drivers or parents), when it came to telling their own stories about accidents, they almost always accepted full responsibility for outcomes of mismanaged risks. Adults also most commonly held themselves to blame for accidents, even if only in a generalized sense of being "careless". At one level, the individualization of risk assessment, through which we are all responsible for managing our risk environments, is irresistible. To claim that we are responsible for our own safety is to claim a very basic social competence: that we are capable of "looking after ourselves". For the children in these discussions, taking on responsibility marked the move on from early childhood when other adults were seen as responsible for your safety. To be a competent social actor, their stories suggested, involved accepting responsibility. For the adults, too, risk assessment was not just a strategy for reducing accidents, it was a technique for constructing an appropriate social identity.

Indeed there is some evidence here that knowledge about accidents and how to prevent them is used in everyday discourse to construct such sociological variables as class, gender and parenthood, rather than simply being an outcome of them. Ellen's comment to Sue (above) that her lack of a stair gate is evidence of "terrible parenting" is a joking insult to a friend, met with laughter in her audience, but it also perhaps indicates a more serious point. It is possible to make the comment, and for it to be taken as a joke, because the group is assumed to share a common knowledge of what proper parenting consists of (that is, installing various safety equipment, not letting young children cross roads alone). Sue's lack of a stair gate is not a serious challenge to this local consensus, in the way that "other people's" might be. Such "other people" might include men, who were perceived as incompetent risk assessors in terms of their children's safety, but also might include those with fewer material resources, who might make different assessments about the necessity of equipment such as stair gates. Further, for these mothers (all with male partners), talk about the "ineptness" of men in adequately assessing risk possibly contributes to the construction of their heterosexual social identities. Wilton (1993), in her account of the functions of heterosexual women's friendships, suggests that accounts of male incompetence or oppressiveness within female friendship groups construct men as "naturally" flawed, and women as inevitably having to cope with them in the context of heterosexual relationships. Talk about men's inability to take responsibility for safety in the home constructs, for these women, not only an identity as a "proper mother" (whose responsibility safety is seen to be) but also an identity as a heterosexual mother, who accepts the inevitability of men's lack of responsibility.

Similarly, the children's accounts of "gender-appropriate" risk-taking behaviour suggest that they are achieving a gendered identity through talk about risk (if not actual risk-taking). Here, for instance, Mehmet tells me why boys have more accidents, and his friend Kenny soon joins in to agree with his account of "boy's games":

Mehmet: Boys normally play wild games, like.

Kenny: No, what do you mean, wild games?

Mehmet: Dangerous, like when you keep on running and like –

Kenny: – yeah, like when we play that wrestling game –

Mehmet: – yeah, like you push and –

Kenny: – you can scrape your hand or even break your hand!

Mehmet: Whenever I play that game I always injure myself. Like I nearly broke my finger, I couldn't move it, last time –

Kenny: – when that boy jumped.

The girls provided rather different accounts of risk taking. First, even the youngest girls (aged seven and eight) were more likely than the boys to tell stories that illustrated their responsibility for the safety of others, such as Vicky's account here of an accident to her brother:

I didn't mean it – mummy said "can you go out and get the washing in please, Vicky?" I said yes, so I was going out, my brother was coming to the back door and he put his thumb in where the door closes and the door opened again so I SLAMMED it closed and it slammed my brother's thumb in the door . . . and as I was coming in I saw my brother's nail stuck in the door. Yeah, like, um, I should have had more responsibility for him because I'm the oldest. (Vicky, aged 8)

Only one boy in the discussions made claims to such feelings of responsibility for other children. However, when he described having to look after a young cousin, and make sure the cousin did not hurt himself jumping from furniture, his friend Mohammed was quick to point out that such feelings were quite unwarranted, and that any accidents that resulted would not be his fault:

. . . but grown-ups has already told them "don't do it [jump off the furniture], it's dangerous". Like, if they do it and something happens, it's no-one's fault, it's their fault, 'cause they already told them. (Mohammed, aged 11)

Girls' accounts of accidents also stressed their responsibility for their own safety in the face of temptations:

JG: Do you ever dare people to do things?

Emma: Yeah, but not dangerous things like [lying in the road].

Tunde: Not dangerous stuff.

JG: If somebody did dare you to do something dangerous, would you do it?

Tunde: No, I wouldn't.

Emma: No, never.

Tunde: No.

Emma: If they dared me to do something dangerous, and I was worried about losing my friends, well they're not my friends really.

189

This story, and others in the transcripts, reveal a sense of coming to some shared consensus about responsibilities through telling stories about accidents and how they should have been prevented. In the children's stories accidents are the point of articulation for concerns about moral issues such as whether one accepts dares or not, or obeys adult injunctions against certain behaviours. Emma and Tunde echo each other's comments – "no, never" – and in doing so reiterate the boundaries that their particular friendship group draws around appropriate risk avoidance behaviour.

Such boundaries are drawn around various groups in terms of their balancing of risks; "other" people are those whose criteria for assessing risks have either not been demonstrated (novice hill walkers) or found wanting (fathers, some teachers). Within the group, individual decisions may be challenged, but a shared rationale for coming to them is assumed.

Calculating the incalculable

The accidental, it was suggested in Chapter 3, provides a provisional explanation for that which is at the limits of rational explanation. Accidents, it seems, remain the remnants of our classificatory system in many ways – they are still the leftovers. This is why it is difficult to define the contents of the category. Its constitution is defined negatively: an event is accidental not because of any innate characteristics, but because it is *not* something else (a suicide, vandalism, child abuse, a push in the playground "done on purpose"). Inevitably, such definitions are provisional, since some other future verdict cannot be precluded and the designation is always, potentially if not overtly, in dispute. Both professionals and lay people use the same logic, that of exclusion, to create a provisional category of events that are "left over" after other possible explanations have been suggested, and to construct some accidents as "preventable".

However, the contemporary accident is not the result of unknown forces, or those for which there is no merit in seeking an explanation. There was no evidence here of specifically "lay" beliefs in the random nature of accidents, or a belief that they were in general unpreventable. On the contrary, these respondents were highly conscious of risks and took many actions to prevent accidents happening, and as Ellen comments:

It always strikes me as amazing how few accidents happen, because potentially there are an enormous range [of risks]. (Ellen)

The astrologer, perhaps unsurprisingly, superstitiously touched the wooden table after describing herself as someone who was not accident-prone. Many other respondents, however, also talked about luck, although only when talking about accidents avoided rather than those suffered. Davison et al. (1991), in their discussion of lay beliefs about heart disease, note that the focus on "risk factors" in health education may make such fatalistic beliefs more salient, as there is no other way of providing meaning for those events (heart attack or accident) that are not in any obvious way the outcome of a specific risk having been taken. However, the fatalism of these respondents did not appear to be a resigned belief about the unpredictable nature of the world, which nothing could be done about. Leroy was the only person interviewed to persist in stating that "accidents were a coincidence" and that therefore nothing could be done about them. His views were marginalized by his friends, who accused him of "using them long words again" and of recklessly ignoring risks. For most, their "fatalism" was specifically produced through the techniques of risk assessment.

First, the very multiplication of possible risks meant that almost all accidents in practice could be attributed to lack of attention to particular risks – even if only humorously, as in Ellen's example above of the advice to "beware of outcrops of granite!", or Amelia's ironic comment that the person who laid the tarmac could be responsible for her cycling accident. Such humour represents perhaps resistance to the dominance of risk assessment as a technology for making sense of accidents, but it also recognizes the possibility that risks can, at least in theory, account for all accidental outcomes. In general, only in abstract or hypothetical ("we could all get run over by a bus tomorrow") cases did accidents "just happen". The only exception, perhaps was the actuary's example of being struck by lightning. This was, however, the only unequivocal example he could think of where no blame would attach. A "bolt from the blue", it seems, can only describe accidents that are literally just that – it no longer has any metaphoric utility in everyday discourse about accidents.

Davison et al. (1991), in their account of knowledge about heart disease, suggest that fatalistic beliefs continue to co-exist with beliefs about the value of preventative action because they explain the distribution, rather than the incidence, of misfortune. Accidents, likewise, must be explained as personal misfortunes, and it was clear to those interviewed here that preventative logic was flawed as a deterministic way of understanding the distribution of accidents. If the outcome is serious, people need to understand why the accident happened to them at that particular moment, as well as understanding why that kind of accident happens in general. However, only the astrologer had an explicit theory that saw accidents as having a "meaning" in a Freudian sense. Neither was fate, for other respondents, a significant factor in explaining the occurrence of misfortunes that were identified as accidents. It did, however, sometimes explain fortune – why certain people did not have accidents, despite the (potentially inexhaustible) range of risks that exist. Again, fate only explained the abstract or hypothetical accidents. In practice, the forensic examination of actual experiences resulted in responsibilities being attributed and meaning attached through the attribution of negligence or even, in some cases, motivation. "Misfortune" often resulted from the (calculable) outcome of a balancing of risks: such as those of mountain climbing against the "risk" of boredom, or those of allowing children to play outside against the "risk" of over-protecting them.

Fatalism reconfigured

The persistence of fatalistic beliefs appeared to be neither unequivocal evidence of the incomplete domination of other discourses, nor of resistance to those discourses. Rather, it could only be understood *with reference* to these other discourses; namely, those of risk and its management. The contours of "fate" and "luck" as explanations for the accidental, for these respondents, were understood through risk. To a large extent, fate could be (theoretically) calculated like any other risk factor for accidents.

It was suggested in Chapter 5 that education may persist as the primary strategy for accident prevention, despite its relative lack of success, because it appeals to a risk-management strategy in which preventative actions can be taken as talismans against misfortune, rather than as a direct attempt to influence risk factors. In the stories about accidents told by these respondents, there is a sense in which safety was ensured by a knowledge of risks, and an expertise in managing them, rather than through direct attempts to reduce the causes of specific accidents. The health visitor, for instance, describes how she burnt her leg on holiday: an accident that in her account is presented as almost unfair, as she had demonstrated a basic knowledge of precautions that seemed in excess of her fellow holiday makers:

> . . . We're on this tiny little motorbike up a mountain – we had a helmet, would you believe – we were the only people in Kos to have a helmet! [laughs], so we took that precaution – but we were wearing only shorts . . . I didn't think it would burn me. (Health Visitor)

The children's "look, listen, learn" mantra, or the Green Cross Code that one mentioned, "look left, look right and look left again", are seen by these respondents as inadequate because they reduce prevention to a general all-purpose technique for safety. Prevention in a contemporary risk society relies on a more sophisticated knowledge of risks, in which the boundaries of the predictable are calculable in theory if not precisely known. Danger arises not from the operation of "fate" but from outside these boundaries – from those who do not calculate risks, and from those whose particular vulnerabilities are not known.

In Hacking's (1987) phrase, chance had largely been tamed in everyday discourse about accidents and their management. However, it had been tamed in ways which were local and contingent. Social groups (children's friendship groups, mothers, climbers) negotiate norms about proper responsibilities that draw on the general logic of risk assessment (to do otherwise would undermine any attempts to create a competent social identity), but which are particular in their local application. Risk assessments were not absolute, and stories about accidents (the outcomes of faulty assessments) served as a local arena for the development of consensus about proper responsibilities. Talk about accidents produces social knowledge about misfortune, how to classify it and how to manage it; also it provides a set of strategies for constructing shared knowledge about responsibilities and appropriate social identity in everyday social interaction.

Chapter 8

Conclusions: towards an archaeology of accidents

Misfortunes are perhaps universal to human society, if ways of classifying them are not. This book began by noting that in late twentieth-century Britain some misfortunes become classified as accidents and that there was nothing inevitable about how this classification happened. A diverse range of misfortunes are identified as accidents, from the trivial to the tragic. The trivial are the subject of considerable everyday conversation, whereas the tragic are the cause of much human misery, and have been identified as a public health priority. Although this suggests accidents as an important subject for sociological study, there has been rather little of this.

In order to explore the shifting conceptual space occupied by accidents, a range of clues have been followed up. They include: examination of written sources, such as the reports of the Registrar-General, writings from the seventeenth century, twentieth-century accident prevention literature; an observation of a coroner's court; qualitative analysis of interview and focus-group transcripts; the recording of everyday sources such as newspaper reports of accidents and folk wisdom. If accidents have been "neglected" by sociology, with a few notable exceptions (such as the work of Figlio 1985; Tombs 1990, 1991, 1992; and Roberts et al. 1992, 1993), this paucity of secondary sources was more than compensated by a wealth of primary data. Accidental misfortunes seem to provide an incitement to discussion and analysis, in both public and private arenas. Inevitably, only a small part of the possible field of data has been utilized here, and

195

there are many clues that have not been followed up, such as English legal cases of accidents, or the many popular media representations of accidents in television dramas and documentaries. Also inevitably, there are many sociological questions of importance that have not been addressed, such as those concerning the social distribution of accidental misfortunes, or the possibilities of a gendered discourse of risk and accidents.

The concern has been with one particular question: what are the general rules by which accidents are socially constructed? Those clues that have been pursued to understand this question have suggested an important place for accidents as a legitimate subject of sociological enquiry. They are not only a pivotal category of misfortune in late twentieth-century Britain, but also a blank slate, on which various contemporary cultural concerns (specifically, those about uncertainty, responsibility and culpability) are inscribed. These concluding remarks will sum up the argument and examine its implications for an understanding of how misfortune is experienced in contemporary culture.

The arguments presented in this book can be summarized by first outlining the discursive shifts that have produced rather different spaces in which the accident has appeared, and by then tracing the relationship of the subjective experience of accidental misfortune to these different discourses.

The place of accidents in our classification of misfortune

Before 1650, an accident was merely a happening or an event, and there appears to have been no space in European discourse for the concept of an event that was neither motivated nor predictable. For Ward (1622), for instance, a universe governed by an omnipotent God precluded any category of misfortunes that were inexplicable. In the middle of the seventeenth century, those shifts in scientific discourse analyzed by Hacking (1975) and Foucault (1989) created new explanatory possibilities, based on evidence, deduction and statistical reasoning. These shifts (which were here characterized as the emergence of rationality) not only opened up a space for accidents, but perhaps also created them as a necessary category of misfortune. Rational explanation inevitably had its limits, in that there were remnants, the local and particular events that did not (at least as yet) fit into a pattern. For Graunt, analyzing Bills of Mortality in 1662, such "accidents" were explicitly omitted, as they promised little reward for a scientific explanation. By the end of the seventeenth century, Petty could confidently dismiss the accident as a despised explanation of misfortune. Rationality, then, produced a space for accidental events at the margins of its explanatory reach. The accident was both necessary, as such explanations could not be all-encompassing, and despised, as the rational project was a comprehensive one, with a goal of exhaustive analysis.

In the middle of the nineteenth century, accidents were constructed in the statistics of the Registrar-General through a specifically moral discourse. In demarcating accidents from other "external" causes of death, Farr (Registrar-General 1862) utilized moral content as the major axis of his classification. Today, accidents are still recorded as such through the medico-legal processes of a coroner's court, which constructs them not in terms of what they are, but in terms of what they are not. That is, a death is recorded as accidental because there is no evidence to suggest any motivation or moral culpability.

At the end of the nineteenth and beginning of the twentieth century, the emergent discipline of sociology is silent on accidents. As part of the rationalist project, sociology cannot construct the accident as a legitimate arena for research, as it is neither predictable nor motivated. However, in the early twentieth century, accidents do appear in European discourse, but in the literatures of anthropology and psychology. In rational cosmologies, the accident (as a marginal, necessary and despised category) is a given, hardly worthy of note. However, it can therefore act as a marker of a self-conscious modernity. As an inevitable outcome of rational classification systems, it becomes visible by its absence in other classificatory systems; in the cosmology of pre-rational people, such as children or "primitives". A belief that some misfortunes are merely accidental becomes definitive of modernity. At this point there are also attempts to reduce the inexplicable margins of rationality; to reduce the number of misfortunes that are "merely" accidental. Freud, for instance, argued that apparent accidents could reveal underlying rational motivations: they were not "really" accidents, in that their occurrence could be explained. In this light, Figlio's (1985) description of the Workmen's Compensation Act of 1887 can also be seen as an attempt to define some workplace accidents as not "really" accidents, as they arise from the negligence of employers.

Until the middle of the twentieth century, however, there continued to be a space occupied by some misfortunes that were merely the result of coincidence and bad luck, and for which there was no profit in seeking further explanation. Accidents were an inevitable feature of a universe understood as obeying rational and probabilistic laws. This space was radically reconfigured in the middle of the twentieth century, when accidents became preventable. In Hacking's (1987) terms, this followed a "probabilistic revolution", in which random events themselves became predictable through the erosion of deterministic laws and their replacement by the autonomous laws of chance. Here, it has been argued that a new space was opened up for accidents by the fracturing of the modernist consensus around rationality, and its explanatory power. Specifically, the emergence of a discourse of risks and their management produced the accident as a predictable, and thus preventable, misfortune. Accidents became both the archetypal outcomes of the mismanagement of risk and, at the same time, the paradigmatic events upon which to demonstrate the success of new techniques. From the margins of an explanatory system, they move to its very centre. Accident prevention became possible as a discrete professional activity when accidents were reconfigured as the outcomes of identifiable and calculable sets of risk factors, which could be manipulated by the potential accident victim, rather than as inevitable events that were to be expected from time to time.

These discursive shifts have not necessarily been uniform. In some senses, the operation of the coroner's court was seen to be a tension between a modernist discourse evident in the formal guidelines for coroners – in which the accident was a given, defined only in its relation to other, more culpable deaths – and the rather more contemporary needs identified by attempted reforms of the court's functions – which suggested that the "moral" function of the court be abandoned in the interests of the accurate record keeping upon which epidemiological knowledge is based. However, it was seen that accidents come to be classified as such through a moral enquiry, in which the court still produces fatal accidents (and therefore fatal accident rates – the very raw material of much risk analysis) as the "leftovers" of medical nosology. A similar tension is evident in the only partially successful attempts by the medical profession to utilize a new vocabulary for accident research, centring on injuries, hosts, vectors and energy transfers. These attempts are undermined, perhaps, by the continuing appeal to the accidental as marginal category for the as-yet unexplained.

The subjective experience of accidents

Managing risks

Most accidents are misfortunes. They are events that we experience and have to make sense of in personal terms, rather than as part of a population risk profile. This book started with a working definition which suggested that a heterogenous class of misfortunes become classified as "accidents" because they are experienced as both unmotivated and unpredictable. The ideal accident is a happening with unwanted outcomes (such as injury or material damage) for which no one can be blamed, as no intention was involved, and which could not have been expected at the particular time and place at which it happened. This ideal is appealed to in the anthropological and psychological discourses of the early twentieth century as one that is uncontested: only the child or the primitive would seek moral or causal explanations for accidental misfortunes. The accident, it is implied, is experienced as an inevitable misfortune over which we have little control. This ideal persists in the initial definitions given in response to the question "What is an accident?"

However, in the late twentieth century this ideal is rarely realized in practice. In the process of the coroner's court and in everyday stories about accidents, for instance, such a definition operates only in the abstract, or to describe hypothetical events. At its logical extreme, a discourse of risk undermines the very existence of accidents in this ideal sense in two ways. First, a growing sophistication in the mapping of potential risk factors makes all events predictable and ultimately preventable. Second, as responsibility is divorced from motivation, all victims of accidents are potentially culpable. Culpability arises not from the motivations of the victim or other agents, but from their ignorance or miscalculation of risks. Risks are the translations of population statistics (the numbers of fatalities or injuries correlated with specific factors) into individual behaviours, such as awareness of climate when mountain climbing, or cycling only with a helmet, or installing guards over electric sockets in the home. As risk management has been, in O'Malley's (1993) word, "privatized", we are all responsible for the surveillance and management of our own risk environments, and held culpable for mismanagement.

An illustration of the different implications of the new regime for the experience of accidents lies perhaps in the comparison of two superficially similar works: Graunt's (1662) observations of the Bills of Mortality and *The BMA guide to living with risk* (1990). Just as Graunt described his project as one of enumerating the risks of death from various causes so that people could "better understand the Hazard they are in" (Graunt 1662: 16), the BMA suggested that one purpose of their guide was to "put risk in perspective, and to put numbers on a selection of risks as far as possible" (BMA 1990: xvii). The similarity, however, ends here. Graunt's faith in rational analysis is a reassuring one: that further knowledge will correct misconceptions, and that the quantification of that knowledge will lead not only to less anxiety but also to greater social justice. His statistical analysis leads him to various suggestions for the improvement of society: that, for instance, beggars should be kept by the state (Graunt 1662: 19). The BMA guide, on the other hand, is profoundly unsettling. "It is not", the authors point out, "possible to make choices for people" (BMA 1990: xviii). People must instead make their own choices; but from a vast array of possible risks, which must be quantified, understood and balanced. Rather than reducing anxiety, knowledge of risks increases it. There are, note the authors, "few things that are certain in this uncertain and complex world" (BMA 1990: xv), and the range of risks to worry about is enormous:

> One might ask, how might it affect me if a nuclear power station was built nearby, rather than a coal-fired one? If I collide with that car over there, would I be safer in it or my own? . . . How often does someone check the brakes of the train I am travelling in tomorrow? (BMA 1990: xv)

Transport, food, leisure activities, work and medical care all involve sets of risks that have been studied, and which the BMA here reports for a lay audience. In a world in which "experts" are no longer trusted to make decisions, risk assessment is an individualized activity, in which we must all constantly engage. The implications for those who suffer accidents are rather bleak. Modernism provided no solace in terms of meaning for an accidental misfortune beyond that of mere coincidence, but implied a certain sympathy for the victim. The accident as an outcome of mismanaged risk is, however, a misfortune that should never have happened in the first place.

Social identity and the management of misfortune

Accident prevention reduces uncertainty by constructing the accident as an event that could be predicted, at least in theory. Another strategy for managing misfortune is the "actuarial" one, which reduces uncertainty by "socializing" the risks of accidents, or at least the financial outcomes of those risks (Ewald 1991, Simon 1988). Thus we can insure against accidental injury or death, sharing the risk with a larger population, and gain some compensation for time in hospital or loss of earnings should an accident happen. Simon (1988) has addressed the ideological effects of practices such as these, and suggests that the subjective identities produced by the insurance industry (and other "actuarial" practices) are "alienating and disempowering". Aggregates are formed through similarities in risk status that may have no social meaning, such as having high blood pressure, being a smoker or living within a certain postcode. Tensions arise, Simon argues, when the boundaries of these actuarial groups apparently coincide with more traditional groups, such as "gender", as a risk group, with "women" as a gender class. Class or status groups share histories, allegiances and social identity, whereas actuarial aggregates are merely "segments of the population . . . that have no patterns of shared experience . . . and no basis for understanding themselves as motivated by a common cause" (Simon 1988). Actuarial categories thus neutralize moral divisions, as they are based on risk profiles that are divorced from any social structural significance.

The rise of insurance as a strategy for managing misfortune in the late twentieth century might, then, suggest that accidents, like other misfortunes (such as being the victim of a crime, or illness), are no longer a site for the production of social identity. However, such "socializing" strategies coexist with those "privatizing" ones that construct responsibility for accident prevention (or crime prevention) as the personal responsibility of every potential victim. In Chapter 7 it was suggested that these privatizing strategies do (in the case of accidents at least) provide one space in which meaningful social identities, allegiances and exclusions are produced.

In the introductory chapter, it was suggested that to label an event as an accident implied a paradox. On the one hand, it suggested that the outcome was no-one's fault, so there could be no moral culpability, on the part of the sufferer or the agent. However, some people were seen to "deserve" accidents. Accidents come to be defined through a process of moral interrogation, formally in the coroner's court, less formally in the everyday social interactions in which accident stories are told and discussed. The accident is the outcome of such negotiation, but is also the vehicle by which these issues are constructed. Thus, "proper, responsible parents" are those who install safety equipment and make sure their children wear a cycle helmet, and stories about accidents are a forum for the social production of this knowledge. Likewise, the stories children tell about playground accidents are an arena in which a local consensus is reached about what kinds of children should take dares, or in which situations parents can be disobeyed. It is at this level, the local one of classifying misfortune and engaging in preventative activity, rather than the global one of amelioration, that social identities are created.

Accidents in the late twentieth century

If accidents have been brought to the centre of contemporary discourse, they have in part been dissolved in the process. An accident (an unpredictable event for which no-one can be blamed) can, in theory, no longer happen. The very act of analyzing accidents disperses them: epidemiological aggregation and risk analysis renders them predictable, respondents in interviews question their original classification of an event as "accidental", and public debate about coroners' verdicts uncovers culpable agents. The category of misfortunes that get provisionally labelled as accidents is a rather amorphous field, shaped by other cultural concerns. The accident in late twentieth-century Britain is a vehicle for constructing uncertainty, responsibility and culpability as much as it is an outcome of them.

It has been suggested that as a society we are becoming less capable of accepting uncertainty and risk (Fox 1980), and more likely to attribute blame to others for our misfortunes (Douglas & Wildavsky 1983). In one sense, the findings reported here might qualify these interpretations, as technologies of risk and its assessment provide a wealth of strategies for coping with uncertainty, and for "privatizing" responsibility for the outcomes of uncertainty, rather than merely blaming others. Although respondents in interviews did sometimes seek to lay responsibility elsewhere for accidents, they accepted personal responsibility for mapping the risks that they faced, which included assessing others' abilities to balance risks on their behalf. Engaging in action that was seen as "preventative", such as wearing a motorbike helmet, or learning about the risks of mountains, or installing a stair gate, offered, for these respondents, a sense of control over a risky environment. Although it was recognized that there were logical limits to the effectiveness of an accident-prevention enterprise, such action served in a social way to demonstrate that proper responsibility had been taken, and that they "had done all they could". The manipulation of risk factors is a talismatic activity, in that it is concerned not with removing the known causes of unwanted effects in a deterministic way, but with the demonstration of adherence to and faith in the possibilities of risk management.

Accidents, within a rational discourse, were a partial answer to the question of culpability, for if a misfortune was an accident, no-one could be blamed. In contemporary Britain, it has been suggested, responsibility and culpability have been divorced. Significantly, Freudenburg (1993) suggested a concept of "recreancy", which described a loss of faith in experts, and is unconnected with motivation. For Figlio (1985), the emergence of negligence was central to the appearance of accidents as a class of misfortunes, as it engendered the notion that responsibility could be held by those who did not intend harm. However, it was suggested here that this is not quite adequate, as some misfortunes that are classified as accidents are not about negligence, or if they are it is a rather more general kind of negligence, rather than one arising from specific contract relationships (for instance, parents' feelings of responsibility for all children's accidents, despite the lack of any recognizable negligent action on their part), and negligent acts were sometimes contrasted to accidents. Negligence, like "fate" or "luck", is merely one more risk factor to take into account, and another potential element in the forensic analysis of accidents in order to attribute responsibility.

As a category of misfortune, the accidental is rather elusive, for it is not easily wrenched from the field of discourses that produce it: risk, uncertainty and responsibility. Indeed, accidents are a key point of articulation for these obsessions of late twentieth-century culture. From being the remnants of modernist explanatory systems, accidents have been transformed into a pivotal category of contemporary ones. To manage accidental misfortune is the ultimate challenge for risk assessment techniques: to predict the unpredictable, and demonstrate that "there is no such thing as an accident". Yet we continue to classify many misfortunes as accidents: that such events still happen demonstrates the limits to risk assessment as a method of reducing uncertainty. It also demonstrates we cannot eliminate misfortune, however sophisticated our strategies for managing it become.

References

Adams, J. 1993. Risk compensation and the problems of measuring children's independent mobility and safety on the roads. In *Children, transport and the quality of life*, M. Hillman (ed.), 44–58. London: Policy Studies Institute.

Adams, J. 1995. *Risk*. London: UCL Press.

Agass, M., D. Mant, A. Fuller, A. Coulter, L. Jones 1990. Childhood accidents: a practice survey using general practitioners' records and parental reports. *British Journal of General Practice* **40**, 202–5.

Alwash, R. & M. McCarthy 1987. How do child accidents happen? *Health Education Journal* **46**, 169–71.

Alwash, R. & M. McCarthy 1988. Accidents in the home among children under 5: ethnic differences or social disadvantage? *British Medical Journal* **296**, 1450–53.

American Public Health Association 1968. *Accidents and homicide*. American Public Health Association, Harvard College.

Ampofo-Boateng, K. & J. A. Thomson 1991. Children's perception of safety and danger on the road. *British Journal of Psychology* **82**, 487–505.

Ansell, J. & F. Wharton 1992. *Risk: analysis, assessment and management*. Chichester, England: John Wiley.

Armstrong, D. 1986. The invention of infant mortality. *Sociology of Health and Illness* **8**, 211–32.

Arnauld, A. & P. Nicole 1851. *The Port-Royal logic*, trans. T. S. Baynes. Edinburgh: Sutherland and Knox.

Arnheim, D. & W. Sinclair 1975. *The clumsy child: a program of motor therapy*. St Louis: CV Mosby.

Atiyah, P. 1983. *Law and modern society*. Oxford: Oxford University Press.

Atkinson, J. M. 1978. *Discovering suicide*. London: Macmillan.

REFERENCES

Backett, K. 1992. Taboos and excesses: lay health moralities in middle-class families. *Sociology of Health and Illness* **14**, 255–74.

Basch, C. 1987. Focus group interview: an underutilised research technique for improving theory and practice in health education. *Health Education Quarterly* **14**, 411–48.

Bauman, Z. 1992. *Intimations of postmodernity*. London: Routledge.

Bayer, R., C. Levine, S. Wolf 1986. HIV screening: an ethical framework for evaluating proposed programs. *Journal of the American Medical Association* **256**, 1768–74.

Beck, U. 1992. *Risk society: towards a new modernity*, trans. R. Ritter. London: Sage.

Bellaby, P. 1990. To risk or not to risk? Uses and limitations of Mary Douglas on risk-acceptability for understanding health and safety at work and road accidents. *Sociological Review* **38**, 465–83.

Berger, P. & T. Luckman 1979. *The social construction of reality*. Harmondsworth: Penguin.

Bergman, D. 1991. Worked to death. The *Guardian*, 23 Oct.

Bijur, P. E., J. Golding, M. Haslum, M. Kurzon 1988. Behavioral predictors of injury in school-age children. *American Journal of Diseases of Children* **142**, 1307–12.

Bijur, P. E., S. Stewart-Brown, N. Butler 1986. Child behavior and accidental injury in 11,966 preschool children. *American Journal of Diseases of Children* **140**, 487–92.

Blaxter, M. 1976. *The meaning of disability*. London: Heinemann.

Blaxter, M. 1983. The cause of disease: women talking. *Social Science and Medicine* **17**, 59–69.

Bloor, D. 1976. *Knowledge and social imagery*. London: Routledge & Kegan Paul.

Bloor, J. M. & G. Horobin 1975. Conflict and conflict resolution in doctor–patient interaction. In *A sociology of medical practice*, C. Cox & A. Mead (eds), 271–84. London: Collier Macmillan.

BMA (British Medical Association) 1990. *The BMA guide to living with risk*. Harmondsworth: Penguin.

Bork, A. 1980. Randomness and the twentieth century. In *Risk and chance: selected readings*, J. Dowie & P. Lefrere (eds), 53–73. Milton Keynes: Open University Press.

Bradley, C., K. S. Lewis, A. M. Jennings, J. D. Ward 1990. Scales to measure perceived control developed specifically for people with tablet-treated diabetes. *Diabetic Medicine* **7**, 685–94.

Brenner, C. 1964. Parapraxis and wit. In *Accident research: methods and approaches*, W. Haddon, E. Suchman, D. Klein (eds), 292–4. New York: Harper & Row.

Broderick Committee 1971 *Report of the Committee on Death Certification and Coroners*. London: HMSO.

Brown, G. & S. Davidson 1978. Social class, psychiatric disorder of mother, and accidents to children. *Lancet* **i**, 378–80.

Bunting, M. 1994. Backing for the dentist who refused to treat children. The *Guardian*, 28 June.

Bunton, R. & R. Burrows 1995. Consumption and health in the "epidemiological" clinic of late modern medicine. See Bunton, Nettleton, Burrows (1995), 206–22.

Bunton, R., S. Nettleton, R. Burrows (eds) 1995. *The sociology of health promotion: critical analyses of consumption, lifestyle and risk*. London: Routledge.

Burchell, G., C. Gordon, P. Miller 1991. *The Foucault effect: studies in governmentality*. London: Harvester Wheatsheaf.

Bury, M. 1986. Social constructionism and the development of medical sociology. *Sociology of Health and Illness* **8**, 137–69.

Bytheway, B. 1978. Accidents and accidents. *New Age* (Spring), 30.

Calnan, M. 1982. The hospital accident and emergency department: what is its role? *Journal of Social Policy* **11**, 483–503.

Cameron, D. & C. Bishop 1992. Farm accidents in adults. *British Medical Journal* **305**, 25–6.

Cameron, D., C. Bishop, J. R. Sibert 1992. Farm accidents in children. *British Medical Journal* **305**, 23–5.

CAPT (Child Accident Prevention Trust) 1989. *Basic principles of child accident prevention*. London: Child Accident Prevention Trust.

Carter, S. 1994. Scientific theories of risk and male work practices – a case study. Paper presented at the British Sociological Association Annual Conference (*Sexualities in Social Context*), University of Central Lancashire, England.

Carter, Y. H. & P. W. Jones 1993. Accidents among children under five years old: a general practice based study in north Staffordshire. *British Journal of General Practice* **43**, 159–63.

Castel, R. 1991. From dangerousness to risk. See Burchell, Gordon, Miller (1991), 281–98.

Cliff, K. S. 1984. *Accidents: causes, prevention and services*. London: Croom Helm.

Comaroff, J. & R. Maguire 1981. Ambiguity and the search for meaning: childhood leukemia in the modern clinical context. *Social Science and Medicine* **15B**, 115–123.

Combes, G. 1991. *You can't watch them twenty-four hours a day: parents' and children's perceptions, understanding and experience of accidents and accident prevention*. London: Child Accident Prevention Trust.

Cooter, R. 1993. *Surgery and society in peace and war: orthopaedics and the organization of modern medicine*. Basingstoke: Macmillan.

Cornwell, J. 1984a. *Health – a coincidence? Accounts of health and illness in a working-class community: the case of Bethnal Green*. PhD thesis, University of London.

Cornwell, J. 1984b. *Hard earned lives: accounts of health and illness from East London*. London: Tavistock Publications.

Crawford, R. 1986. Individual responsibility and health politics. In *The sociology of health and illness: critical perspectives*, P. Conrad & R. Kern (eds), 369–77. New York: St Martins Press.

Croft, A. & J. Sibert 1992. Accident prevention – environmental change and education. In *Accidents and emergencies in childhood*, J. Sibert (ed.), 1–8. London: Royal College of Physicians.

Daniels, A. 1987. The captive professional: bureaucratic limitations in the practice of military psychiatry. In *Encounters between patients and doctors*, J. Stoeckle (ed.), 235–51. Cambridge, Mass.: MIT Press.

Daston, L. 1987. The domestication of risk: mathematical probability and insurance 1650–1830. In *The probabilistic revolution: vol 1 (Ideas in history)*, L. Krüger, L. Daston, M. Heidelberger (eds), 237–60. Cambridge, Mass.: MIT Press.

Davison, C., G. Davey-Smith, S. Frankel 1991. Lay epidemiology and the prevention paradox: the implications of coronary candidacy for health education. *Sociology of Health and Illness* **13**, 1–19.

DHSS (Department of Health and Social Security) 1980. *Inequalities in health*. London: HMSO.

Dingwall, R., J. Eekelaar, T. Murray 1983. *The protection of children: state intervention and family life*. Oxford: Basil Blackwell.

Doege, T. C. 1978. An injury is no accident. *New England Journal of Medicine* **298**, 509–10.

DOH (Department of Health) 1992. *The health of the nation: a strategy for health in England*. London: HMSO.

DOH (Department of Health) 1993. *The health of the nation key area handbook: accidents*. Leeds: Department of Health.

Donaldson, M. 1978. *Children's minds*. London: Croom Helm.

DoT (Department of Trade) 1980. *The HASS 1979 – a presentation of twelve months data*. London: HMSO.

DOT (Department of Transport) 1985. *Compulsory seat belt wearing*. London: HMSO.

DOT (Department of Transport) 1993. *Road accidents Great Britain 1992: the casualty report*. London: HMSO.

DOT/MAIB (Department of Transport/Marine Accident Investigation Branch) 1991. *Report of the Chief Inspector of Marine Accidents into the collision between the passenger launch Marchioness and MV Bowbelle*. London: HMSO.

Douglas, J. 1967. *The social meanings of suicide*. Princeton, New Jersey: Princeton University Press.

Douglas, M. 1973. *Natural symbols: explorations in cosmology*, 2nd ed. London: Barrie & Jenkins.

Douglas, M. 1984. *Purity and danger: an analysis of the concepts of pollution and taboo*. London: Ark.

Douglas, M. 1986. *Risk acceptability according to the social sciences*. London: Routledge & Kegan Paul.

Douglas, M. 1992. *Risk and blame: essays in cultural theory*. London: Routledge.

Douglas, M. & A. Wildavsky 1983. *Risk and culture*. Berkeley and Los Angeles: University of California Press.

Durkheim, E. 1950. *The rules of sociological method*, trans. S. A. Solouay & J. M. Mueller. Glencoe: Free Press.

Durkheim, E. 1963. *Suicide: a study in sociology*, trans. J. Spaulding & G. Simpson. London: Routledge & Kegan Paul.

Durkheim, E. & M. Mauss 1963. *Primitive classification*, trans. R. Needham. London: Cohen & West.

Elias, N. 1985. *The loneliness of the dying*, trans. E. Jephcott. Oxford: Basil Blackwell.

Engel, M. 1994. Death and the risk business. The *Guardian*, 4 May.

Evans, L. 1993. Medical accidents: no such thing? *British Medical Journal* **307**, 1438–9.

Evans-Pritchard, E. E. 1937. *Witchcraft, oracles and magic among the Azande*. Oxford: Clarendon Press.

Evelyn, J. 1819. *Memoirs of John Evelyn, FRS*. London: Henry Colborn.

Ewald, F. 1991. Insurance and risk. See Burchell, Gordon, Miller (1991), 197–210.

Featherstone, M. 1988. In pursuit of the post-modern: an introduction. *Theory, Culture and Society* **5**, 195–215.

Feyerabend, P. 1987. *Farewell to reason*. London: Verso.

Figlio, K. 1985. What is an accident? In *The social history of occupational health*, P. Weindling (ed.), 180–206. London: Croom Helm.

Fo, D. 1980. *The accidental death of an anarchist: a farce*, (adapted by G. Richards). London: Pluto.

Forbes, T. 1985. *Surgeons at the Bailey*. New Haven, Conn.: Yale University Press.

Fordham, F. 1966. *An introduction to Jung's psychology*. Harmondsworth: Penguin.

Foucault, M. 1974. *The archaeology of knowledge*. London: Tavistock.

Foucault, M. 1979. *Discipline and punish*. Harmondsworth: Penguin.

Foucault, M. 1984. Nietzsche, genealogy, history. In *The Foucault reader*, P. Rabinow (ed.), 76–100. Harmondsworth: Penguin.

Foucault, M. 1989. *The order of things: an archaeology of the human sciences*. London: Routledge.

Foucault, M. 1991. Questions of method. See Burchell, Gordon, Miller (1991), 73–86.

Fox, R. 1980. The evolution of medical uncertainty. *Milbank Memorial Fund Quarterly/Health and Society* **58**, 1–49.

Frankenberg, R. 1974. Functionalism and after? Theory and developments in social science applied to the health field. *International Journal of the Health Services* **4**, 411–27.

Freidson, E. 1970. *Profession of medicine*. New York: Dodd Mead.

Freud, S. 1938. *The psychopathology of everyday life*. Harmondsworth: Penguin.

Freudenburg, W. R. 1993. Risk and recreancy: Weber, the division of labor, and the rationality of risk perception. *Social Forces* **71**, 909–32.

Gabbay, J. 1982. Asthma attacked? Tactics for the reconstruction of a disease concept. See Wright & Treacher (1982), 23–48.

Gallagher, E. 1976. Lines of reconstruction and extension in the Parsonian sociology of illness. *Social Science and Medicine* **10**, 207–18.

Genn, H. 1987. *Hard bargaining*. Oxford: Clarendon Press.

Genn, H. & S. Burman 1977. Some social and legal consequences of accidents in the home. In *Accidents in the home*, S. Burman & H. Genn (eds), 116–34. London: Croom Helm.

Gerhardt, U. 1979. The Parsonian paradigm and the identity of medical sociology. *Sociological Review* **27**, 229–51.

Gerhardt, U. 1990. Qualitative research on chronic illness: the issue and the story. *Social Science and Medicine* **30**, 1149–59.

Giddens, A. 1991. *Modernity and self-identity: self and society in the late modern age.* Cambridge: Polity Press.

Gillies, E. 1976. "Introduction" to E. E. Evans-Pritchard, *Witchcraft, oracles and magic among the Azande,* abridged ed. Oxford: Clarendon Press.

Gonzalez-Crussi, F. 1986. *Three forms of sudden death.* London: Pan Books.

Gordon, C. 1991. Governmental rationality: an introduction. See Burchell, Gordon, Miller (1991), 1–52.

Gordon, J. E. 1964. The epidemiology of accidents. In *Accident research: methods and approaches*, W. Haddon, E. Suchman, D. Klein (eds), 15–40. New York: Harper & Row.

Graham, H. J. & J. Firth 1992. Home accidents in older people: role of primary health care team. *British Medical Journal* **305**, 30–32.

Graunt, J. 1662. *Natural and political observations mentioned in a following index, and made upon the Bills of Mortality.* London.

Green, J. 1992. The medico-legal production of fatal accidents. *Sociology of Health and Illness* **14**, 373–90.

Green, J. 1995. *Risk, rationality and misfortune: towards a sociology of accidents.* PhD thesis, University of London.

Green, J. & L. Hart 1996. *Children and risk.* Research Reports No. 1. London: South Bank University.

Greenwood, M., W. J. Martin, W. T. Russell 1941. Deaths by violence, 1837–1937. *Journal of the Royal Statistical Society* **104** (part II), 146–71.

Greil, A., K. Porter, T. Leitko, C. Riscilli 1989. Why me? Theodicies of infertile men and women. *Sociology of Health and Illness* **11**, 213–29.

The *Guardian*. 1991. Accident verdict on injected patient. 26 October.

The *Guardian*. 1993. Hillsborough boy need not have died, judges told. 3 November.

Guildhall Library MS 126. *Rotuli Coronatorum.* Medieval Coroners' rolls, transcribed and translated by R. Sharpe.

Hacking, I. 1975. *The emergence of probability.* Cambridge: Cambridge University Press.

Hacking, I. 1987. Was there a probabilistic revolution 1800–1930? In *The probabilistic revolution, vol. 1*; (*Ideas in history*), L. Krüger, L. Daston, M. Heidelberger (eds), 45–8. Cambridge, Mass.: MIT Press.

Haddon, W., E. Suchman, D. Klein (eds) 1964. *Accident research: methods and approaches.* New York: Harper & Row.

Henwood, M. 1992. *Accident prevention and public health: a study of the annual reports of Directors of Public Health.* Birmingham: RoSPA.

Hillman, M., J. Adams, J. Whitelegg 1990. *One false move . . . A study of children's independent mobility.* London: Policy Studies Institute.

Hindess, B. 1988. *Choice, rationality and social theory.* London: Unwin Hyman.

Holdsworth, W. 1936. *A history of English law,* vol. II. London: Methuen.

Hollis, M. 1982. The social destruction of reality. See Hollis & Lukes (1982), 67–86.

Hollis, M. & S. Lukes (eds) 1982. *Rationality and relativism.* Oxford: Basil Blackwell.

Horton, R. 1970. African traditional thought and Western science. See Wilson (1970), 131–71.

Hume, D. 1739. *A Treatise of Human Nature: being an attempt to introduce the experimental method of reasoning into moral subjects.* London: John Noon.

Hunnisett, R. 1961. *The medieval coroner.* Cambridge: Cambridge University Press.

Hunnisett, R. 1985. *Sussex coroners' inquests.* Sussex Record Society, vol. 74.

Husband, P. 1973. The accident-prone child. *The Practitioner* **211**, 335–44.

Illich, I. 1976. *Medical nemesis: the expropriation of health.* New York: Pantheon.

Ingleby, D. 1982. The social construction of mental illness. See Wright & Treacher (1982), 123–43.

Jackson, N. & P. Carter, 1992. The perception of risk. See Ansell & Wharton (1992), 41–54.

Jackson, R. M. 1977. *Children, the environment and accidents.* London: Pitman Medical.

Jeffrey, R. 1979. Normal rubbish: deviant patients in casualty departments. *Sociology of Health and Illness* **1**, 90–107.

Jervis, Sir J. 1986. *On the office and duties of coroners.* P. Matthews & J. Foreman (eds). London: Sweet & Maxwell.

Jones, D. R. 1986. Flying and danger, joy and fear. *Aviation, Space and Environmental Medicine* **57**, 131–6.

Jung, C. G. 1955. *Synchronicity: an acausal connecting principle,* trans. R. F. C. Hull. London: Routledge & Kegan Paul.

Kammerer, P. 1919. *Das Gesetz der Serie: Eine Lehre von den Wiederholungen im Lebens- und im Weltgeschehen.* Stuttgart: Deutsche Verlags-Anstalt.

Kavanagh, G. 1985. *The coroners rules and statutes.* London: Sweet & Maxwell.

Kemp, A. & J. R. Sibert 1992. Drowning and near drowning in children in the United Kingdom: lessons for prevention. *British Medical Journal* **304**, 1143–6.

Kendrick, D. 1993. Accidental injury attendances as predictors of future admission. *Journal of Public Health Medicine* 15, 171–4.

Kendrick, D., P. Marsh, E. I. Williams 1995. General practitioners: child accident prevention and "The Health of the Nation". *Health Education Research* 10, 345–53.

Kickbusch, I. 1988. New perspectives for research in health behaviour. In *Health behaviour research and health promotion*, R. Anderson (ed.), 237–43. Oxford University Press.

Kister, M. C. & C. J. Patterson 1980. Children's conceptions of the causes of illness: understanding of contagion and use of immanent justice. *Child Development* 51, 839–46.

Kitzinger, J. 1994. The methodology of focus groups. *Sociology of Health and Illness* 16, 103–21.

Koestler, A. 1975. *The case of the midwife toad*. London: Pan Books.

Kuhn, T. 1970. *The structure of scientific revolutions*, 2nd edn. Chicago: University of Chicago Press.

Lane, R. 1979. *Violent death in the city: suicide, accident and murder in nineteenth century Philadelphia*. Cambridge, Mass.: Harvard University Press.

Langley, J. 1982. The "accident-prone" child – the perpetuation of a myth. *Australian Paediatric Journal* 18, 243–6.

Lash, S. & S. Whimster 1987. *Max Weber, rationality and modernity*. London: Allen & Unwin.

Laungani, P. 1989. Accidents in children – an Asian perspective. *Public Health* 103, 171–6.

LDSAMRA (Lake District Search and Mountain Rescue Association) *c.* 1992. *Mountain Accidents 1991*. Kendal: Lake District Search and Mountain Rescue Association.

Lee, A. M. 1992. Some recent English transportation accidents. See Ansell & Wharton (1992), 123–36.

Lévy-Bruhl, L. 1923. *Primitive mentality*. London: George Allen & Unwin.

Lodge, T. 1603. *A Treatise of the plague, containing the nature, signes and accidents of the same*. London: E White and NL.

Luker, K. 1975. *Taking chances: abortion and the decision not to contracept*. Los Angeles: University of California Press.

Lukes, S. 1982. Relativism in its place. See Hollis & Lukes (1982), 261–305.

Lyotard, J. 1986. *The postmodern condition: a report on knowledge*. Manchester: Manchester University Press.

Matthews, P. 1988. *1st Supplement to 10th Edition of Jervis*. London: Sweet & Maxwell.

Mayall, B. 1993. Keeping healthy at home and school. *Sociology of Health and Illness* 15, 447–63.

Mead, M. 1931. *Growing up in New Guinea: a comparative study of primitive education*. London: George Routledge.

Melia, R. J. W., D. Morrell, A. V. Swan, J. Bartholomew 1989. A health visitor investigation of home accidents in pre-school children. *Health visitor* (June), **62**, 181–3.

Ministry of Health 1944. *A National Health Service*. London: HMSO.

Ministry of Reconstruction 1919. *Reconstruction problems 23: public health*. London: HMSO.

Ministry of Works 1950. *An inquiry into accidents in the home*. London: HMSO.

Myers, P. 1994. Death of a man crushed by police car in ditch ruled "accidental". The *Guardian*, 28 May.

NAHA/RoSPA Strategy Group 1990. *Action on accidents: the unique role of the health services*. Birmingham: NAHA/RoSPA.

Naidoo, J. 1986. Limits to individualism. In *The politics of health education*, S. Rodmell & A. Watt (eds), 17–37. London: Routledge & Kegan Paul.

National Research Council Division of Medical Sciences 1966. *Accidental death and disability: the neglected disease of modern society*. Washington, DC: National Research Council.

National Safety Council 1949. *Accident facts*. Chicago: National Safety Council.

Nichols, T. 1989. On the analysis of size effects and "accidents". *Industrial Relations Journal* (Spring), 62–5.

Nichols, T. 1991. Industrial injuries in British manufacturing industry and cyclical effects: continuities and discontinuities in industrial injury research. *The Sociological Review* **39**, 131–9.

Nichols, T. & P. Armstrong 1973. *Safety or profit*. Bristol: Falling Wall Press.

NSPCC (National Society for the Prevention of Cruelty to Children) Battered Child Research Team 1976. *At risk*. London: Routledge & Kegan Paul.

O'Malley, P. 1992. Risk, power and crime prevention. *Economy and Society* **21**, 252–73.

O'Malley, P. 1993. Risk, power and crime prevention. Paper presented to the *History of the present network* Seminar, London School of Economics.

OPCS (Office of Population Censuses and Surveys) 1976. *1974 Mortality statistics: accidents and violence*. London: HMSO.

OPCS (Office of Population Censuses and Surveys) 1978. *Occupational mortality 1970–72*. London: HMSO.

OPCS (Office of Population Censuses and Surveys) 1982. Studies in sudden infant death. In *Studies on medical and population subjects no. 45*. London: HMSO.

OPCS (Office of Population Censuses and Surveys) 1991. *1989 mortality statistics: accidents and violence*. DH4 no. 15. London: HMSO.

OPCS (Office of Population Censuses and Surveys) 1992a. *1990 Mortality statistics: injury and poisoning*. DH4 no. 16. London: HMSO.

OPCS (Office of Population Censuses and Surveys) 1992b. *1841–1990 Mortality statistics: serial tables*. London: HMSO.

OPCS (Office of Population Censuses and Surveys) 1994a. *1992 Mortality statistics: childhood*. DH6 no. 6. London: HMSO.

OPCS (Office of Population Censuses and Surveys) 1994b. *1992 Mortality statistics: injury and poisoning.* DH4 no. 18. London: HMSO.

Overing, J. (ed.) 1985. *Reason and morality.* London: Tavistock.

Palmer, T. 1992. A weather eye on unpredictability. In *The* New Scientist *guide to chaos*, N. Hall (ed.), 69–81. Harmondsworth: Penguin.

Pareto, V. 1976. *Sociological writings,* trans. D. Mirfin. Oxford: Basil Blackwell.

Parsons, T. 1951a. *The social system.* London: Routledge & Kegan Paul.

Parsons, T. 1951b. Illness and the role of the physician: a sociological perspective. *American Journal of Psychiatry* **21**, 452–60.

Parsons, T. 1975. The sick role and the role of the physician reconsidered. *Milbank Memorial Fund/Health and Society* **53**, 257–78.

Patton, C. 1985. *Sex and germs.* Boston: South End Press.

Percival, I. 1992. Chaos: a science for the real world. In *The* New Scientist *guide to chaos*, N. Hall (ed.), 11–21. Harmondsworth: Penguin.

Perrow, C. 1984. *Normal accidents: living with high risk technologies.* New York: Basic Books.

Petty, W. 1687. *Two essays in political arithmetick, concerning the people, housing, hospitals etc of London and Paris.* London: John Lloyd.

Petty, W. 1699. *Several essays in political arithmetick.* London: R. Clavel and H. Mortlock.

Philipp, R. & E. Philipp, 1988. Can we help to prevent skiing accidents? *Health Education Journal* **47**, 141–3.

Piaget, J. 1930. *The child's conception of physical causality.* London: Kegan Paul, Trench, Trubner & Co.

Piaget, J. 1932. *The moral judgement of the child.* London: Kegan Paul, Trench, Trubner & Co.

Piaget, J. & B. Inholden 1975. *On the origin of the idea of chance in children.* London: Routledge & Kegan Paul.

Pill, R. & N. C. H. Stott 1982. Concepts of illness causation and responsibility: some preliminary data from a sample of working-class mothers. *Social Science & Medicine* **16**, 43–52.

Plant, M. & M. Plant 1993. *Risk takers: alcohol, drugs, sex and youth.* London: Routledge.

Polnay, L. 1992. Is neglect neglected? In *Accidents and emergencies in childhood*, J. Sibert (ed.), 105–24. London: Royal College of Physicians.

Popay, J. & A. Young (eds) 1993. *Reducing accidental death and injury in children: a report produced for NWRHA Public Health Working Group on Child Accidents.* Manchester: PHRC.

Popper, K. 1959. *The logic of scientific discovery.* London: Hutchinson.

Popper, K. 1960. *The poverty of historicism.* London: Routledge & Kegan Paul.

Popper, K. 1974. *Objective knowledge.* Oxford: Clarendon Press.

Porter, T. 1986. *The rise of statistical thinking 1820–1900.* Princeton: Princeton University Press.

Powell, P. 1971. *2000 accidents: a shop floor study of their causes.* London: National Institute of Industrial Psychology.

Prior, L. 1989. *The social organisation of death: medical discourses and social practices in Belfast.* London: Macmillan.

Prior, L. 1995. Chance and modernity: accidents as a public health problem. See Bunton, Nettleton & Burrows (1995), 206–22.

Rafnsson, V. & H. Gunnarsdottir 1993. Risk of fatal accidents occurring other than at sea among Icelandic seamen. *British Medical Journal* **306**, 1379–81.

Registrar-General 1839, 1840, 1848, 1854, 1856 and 1862. *Annual Report of Births, Marriages and Deaths.* London: HMSO.

Registrar-General 1957. *Statistical Review of England and Wales 1954–6 Part III.* London: HMSO.

van Reijen, W. & D. Veerman 1988. An interview with Jean-François Lyotard. *Theory, Culture and Society* **5**, 277–309.

Richards, S. 1985. *Luck, chance and coincidence.* Wellingborough: The Aquarian Press.

Roberts, H., S. Smith, C. Bryce 1993. Prevention is better. . . *Sociology of Health and Illness* **15**, 447–63.

Roberts, H., S. Smith, M. Lloyd 1992. Safety as social value: a community approach. In *Private risks and public dangers*, S. Scott, G. Williams, S. Platt, H. Thomas (eds), 184–200. Aldershot: Avebury.

Roberts, I. 1993. Why have child pedestrian death rates fallen? *British Medical Journal* **306**, 1737–9.

Robertson, L. 1983. *Injuries: causes, control strategies and public policy.* Lexington, Mass.: DC Heath.

Rogers, A. & D. Pilgrim 1995. The risk of resistance: perspectives on the mass childhood immunization programme. In *Medicine, health and risk*, J. Gabe (ed.), 73–90. Oxford: Blackwell Scientific.

Rorty, R. 1986. Foucault and epistemology. In *Foucault: a critical reader*, D. Couzens Hoy (ed.), 41–50. Oxford: Basil Blackwell.

RoSPA (Royal Society for the Prevention of Accidents) 1984. *First steps to safety: a child's guide to parents . . . and a reminder to grandparents.* London: RoSPA.

RoSPA (Royal Society for the Prevention of Accidents) 1992. *RoSPA 75th Anniversary: past, present and future.* Birmingham: RoSPA.

Roth, J. 1972. Some contingencies of the moral evaluation and control of clientele. *American Journal of Sociology* **77**, 839–59.

Rotter, J. 1966. Generalised expectancies for internal versus external control of reinforcements. *Psychological Monographs* **80**, 1–28.

Rotter, J. 1982. *The development and application of social learning theory.* New York: Praeger.

Royal College of Physicians 1991. *Prevention medicine: a report of the working party of the Royal College of Physicians.* London: Royal College of Physicians.

Royal College of Surgeons *c.* 1963. *Working party on accident prevention and life saving*

1961–1963. London: Royal College of Surgeons.

Russell, B. 1946. *A history of Western philosophy*. London: George Allen & Unwin.

Sandels, S. 1975. *Children in traffic*. London: Paul Elek.

Scheppele, K. L. 1991. Law without accidents. In *Social theory for a changing society*, P. Bourdieu & J. S. Coleman (eds), 267–93. Oxford: Westview Press.

Schroeder, R. 1987. Nietzsche and Weber: two "prophets of the modern world". In *Max Weber, rationality and modernity*, S. Lash & S. Whimster (eds), 207–21. London: Allen & Unwin.

Sharpe, R. 1913. *Calendar of Coroners' Rolls of the City of London AD 1300–1378*. London: Richard Clay.

Shaver, K. G. & D. Drown 1986. On causality, responsibility and self-blame: a theoretical note. *Journal of Personality and Social Psychology* **50**, 697–702.

Sibert, J. R. 1975. Stress in families of children who have ingested poison. *British Medical Journal* **3**, 87–9.

Sibert, J. R., A. W. Croft, R. M. Jackson 1977. Child-resistant packaging and accidental child poisoning. *Lancet* **ii**, 289–90.

Sibert, J. R., G. B. Maddocks, B. M. Brown 1981. Childhood accidents – an endemic of epidemic proportions. *Archives of Diseases in Childhood* **56**, 225–34.

Sica, A. 1988. *Weber, irrationality and social order*. Berkeley: University of California Press.

Simon, J. 1988. The ideological effects of actuarial practices. *Law and Society Review* **22**, 772–800.

Simpson, K. & B. Knight 1985. *Forensic medicine*, 9th edn. London: Edward Arnold.

Smart, B. 1990. On the disorder of things: sociology, postmodernity and "the end of the social". *Sociology* **24**, 397–416.

Smith, M. 1993. Changing sociological perspectives on chance. *Sociology* **27**, 513–31.

Smith, M. & I. Smith 1991. *How to save your child's life: the unique guide to help children survive, 24 hours a day*. London: Grafton Books.

Smith, T. 1987. AIDS: a doctor's duty. *British Medical Journal* **294**, 6.

Smithson, M. 1985. Toward a social theory of ignorance. *Journal for the Theory of Social Behaviour* **15**, 151–72.

Sontag, S. 1979. *Illness as metaphor*. London: Allen Lane.

Sontag, S. 1989. *AIDS and its metaphors*. London: Allen Lane.

Spiegel, C. N. & F. C. Lindaman 1977. Children can't fly: a program to prevent childhood morbidity and mortality from window falls. *American Journal of Public Health* **67**, 1143–7.

Springett, P. 1994. Nightmare on Lime Street. The *Guardian* 26 April.

Stapleton, J. 1986. *Disease and the compensation debate*. Oxford: Clarendon Press.

Stewart-Brown, S., T. J. Peters, J. Golding, P. Bijur 1986. Case definition in childhood accident studies: a vital factor in determining results. *International Journal of Epidemiology* **15**, 352–60.

Stone, D. 1991. Preventing accidents – a high priority target. *Medical Monitor* (24 May), 61–5.

Stone, D. 1993. Implementing a strategy for accident prevention. *Medical Monitor* (7 April), 50–52.

Sutherland, R. 1992. Preventing child traffic injuries. In *Accidents and emergencies in childhood*, J. Sibert (ed.), 33–8. London: Royal College of Physicians.

Szasz, T. 1961. *The myth of mental illness*. New York: Hocbar/Harper.

Szasz, T. & M. Hollander 1956. A contribution to the philosophy of medicine: the basic models of the doctor–patient relationship. *Archives of Internal Medicine* **97**, 585–92.

Taylor, C. 1982. Rationality. See Hollis & Lukes (1982), 87–105.

Teanby, D. 1992. Underreporting of pedestrian road accidents. *British Medical Journal* **304**, 422.

Tennen, H. & G. Affleck 1990. Blaming others for threatening events. *Psychological Bulletin* **108**, 209–32.

Thomas, K. 1978. *Religion and the decline of magic*. Harmondsworth: Penguin.

Tombs, S. 1989. Deviant workplaces and dumb managements? Understanding and preventing accidents in the chemical industry. *Industrial Crisis Quarterly* **3**, 191–211.

Tombs, S. 1990. Industrial injuries in British manufacturing. *The Sociological Review* **38**, 324–45.

Tombs, S. 1991. Injury and ill health in the chemical industry: decentering the accident-prone victim. *Industrial Crisis Quarterly* **5**, 59–75.

Tombs, S. 1992. Safety, statistics and business cycles: a response to Nichols. *The Sociological Review* **40**, 132–45.

Turner, B. A. 1978. *Man-made disasters*. London: Wykeham Publications.

Turner, K. 1989. Safety, discipline and the manager: building a "higher class of men". *Sociology* **23**, 611–28.

Wallston, K. A., B. S. Wallston, R. De Villis 1978. Development of the multidimensional health locus of control (MHLC) scales. *Health Education Monographs* **6**, 160–70.

Walsh, S. S. & S. N. Jarvis 1992. Measuring the frequency of "severe" accidental injury in children. *Journal of Epidemiology and Community Health* **46**, 26–32.

Ward, S. 1622. *Woe to drunkards: a sermon*. London: John Marriott & John Grismand.

Warwick, I., P. Aggleton, H. Homans 1988. Constructing commonsense – young people's beliefs about AIDS. *Sociology of Health and Illness* **10**, 213–33.

Weber, M. 1930. *The Protestant ethic and the spirit of capitalism*, trans. T. Parsons. London: George Allen & Unwin.

Weber, M. 1948. Science as a vocation. In *From Max Weber: essays in sociology*, H. H. Gerth & C. Wright Mills (eds), 139. London: Routledge & Kegan Paul.

Weber, M. 1968. *On charisma and institution building*. Chicago: University of Chicago Press.

REFERENCES

Weber, M. 1978 *Economy and society: an outline of interpretive sociology*, vol. I ed. G. Roth & C. Wittich. Berkeley: University of California Press.

WHO (World Health Organization) 1957. *Accidents in childhood: Facts as a basis for prevention*. (Report of an advisory group) Technical Report Series no. 118. Geneva: WHO.

WHO (World Health Organization) 1967. *Manual of the international statistical classification of diseases, injuries and causes of death*. Geneva: WHO.

WHO (World Health Organization) 1977. *Manual of the international statistical classification of diseases, injuries and causes of death*. Geneva: WHO.

WHO (World Health Organization) 1981. *Psychosocial factors related to accidents in childhood and adolescence*. Geneva: WHO.

WHO (World Health Organization) Regional Office for Europe 1985. *Targets for Health for All 2000*. Copenhagen: WHO.

WHO (World Health Organization) 1992. *Manual of the international statistical classification of disease and related health problems*. Geneva: WHO.

Williams, H. & J. R. Sibert 1983. Medicine and the media. *British Medical Journal* **286**, 1893.

Wilson, B. 1970. *Rationality*. Oxford: Basil Blackwell.

Wilton, T. 1993. Sisterhood in the service of patriarchy: heterosexual women's friendships and male power. In *Heterosexuality and patriarchy: a feminism and psychology reader*, S. Wilkinson & C. Kitzinger (eds), 273–6. London: Sage.

Winch, P. 1964. Understanding a primitive culture. *American Philosophical Quarterly* **1**, 307–24.

Wolff, S. 1969. *Children under stress*. London: Allen Lane.

Woodroffe, C., M. Glickman, M. Barker, C. Power 1993. *Children, teenagers and health: the key data*. Buckingham: Open University Press.

Wright, P. 1979. A study in the legitimation of knowledge: the "success" of medicine and the "failure" of astrology. In *On the margins of science: the social construction of rejected knowledge*, P. Wright (ed.), 85–101. Sociological Review Monograph 27, University of Keele.

Wright, P. & A. Treacher 1982. *The problem of medical knowledge: examining the social construction of medicine*. Edinburgh: Edinburgh University Press.

Zola, I. K. 1972. Medicine as an institution of social control. *The Sociological Review* **20**, 487–504.

Zola, I. 1975. In the name of health and illness. *Social Science and Medicine* **9**, 83–7.

Index